Why would a well-educated, middle-aged Ukrainian woman leave behind a beloved child or grandchild to care for elderly clients in Italy and the U.S. – not to return, in some instances, for many years? Taking a fresh approach to a forgotten type of global woman, Solari offers a poignant account of displaced grandmothers and the dreams attached to their hard-earned remittances. This is a highly illuminating and original book.

Arlie Russell Hochschild, author of Strangers in Their Own Land: Anger and Mourning on the American Right

A meticulously researched and beautifully written ethnography about how migration transforms nations from the outside in. Solari tells the compelling story of how Ukranian grandmothers living in "exodus" in California and in "exile" in Italy helped create the post-Soviet, newly capitalist Ukraine. Her narrative challenges much of the conventional wisdom about gender, migration, and nations.

Peggy Levitt, author of Artifacts and Allegiances: How Museums Put the Nation and the World on Display

In this brilliantly conceptualized and well-researched book, we learn to see how motherhood is a key foundation for nation-state building in Ukraine. Solari's examination of post-Soviet life for Ukrainian women and their families shows how newly idealized neoliberal versions of the nuclear family are made possible by the migrant labor and sacrifices of a generation of middle-aged and older women, *babushka* grandmothers who migrate across continents to earn remittances that will sustain nuclear families back home. Balancing original theoretical insights with riveting ethnographic portraits of diverse Ukrainian women, the book offers new insights into the relations between gender, nation, and migrant domestic work.

Pierrette Hondagneu-Sotelo, author of Paradise Transplanted: Migration and the Making of California Gardens

Focusing on case studies of female migrant domestic and care workers from Ukraine to Italy and the U.S., Solari conveys a vivid insight into the issues, exertions, and contradictions of transnational family life in post-socialist times. Solari convincingly combines three thematic areas which otherwise are treated separately: gender relations, migration, and nationalism and shows that an analysis of their interaction is indispensable for the understanding of Ukraine's development and current situation. The book is a must read for students and scholars studying gender, migration, and nationalism in the twenty-first century. It deserves to become an integral part of the global migration studies syllabus.

Helma Lutz, author of The New Maids. Transnational
Women and the Care Economy

Combining the strengths of personal narratives and sophisticated theory, Cinzia Solari challenges traditional categories in her compelling study of a mass emigration movement out of Ukraine after 1991. These diverse migrations, headed by largely middle-aged women in search of employment opportunities, are creating the building blocks of a new Ukrainian nation-state from the outside in. In her examination of the effects of this process, Solari charts a bold new course for an innovative study of post-socialist societies in transition.

Marian Rubchak, author of New Imaginaries: Youthful Reinvention of
Ukraine's Cultural Paradigm

ON THE SHOULDERS OF GRANDMOTHERS

On the Shoulders of Grandmothers is a global ethnography of Ukrainian transnational migration. Gendered migrant subjectivities are a key site for understanding the production of neoliberal capitalism and Ukrainian nation-state building, a fraught process that places Ukraine precariously between Europe and Russia with dramatic implications for the political economy of the region. However, processes of gender and migration that undergird transnational nation-state building require further attention. Solari compares two patterns of Ukrainian migration: the "forced" exile of middle-aged women, mostly grandmothers, to Italy and the "voluntary" exodus of families, led by the same cohort of middle-aged women, to the United States. In both receiving sites these migrants are caregivers to the elderly.

Using in-depth interviews and ethnographic data collected in three countries, Solari shows that Ukrainian nation-state building occurs transnationally. She examines the collective practices of migrants who are building the "new" Ukraine from the outside in and shaping both Italy and the United States as well. The Ukrainian state, in order to fulfill its First World aspirations of joining Europe and distancing itself from all things Soviet, is pursuing a gendered reorganization of family and work structures to achieve a transition from socialism to capitalism. This has created a labor force of migrant grandmothers who carry the new Ukraine on their shoulders. Solari shows that this post-Soviet economic transformation requires a change in the moral order as migrant women struggle to understand how to be "good" mothers and grandmothers and men join women in attempts to teach their children to be successful and honorable people, now that the social rules have drastically changed.

Looking at individual migrant women and men and their families in Ukraine allows us to see the production of neoliberal capitalism and new nationalism from the ground up and the outside in for a region that promises to be a flashpoint in our century.

Cinzia D. Solari is Assistant Professor of Sociology at the University of Massachusetts, Boston.

ON THE SHOULDERS OF GRANDMOTHERS

Gender, Migration, and Post-Soviet Nation-State Building

Cinzia D. Solari

Routledge
Taylor & Francis Group

NEW YORK AND LONDON

First published 2017
by Routledge
711 Third Avenue, New York, NY 10017

and by Routledge
2 Park Square, Milton Park, Abingdon, Oxon OX14 4RN

Routledge is an imprint of the Taylor & Francis Group, an informa business

Library of Congress Cataloging in Publication Data
A catalog record for this book has been requested

ISBN: 978-1-138-70703-0 (hbk)
ISBN: 978-1-138-70704-7 (pbk)
ISBN: 978-1-315-20152-8 (ebk)

Typeset in Bembo
by Taylor & Francis Books

CONTENTS

PART III
Exodus: The United States

ILLUSTRATIONS

Figures

Tables

ACKNOWLEDGMENTS

I am often asked how the child of Italian immigrants ends up with a regional focus on the former Soviet Union. It was a long road, and it began in third grade social studies. I was asked to pick a historical figure, pretend they were alive and sitting across the table from me, and write the conversation we would have. I picked Catherine the Great, because I thought it wonderful that a woman's last name could be "The Great." As I read biography after biography, I attempted to convince Catherine to free the serfs and marveled at the power a woman could possess and the heights she could reach. This began my love affair with the region. After the public schools in our Boston suburb announced that, as an immigrant kid of parents without high school diplomas, I was not "college material," my mother convinced Dana Hall School to take me on scholarship the summer before my junior year of high school. I am grateful to Dana Hall, and to my extraordinary mother, for altering the course of my life. I thank the amazing teachers I had at Dana who nurtured my curiosity for the region, even allowing me to write my American history paper on the Cuban missile crisis, if I promised to write it from the U.S. perspective. I owe a special thanks to Helen Burke Montague, my college counselor, who convinced me that not only was I college material, but I was headed to the Ivy League. Thank you also to Peggy Sweeney in college counseling who has cheered me and so many young women on to great things though her kindness and hard work.

During my undergraduate years at Brown University, I studied Russian language and history and thank my mentor and Russian historian Abbott Gleason for his wonderful seminars (I am sure I took them all) and for his support. You are missed. During my time at Brown, I often imagined the possible world orders had Stalin never existed. It was not until I decided to apply for graduate school in history that I realized that my fascination with the region was also fueled by the idea that social institutions can so dramatically shape how a society is organized, the life chances of individuals born into different social circumstances, and what individuals think is possible and desirable. I worried that with the collapse of the Soviet Union, there would be a dearth of studies rooted in the region. I worried that to no longer have the Soviet Union, both its good and its bad, as an alternative example to our capitalist world, would impoverish our imaginations.

When I arrived at Berkeley to begin my Ph.D. in Sociology, however, I feared I was finally in over my head. I felt my working-class background simply did not provide me with the cultural capital to navigate graduate school. I must have looked as lost as I felt walking through Barrows Hall that first year of graduate school, because Michael Burawoy walked over to me in the hallway one day and said: "I'd like you to sign up for office hours with me once a week." And once again the course of my life was altered. My mother was fond of saying, as we battled the public schools to treat my siblings and me fairly, that "a teacher can lift you up, or a teacher can bring you down." I am deeply grateful to Michael, my mentor, dissertation advisor, and inspiration for how to lift students up. I try to emulate Michael's ability to lift students up with my own students at the University of Massachusetts, Boston. Many of my students have backgrounds that look like mine, but did not get the lucky breaks that sent me down my particular path. Thanks to my undergraduate and graduate students who continue to inspire me, even as I attempt to inspire them.

I am also grateful to Raka Ray and Barrie Thorne for introducing me to and legitimating feminist theory as one way to name and explain the workings of power. Thanks also to Edward Walker at Berkeley's post-Soviet Center. In addition to Raka and Michael, Irene Bloemraad and Victoria Bonnell were outstanding dissertation committee members, thank you. It was in a combination of seminars, including a Sociology of Work seminar co-taught by Kim Voss and Raka Ray as well as Ann Swidler and Gil Eyal's theory seminars, where I realized that migrant domestic workers, as an object of study, suffered from what Kimberlé Crenshaw calls "intersectional disempowerment." Migrant domestic workers fall in between many vectors of power and of disciplinary study. Therefore, migration scholars tend to leave the study of migrant domestic workers to gender scholars; scholars of work tend to leave the study of domestic workers to those studying social movements and unionization; yet these scholars leave the study of migrant domestic worker lives to race scholars. In this way, the experiences of subject formation of migrant domestic workers is "chopped up" in the scholarly literature. Their oppression becomes compounded by simply adding modifiers to the noun "domestic worker": migrant, woman, undocumented, racialized, and so forth until I was unable to recognize the lives of domestic workers I knew from my personal life (many family members) in the narratives the literature provided. Combined with my interest in the former Soviet Union, searching for an intersectional understanding of my participants as migrant domestic workers in the context of lives that have experienced significant historical change from Soviet to post-Soviet social worlds was the original impetus for this project.

I am deeply in the debt of all the participants in Italy, California, and Ukraine who shared their lives with me despite great obstacles and allowed me to carry their hopes and joy, but also their pain for the time they welcomed me on their journeys. Their narratives expanded my capacity for empathy and made me a better person as well as a better scholar. I also thank the many Italian migration scholars who provided me with advice as I laid the groundwork for this project on a preliminary trip to Italy. At the University of Trento and the University of Bologna I thank Asher Colombo, Francesca Decima, Gianfranco Poggi, Carlo Ruzza, and Giuseppe Sciortino. In Rome I am especially grateful to Ferruccio Pastore who shared knowledge and contacts gained from his work at *Centro Studi Politica Internazionale* where he worked on migration policy. In L'viv I thank the nuns who hosted me and provided me with care, professors at the University of L'viv who encouraged their students to speak with me, and the brave young adults who shared their hopes and fears for their families and their country. In San Francisco I thank my contacts at the IHSS and the SEIU offices. Without their help the California interviews would not have materialized. I also thank all the Ukrainian, Italian, and American community leaders who shared their thoughts with me. Their perspectives enrich this book.

Many sincere thanks to Smitha Radhakrishnan, my graduate school friend and confidant for years of sustained support and encouragement in life and in work. I also thank her for her feedback on this project at all stages. I thank members of my Boston-area writing groups for their feedback and support including Helen Marrow, Natasha Kumar Warikoo, Bart Bonikowski, Caitryn Lynch, Sarah Lamb, and Elizabeth Ferry. I thank all the colleagues who supported my work at UMass Boston, and I offer a special thank you to Andrea Leverentz who has always gone above and beyond. I am also fortunate to be part of an amazing reading group of Boston-area gender scholars, and I especially thank Margaret Andersen who offered me professional advice with skill and laughter. Finally, I benefited from the insights of graduate school colleagues and friends such as Kerry Woodward, Marcel Paret, Ofer Sharone, Fareen Parvez, Laleh Behnehanian, Jane Zavisca, and Keyvan Kashkooli, and many more who contributed toward improving this book. Thanks to Jennifer Utrata who provided helpful edits to a book chapter.

This project has also benefited from many funding sources. The UC Berkeley Institute of Slavic, East European and Eurasian Studies as well as the Foreign Language and Area Studies grants through the U.S. Department of Education funded the early stages of this project. University of California's Labor and Employment Institute, the Center for Working Families, and the Department of Sociology helped fund field research in three countries. I was fortunate to be a Katz Fellow, a Leo Lowenthal Fellow, and recipient of a UC California Chancellor's Dissertation grant which helped fund transcription, data analysis, and time to write.

I dedicate this book to my family: To my husband Davide Cis whose support for all I do has never wavered – even when it meant spending our first wedding anniversary apart while I was in Russia, being on his own while I was in the field, or caring for me and our children when chronic, debilitating migraines made it seem this book and life might not move forward. He has also helped edit these pages and locate statistical data, and thus improved this book. Words cannot express my love and gratitude. Thank you Davide; to my sister Claudia Solari, a UCLA-trained sociologist, who scoured census data and crunched numbers as well as did final read-throughs of chapters that benefited the book and for which I am grateful; to my children Selene and Eliano Solari-Cis without whom nothing has meaning; and especially to my parents Rosetta and Giancarlo Solari who made incredible sacrifices and fought fiercely to ensure that their children got the education they merited. They turned out two daughters with Ph.D.s and a son with an M.D., which I, and any sociologist, would consider remarkable. They never wavered from the belief that we could do anything we put our minds to. I love you mamma and papa.

NOTES ON TRANSLITERATION AND PARTICIPANTS

I follow the U.S. Library of Congress system of transliteration of Russian and Ukrainian Cyrillic letters. Most transliterated words are Russian, however a few words were commonly said in Ukrainian in the field, and I therefore transliterated the Ukrainian word. Please note that many of the foreign words in Chapter 2 are Italian.

The names of participants are pseudonyms. At times I omit or change some of the identifying details to protect participants' anonymity, however my description of people and places are factually accurate and based on field notes and interview transcripts. There are different ways of transliterating Ukrainian and Russian names and this can have political implications. Although English-speakers are used to seeing "Ludmila," the Ukrainian spelling is "Lydmyla" and "Yuri" is spelled Yuriy. This transliteration is complicated by the fact that the letter "y" is not part of the official Italian alphabet. Some participants in Italy did not use the letter "y" in the transliteration of their names, despite patriotic convictions, for the ease of Italians. Others, however, chose to use what felt like a more Ukrainian transliteration regardless. Many of the participants I never communicated with in writing and so I simply do not know which transliteration they preferred. Other participants were proud of their Russian language and this was also reflected in the transliteration of their name. Given this complexity, I transliterated names in ways that made sense to me given what I know about the participant, and I ask for patience from readers who are familiar with the languages and politics of the region with what can seem like inconsistencies in the transliteration of names.

INTRODUCTION

"Gulag" versus "Promised Land": Metaphors of Destination and Transnational Social Fields

A Sunday in Rome's Garbatella

On a Sunday morning in November 2004, I took Rome's metro from St. Peter's Square and rode 40 minutes outside the city center to the Garbatella metro stop. Among post-1991 Ukrainian migrants in Rome (those who migrated after the dissolution of the Soviet Union and the declaration of Ukrainian independence), "the Garbatella" also referred to a large parking lot behind the station where every Sunday, 50 Soviet-era courier vans arrived from all over Ukraine filled with photographs, letters, and Ukrainian products sent from family members in Ukraine to those working as caregivers to the elderly in Italy. Over 5,000 Ukrainians, most undocumented, visited the Garbatella every Sunday.

This morning I am with Tanya, an energetic woman in her 50s. As Tanya and I exited the metro, we paused on a platform that overlooked the Garbatella. Looking out over the crowd, it was immediately obvious that those below were almost all women. Even more interesting, whereas most migrant populations around the world tend to be in their 20s or 30s, these women were in their 40s, 50s, and 60s, many of them *babushki* (the plural of *babushka* meaning grandmother). Tanya sighed and said in Russian, "Do you see all those women down there? They carry Ukraine on their shoulders and don't think they don't know it … and don't think they are happy about it either." Although I certainly witnessed and participated in moments of happiness with Ukrainian domestic workers in Rome, overwhelmingly the women and men I encountered used phrases that suggested "forced" exile such as "forced out of Ukraine," "stuck in prison," and "gulag" to speak about their migration to Italy. Many I spoke with had personal or familial experiences with relocation to Soviet-era gulags. "Gulag" expansively refers to a system of forced labor camps that peaked in the 1930s–1950s under Stalin and continued to exist in limited form into the 1980s. Perceived offenses against the Soviet state were punished with exile to labor camps, often in remote, underpopulated regions with brutal living conditions. Ukrainians constituted the second most numerous ethnic group among the gulag population.[1] Therefore, the "gulag" was a ready-made metaphor for migrants in Italy who described working abroad as a forced, *post*-Soviet exile to the labor camps.

Entering the Garbatella, I walked among the throngs of people. Most Sundays, women shared with me photographs from home. These included pictures of cars, computers, kitchen remodels, or fashionable clothes bought with the monetary remittances they sent back to their families. Migrants often told me that these photographs were "proof" that Ukraine is "Europe." As they pointed to objects bought with their remittances, women often said things like, "We may be in Italy, but we are still working for the new Ukraine!" It was not only consumer products that participants on the Garbatella pointed to as symbols of Ukraine's European standing, but also the behaviors of children who were studying "international business" or joined protests for a European Ukraine. Ethnographic experiences such as these highlighted a *gendered migrant subjectivity* forged by a particular intersection between gender, migration, and post-Soviet economic transformation. A deep, and even tortured, relationship to Ukraine emerged from my interviews with Ukrainian migrant domestic workers. The angst-filled discussions migrants had with me and each other about the life choices their migration made possible for their children and grandchildren back in Ukraine and the kind of nation the new Ukraine would become dominated Ukrainian spaces in Rome.

A Domestic Worker's Meeting in San Francisco

In San Francisco, the migration narratives Ukrainians told me were strikingly different. Here post-1991 migrants from Ukraine spoke about how "lucky" they were to come to the United States and presented their migration as a "voluntary" exodus.[2] Most were sponsored legally through family reunification visas and later became naturalized U.S. citizens. Migrants spoke, at times sarcastically but mostly emphatically, about coming to "the Promised Land," "the land of opportunity," or simply "America" with all the potential for self-realization and economic betterment the phrases imply.

Like in Italy, migrants I spoke with were domestic workers. One of the regularly organized gatherings for post-1991 migrants in San Francisco were homecare worker union meetings run by Svitlana, herself a Ukrainian migrant. Homecare workers are paid through a California state agency to provide in-home care to low-income elderly and disabled persons.[3] Migrants reported feeling a connection to the U.S. state as "government workers" and described domestic work as a site of integration. I observed this framing during a homecare workers union meeting I attended.

Viktoria gave a presentation in Russian to about 20 people sitting around the table at the Service Employees International Union (SEIU) office on how to vote in the upcoming election for city supervisor. Formerly a literature teacher in Ukraine, Viktoria, 58, blended into this crowd of middle-aged careworkers from the former Soviet Union. In addition to homecare work, Viktoria also worked for the voter registration office during election cycles. As she walked her coworkers through a sample ballot, they lost interest and began chatting in Russian. Yuliana, a large, animated woman with a blond beehive hairdo said with a sparkle in her eye, "Ladies, ladies – oh, excuse me, and gentlemen," winking and smiling at the two men in attendance. "Quiet! This is important. We are government workers for the United States of America. We must learn how to vote!" Viktoria continued, "Yes, Yuliana is right. We are American citizens now, and it is our duty to vote." Galina, a woman in her early 60s, piped up in an exaggeratedly whiny voice, "But Vika,[4] how do we know who to vote for? They all seem the same." Heads nodded and people laughed. "I cannot tell you who to vote for, this is America. Right, Cinzia? Don't say I am not doing my job properly!" Viktoria exclaimed, turning to me. I feigned shock and replied, "Who me? Never!" Viktoria smiled and said, as if relaying a secret, "But I can tell you who our union is supporting." Galina clasped her hands over her chest and looked at the people seated around the large meeting table. She said with a smile, "We must come here [to the union office] to learn how to be Americans! It's not so different [from the Soviet Union]. They still tell us how to vote!" The group erupted into laughter.

★★★★★★★★

On the Shoulders of Grandmothers draws on 160 interviews and two years of ethnographic research I conducted with migrant Ukrainian domestic workers in Italy, California, and their children in Ukraine as well as community leaders. It seeks to answer three questions raised by the contrasting ethnographic experiences illustrated in the above vignettes. First, grandmother-led migrations are both striking and unusual.[5] Why are specifically middle-aged women leaving Ukraine to perform domestic labor abroad? Second, these migrants all have high levels of education, similar economic hardships, and experienced the same "push factors." Why then did migrants in Italy feel they had been "forced" into exile to the Italian "gulag," while migrants in California felt they had left for "voluntary" exodus to the "Promised Land" and how did this impact the behaviors of migrants?[6] Finally, how do migrants in exile to Italy and exodus to California have different effects on Ukrainian nation-state building?

In order to understand why the behavior of migrants at the California union meeting concerned with the rights and obligations of U.S. citizenship differed so drastically from the migrants, whom Tanya called the "*babushki* brigade," that gathered weekly at Italy's Garbatella to discuss their new obligations of Ukrainian instead of Italian citizenship, we must include where migrants came from in our analysis. Therefore, to answer the questions posed above, we must first learn something about Ukraine, specifically its gendered transformation from a socialist economy under the Soviet Union to something resembling a capitalist economy. The next section provides a brief overview of the Ukrainian context in order to situate the contributions of *On the Shoulders of Grandmothers*. Chapter 1 provides a fuller account of how Ukraine became one of the world's top five emigration countries and the genesis of the divergent migrations to Italy and California.

From Soviet to Post-Soviet Ukraine

The Soviet Union or the Union of Soviet Socialist Republics (USSR), established in 1922, was a federal union that grew to encompass 15 republics, including Ukraine, with Moscow as its capital. The Soviet state was the apparatus that governed this federation which spanned West and North Asia, as well as Eastern Europe before it was dissolved in 1991. The Soviet Union had a socialist economy that depended on manufacturing. As a result, the Soviet State needed both men and women in the factories to keep production output high. There was virtually no unemployment in the Soviet Union. In order to achieve near full participation rates for women, the Soviet state provided social benefits including paid maternity leave, free or low-cost childcare, free healthcare, and free higher education. Women had a direct relationship to the Soviet state through subsidies, while men's relationship to the state was vis-à-vis their work category where they were expected to contribute to and lead state enterprises. Men were expected to provide a paycheck to their family, but were otherwise peripheral to family life, because men were not encouraged to participate in childrearing or other domestic tasks.

The Soviet state advocated for gender egalitarianism, although this was never realized. The Soviet state did, however, undermine patriarchal authority in the home to some extent, and installed the state, not individual men, as the head of the Soviet family.[7] The state also made mothering a public service and exalted women as "mother-workers" building socialism alongside men. However, the state did not take on all of women's reproductive labor, leaving women ultimately responsible for childrearing, housework, and wage labor.[8] Thus the socialist economy depended on an extended family household in which young grandmothers, who retired at age 55, were the primary caregivers to children and took care of the home so that young women could participate in the formal labor market.[9] Grandmothers were indeed young because in the Soviet period (as well as in present-day Ukraine) most women expected to have a child between 18–22 years old. This means women in their early 40s are likely already *babushki*. In many cultural contexts, women in their 40s and 50s are not considered "older women," which in Western culture can be perceived as a derogatory term because age, gender, and power intersect to bestow status on older men and disparagement or invisibility on older women. Ukrainian participants, however, embraced both their 40s and grandmotherhood as a life transition in which they thought of themselves as "older women" and their adult children referred to them as the "older generation." Given early retirement ages and relatively low life expectancy (see Conclusion), participants felt they were approaching the end of their professional careers and nearly the end of their lives. The Soviet bodies of my participants often looked older to my and other Westerners' eyes compared to Italian or U.S. bodies of the same age. This is likely the result of the hardships and deprivation many participants reported experiencing under socialism and later the institutional collapse of the Soviet Union. Nevertheless, I will follow the convention of demographers and refer to women in this age group as "middle-aged."

When the Soviet Union was dissolved in 1991, the socialist economy was dismantled, and a newly independent Ukraine opened itself to global capitalism. Three processes occurred simultaneously and intersected to reify young women as mothers and expel many middle-aged women from Ukraine: (1) the reorganization of the economy and labor market according to the adoption of neoliberal capitalist principles; (2) the construction of a new gender order in which women went from "mother-workers" to "housewives" and Soviet extended families moved toward "capitalist" nuclear families; and (3) the rise of *ethnonationalism*, whereby the nation was increasingly defined by a common ethnic heritage, language, and faith, among Ukrainian policymakers and elite.

The previous stability of guaranteed Soviet employment evaporated when Ukraine joined global capitalist markets. Inside Ukraine, unemployment, economic inequality, and poverty rapidly increased in the 1990s during the first decade of independence. Ukrainian women of all ages experienced a loss in livelihood but middle-aged, professional women were particularly affected, because they were concentrated in state-run services and enterprises such as education, healthcare, and scientific research institutes that were shut down or greatly diminished by state collapse.[10] Additionally, post-Soviet discourse constructed market capitalism as "masculine" and fostered an understanding that the limited available jobs were reserved for men who needed to be breadwinners for their families, whereas women should return to the home as wives and mothers.[11]

Just as the socialist economy relied on an extended family unit comprised of "mother-workers," peripheral men, and strong *babushki*, the post-Soviet economy aspired to capitalism and therefore based itself on a new ideal family structure with mother-housewives, father-breadwinners, and absent *babushki*. The American sociologist Talcott Parsons influenced Ukrainian policymakers' conclusion that Ukraine had to transform its family structure and gender relations.[12] Parsons believed that a nuclear family with men and women performing "instrumental" and "affective" roles, respectively, was necessary for the creation of a capitalist economy.[13] Parsons further argued that capitalism required nuclear families with a single breadwinner, because nuclear families were more geographically mobile.

Other family formations with two wage-earners or extended families in which grandparents or other relatives provided childcare were less easy to uproot. Instead, according to Parsons, a nuclear family with one male wage-earner allowed families to move where the best jobs were and provided the flexibility private industry required for economic growth. Therefore, according to Ukrainian nationalism discourse, the Ukrainian state "liberated" women from their Soviet obligation to work and exalted young women for their "biologically determined" role as mothers. As we will see, there was significant variation among respondents who, although forced to engage with this dominant discourse, contested, resisted, accepted, and struggled with this vision of the post-Soviet, ethnic Ukrainian family in their own lives.

Structural changes in the labor market made the discourse of "women returning to the home" appear desirable.[14] Women experienced increased gender discrimination in the labor market, because "business" was constructed as a difficult and even dangerous endeavor unsuited to women in these early days of "Wild West" capitalism plagued by corruption. Additionally, the adoption by the state and elites of neoliberal ideology dramatically reduced state services, such as childcare, that facilitated women's employment in the Soviet era. Anthropologist Nina Glick Schiller defines neoliberalism as:

> a series of projects of capital accumulation that have reconstituted social relations of production in ways that dramatically curtail state investment in public activities, resulting in the reduction of state services and benefits, and the diversion of public monies and resources to develop private service-orientated industries from healthcare to housing.[15]

In Ukraine and the former Soviet Union more broadly, the neoliberal project of divesting in state services and benefits has resulted in the privatization of motherhood and the transfer of responsibility for reproductive labor, once shared with the state, onto the shoulders of individual women.[16]

These changes in the labor market, economy, and family were also supported by Ukraine's urgent process of nation-state building which sought to establish its separation from Russia and the former Soviet Union and legitimize its claims to an independent and ethnically Ukrainian nation and state. In post-Soviet Ukraine, ethnonationalism was articulated in gendered terms. Because of the great diversity within the category "Ukrainian" (see Chapter 1), not all Ukrainians saw Russia as radically different from them. Given Ukraine's long colonial relationship with Russia, still a powerful regional neighbor, this was problematic for establishing an independent Ukrainian state. However, the Soviet Union was so fully discredited as a system after its collapse, that all Ukrainians do agree that they are *not* Soviet.

Perhaps the most condemned aspect of the Soviet Union was its gender order. In post-Soviet discourse, the Soviet Union "distorted" the true biological nature of women and men through policies of gender egalitarianism. The Soviet gender order produced what is now considered an illegitimate family structure of "strong," "masculine" women who neglected familial responsibilities in favor of paid work; "weak," "effeminate" men given to alcoholism and emasculated by controlling wives; and "matriarchal" *babushki* running the extended household. Post-Soviet Ukraine, in its aspirations to be "European" and "capitalist," has instead reified women as housewives and men as breadwinners. Many young women, finding structural obstacles to entering the paid labor market, aspire to fulfill the status ideals of new Ukrainian womanhood by staying home and caring for children or, even if they continue to work, now feel conflicted as they learn from new nationalist discourses that primary childcare is their responsibility and not *babushka*'s.[17]

Therefore, in this new, European, capitalist Ukraine, middle-aged women's jobs have been eliminated or greatly reduced by the collapse of the Soviet state, and young women are now expected to stay home and raise children, previously the anticipated role of *babushki*. As a result, middle-aged women have been *doubly marginalized* from both the labor market and their familial role. However, men's wages remained low and prevented them from supporting their families as breadwinners.[18] *Babushki* realized that their children did not need them to care for grandchildren; they needed money. With their work and family positions eliminated or reduced inside Ukraine, many middle-aged women felt the only way for them to acquire money was to go to work abroad. The lives and experiences of middle-aged women in Western societies inhabit a marginalized position in public imaginaries, and this is compounded in the New Ukraine where the gap between generations is also one between Soviet people (understood as the past) and a younger generation more profoundly shaped by neoliberal capitalism and new Ukrainian nationalisms (understood as the future). Although young sex workers are a small percentage of labor migrants from Ukraine, they receive substantial scholarly and public attention; yet this significantly larger migration of grandmothers by comparison is invisible.[19] Even middle-aged women who remained in Ukraine must nevertheless negotiate this double marginalization and be able to justify to themselves and others why they too were not abroad.[20] For those who emigrated, whether they made their way to Rome or San Francisco was a matter of chance. However, the middle-aged women who led these migrations became part of contrasting *transnational social fields*: exile to Italy and exodus to California.

Peggy Levitt and Nina Glick Schiller define transnational social fields as "a set of multiple interlocking networks of social relationships through which ideas, practices and resources are unequally exchanged, organized, and transformed" and which connects actors across borders.[21] Therefore, transnational social fields include social remittances, which are ideas, behaviors, identities, and knowledge that flow between receiving sending sites; family members who do not migrate but whose lives are deeply transformed by migration; and economic processes that shape the terrain of possibilities for individual actors.[22] However, even scholars who adopt a transnational lens have struggled to delineate the contours of a transnational social field in relation to ethnographic data. Some continue to focus on the structural aspects of the transnational social field, for example focusing on the circulation of bodies between sending and receiving sites.[23] Others, particularly anthropologists, focus on the subjective dimension, arguing that migrants have "transnational imaginaries" that connect them to their homelands even if they never physically return. The first approach risks conceptualizing transnationalism too narrowly and the second too broadly. I propose exile and exodus, as contrasting transnational social fields, to allow us to see the specificity of both the structural dimension as well as the divergent gendered migrant subjects that are building the new Ukraine from the outside in.

Building Post-Soviet Ukraine Transnationally

In 2010, Ukraine had 14.4 percent of its population abroad exceeding both the Philippines and Mexico which had 4.6 percent and 10.7 percent of the total population abroad respectively.[24] Ukraine ranks fifth among top emigration countries.[25] Therefore, migration flows out of Ukraine have material consequences for the trajectory of post-Soviet transformation in Ukraine and the region. In Ukraine, like in many other national contexts, how women behave has both symbolic and structural significance for the nation, and this is heightened in moments of mass emigration.[26] *On the Shoulders of Grandmothers* shows how nation-state building and large-scale economic transformation in Ukraine are produced by the collective actions of individuals acting transnationally. In this context, *gendered migrant subjectivities* are a key site for understanding the production of transnational social fields, nation-state building, neoliberalism, and the workings of global capitalism. For this reason, I present much of the rich ethnographic and interview data through ten narratives that share the experiences of migrants and connects them to the aspirations and trajectories of their family members both in the receiving countries and in Ukraine. Taken together, these narratives illustrate how globalization is produced both from the bottom up inside Ukraine and transnationally from the outside in through migration.

Contexts of Reception in Transnational Social Fields

Migration scholars often study *either* the sending *or* the receiving country.[27] A small but growing literature on sending countries investigates why people migrate and how states manage their population abroad.[28] U.S.-based migration scholars often study receiving countries, particularly the United States, to understand migrant economic, occupational, and political integration. Even those who discuss both "contexts of exit" and "receiving contexts" tend not to analyze them in relation to each other.[29] Rather, once the "push factors" of migration such as poverty or war are mentioned, migration scholars often explain variation in migrant outcomes and experiences by looking at the contexts of reception, which includes the institutional landscape, immigration laws, labor market conditions, and local gender and racial hierarchies of the receiving site.

The contexts of reception are undoubtedly important. They help explain many of the differences between exile to Italy and exodus to California (see Chapters 2 and 4) – but not all of them. Contexts of reception do not explain why middle-aged women are driving the migrations. In fact, scholars use the contexts of reception to explain why most migrants are young women. They note that rising demands for domestic work in wealthy countries is driving the increase in women migrants worldwide and that domestic work is physically grueling, and therefore excludes middle-aged women.[30] Teresa, a Filipina woman in her mid-30s and my contact in one of Rome's domestic workers' unions, found the masses of Ukrainian grandmothers baffling. With a moralizing tone she told me:

> I just don't understand. Lots of the Ukrainian women who come here to care for the elderly look like *they* could use a caregiver! What is wrong with their daughters that they send their elderly mothers abroad to work instead of going themselves? … Filipinas or South American women would never send their mothers.

Teresa and others providing social services to migrants in Italy suggested the reasons must be cultural. However, I uncovered that Ukraine was inserted into *structural* processes of late neoliberal capitalism that constructed this particular generation of women as potential migrants despite conditions in the receiving context that may create preferences for younger women. I also found that in order to explain the unevenness of the process of stage migration to California, the sending country matters, not only for understanding the sending side of migration, but also the receiving side. In approaching my data through a global and transnational lens, I found that the relevant comparison was not between receiving sites.[31] Instead, the transnational social fields of "forced" exile to Italy and "voluntary" exodus to the United States are the central comparison of this book.

Methodological Nationalism and Nation-state building

Migration is often ignored in studies of nation-state building, because we frequently assume that nation-state building is a process internal to a country. This perspective is influenced by what Glick Schiller calls "methodological nationalism" or "an ideological orientation that approaches the study of social and historical processes as if they were contained within the borders of individual nation-states."[32] This narrow frame has erased the role that migration and transnational processes played in the nation-state building processes of Western Europe and the

United States, making it seem they developed modern states and national identities that defined "the people" of the nation within their own territories rather than in relationship to global flows of people and ideas.[33] In fact, many European countries and the United States built industrialized economies with the help of billions of migrants, part of the Great European Migrations of the late nineteenth century, who worked in factories, fields, and mines unimpeded by passport or visa regimes that were largely abolished to facilitate this movement of labor.[34] Migrants also helped shape modern nation-states in these countries.

Today, however, Ukrainian migrants face a world order in which nation-states are understood as "pre-existing" and "natural." For individual migrants and non-migrants, the stakes for nation-state membership have steadily increased at the same time that the barriers to citizenship have also increased. Democratic rights and social benefits are currently tied to individual membership to a nation-state. As a result, the respect and privileges warranted an individual are conflated with membership to a nation-state and its status in the global hierarchy of nations. This often gives migrants, especially those excluded from the political and welfare system of the receiving country, such as Ukrainian migrants in exile to Italy, an urgent personal stake in the nation-state building processes of their sending state and can encourage transnational practices. Poor migrant-sending states frequently also have an increasing stake in fostering ties based on nationalist sentiment among their population abroad. This is because both the sheer percentage of the population of poor migrant-sending states abroad has increased and sending states are increasingly dependent on migrants' monetary remittances as an economic development strategy.[35] These forces intensify the connection between migrants and sending states making a global and transnational analysis that denaturalizes nation-states all the more important.

On the Shoulders of Grandmothers looks at sending and receiving countries as dynamic sites that are interacting with and shaping each other.[36] Gender is a useful idiom for this global and transnational approach precisely because gender is central to articulating and maintaining global economic and cultural systems.[37] Ukraine, the United States, and Italy are connected by large-scale processes of migration and global economic transformations that are fundamentally gendered processes with significant consequence for politics "internal" to Ukraine as well as migrant practices in the receiving countries. I excavate these macro-level processes on the ground through the experiences and subjectivities of migrant domestic workers and their families.

Making Capitalist Subjects through Gendered Migration

The post-Soviet world is a unique site of globalization. With the collapse of the Iron Curtain, global capital, market relations, capitalist moralities, and "Western" ideals flooded into Ukraine and heightened the visibility of global processes on the ground. Scholars studying the region often focus on top-down economic transformations. They study the "transition to capitalism" by looking at elite players such as the "Oligarchs" who are wealthy businessmen with extraordinary political influence.[38] Instead, *On the Shoulders of Grandmothers* studies globalization from the bottom up starting with gendered migrant subjectivities. Yet, how is it possible to extrapolate from subject formation to macro-level processes? And what is a "migrant subject"?

According to Michel Foucault, we are each individuated subjects produced through the specific constellations of power that act upon us.[39] Yet individuals often create identities and engage in behaviors in groups when they are subjected to similar constellations of power that Foucault calls "discourse."[40] For Foucault, discourse is a structured set of statements, rooted in a system of social networks that keep the statements bundled together through repetition so that discourses become truth-making mechanisms. Discourse is power because it creates its own actors or subjects. Following Foucault, Rhacel Parreñas argues that migration is a process of subject formation and that an analysis of subjectivities "moves beneath the structural and institutional bases of social processes to deconstruct their minute effects on the subject."[41] However, through the study of gendered migrant subjectivities, we can also scale up our analysis and follow discourses and relationships of power from the micro-level of individual subjects to the meso-level of social and cultural relations, such as transnational nation-state building, and the macro-level of larger structures, such as the production of neoliberal capitalism.

Neoliberalism is an example of a global discourse that keeps bundled together a set of ideas about the relationship between the state, the economy, the population, and the underlying gender order. Therefore, neoliberalism can similarly shape the beliefs and behaviors of individuals despite varied local histories across world regions.[42] In Ukraine, this shift from socialist to neoliberal economics has also ushered in a new set of moralities. During my fieldwork, many participants explained this idea of subject formation to me in colloquial language by noting that "Soviet" and "capitalist" people had different "mentalities." Ukrainian migrants and their children struggled with these questions about "Soviet" versus "capitalist" subjectivities and their negotiations show how economic structures are tied to family structures and gendered discourses. What an individual must do to be considered a successful and honorable person varies dramatically under socialism and capitalism which have different systems of rewards and punishments and therefore produce contrasting subjects.[43] These new capitalist moralities created painful contradictions for migrants in this study who came of age under the Soviet Union and identified themselves as Soviet people. They worried, therefore, that they lacked the knowledge necessary to teach their children how to be "capitalist" subjects and live economically stable and emotionally fulfilling lives in this new, post-Soviet world.

Young adults I interviewed in Ukraine were also concerned about the production of capitalist subjects. They worried that economic reforms enacted by elites from above, without changing the "Soviet mentality" of the people on the ground, would not be enough to produce a capitalist Ukraine. They wondered how Ukraine could become a capitalist country if its citizens were still Soviet. Twenty-two-year-old Bohdan asserted this view in stark terms over tea in L'viv's city center. He said, "The older generation, they have a Soviet mentality. In order for Ukraine to become a capitalist country, we are waiting for this generation to die." Despite the devaluation of Ukraine's Soviet generation, and middle-aged men are not excluded from this devaluation (see Conclusion), sending some of this generation abroad is accomplishing Bohdan's goal of producing capitalist citizens in an increasingly European Ukraine even though this work and the middle-aged women who perform it are invisible to Bohdan.

Migrants in this study contributed to fundamental structural changes in Ukraine. Simply their physical absence from households, whether it was to go to Italy or the United States, altered the labor market and family structure in Ukraine. It also contributed to the creation of the post-Soviet gender order, which is the basis of Ukraine's ongoing economic transformation. The monetary remittances migrants sent from their labor abroad made it possible for their daughters and daughters-in-law to be or aspire to be stay-at-home mothers to fulfill the new ideals of authentic, ethnic Ukrainian womanhood, even if migrants were often conflicted about the younger generation's rejection of the Soviet fight for gender egalitarianism they held so dear. Migrants often harbored hopes that the younger generation of women would have families with involved husbands *and* fulfilling work lives (see Chapter 1). Simultaneously, remittances allowed their sons to navigate masculinized capitalist markets, which was also fraught with tension (see Chapter 5, Zhanna and Conclusion).

Migrants sent monetary remittances but also social remittances back to Ukraine. Migrants were consciously engaged in processes of subject formation spurred by their migration experiences. Living abroad heightened their awareness of their own "Soviet mentality," and they sought to cultivate a "capitalist self" and "reinvent" themselves in order to help teach their children how to succeed in this new social landscape. Migrants in Italy and the United States with children in Ukraine sent back knowledge about capitalist understandings, practices, and institutions. An examination of gendered migrant subjectivities shows that fundamental institutional change, key to the nation-state building process, was produced through these grandmother-led migrations.

Exile and Exodus: Conceptual Tools

Exile and exodus, as conceptual tools, can be applied to the transnational social fields created by migrations from any country in order to highlight global and transnational processes.[44] They are particularly useful concepts in comparing migrations from a single sending country to multiple destination countries. Exile and exodus are synthesizing concepts that make evident: (1) the link between the structural and experiential dimensions of migration, and (2) the social and institutional infrastructure between sending and receiving countries. These distinct transnational social fields contain both a structural and discursive dimension and span sending and receiving sites. The structural and discursive content of exile and exodus is outlined in Table 0.1.

The structural dimension is descriptive and includes the demographic characteristics of the migrants, citizenship status, the reception migrants experience by the receiving state, and temporal aspects of the transnational social field. The structural dimension is implicated in Ukrainian nation-state building. As we have seen, both exile and exodus helped to transform Ukraine's work and family structures by the physical removal of middle-aged women through migration as well as the social and monetary remittances they send back from labor and learning abroad. Although exodus to the United States produced transnational families living across borders, the ultimate goal of migrants in exodus was to reunite their family in the United States permanently, even if it took years or decades. In contrast, transnational families were built into the structure of exile to Italy. Therefore, exile is constitutive of the transformation from "Soviet," extended family households to "capitalist," nuclear family units. This transnational social field continues to produce, both structurally and discursively, features of a "European" Ukraine.

The concepts of exile and exodus also reveal the subjective dimension of the transnational social field. The intersections of sending and receiving contexts

TABLE 0.1 Comparison of key structural and subjective dimensions of exile versus exodus

		Exile (Italy)	*Exodus (California)*
Structural dimension		1. Middle-aged women (Soviet generation) 2. Individual migration 3. Temporary migrants 4. Exclusion by Italian state	1. Women and men of all ages (led by middle-aged women of Soviet generation) 2. Family migration 3. Permanent migration 4. Inclusion by U.S. state (exclusion by previous waves of Ukrainian migrants)
Subjective dimension		1. Forced connection to sending country 2. Domestic work tied to sending country (Europeanization project) 3. Motherhood discourses: "Prostitutes" and "bad mothers"	1. Connection to sending country was individualized choice 2. Domestic work tied to receiving country (vehicle for integration) 3. Motherhood discourses: "Good mothers" and "Soviet" versus "American" parenting norms

shape which discourses are available and resonate with migrants in transnational social fields. Whether migrants experience their migration as "forced" exile to the post-Soviet "gulag" or a "lucky opportunity" for exodus to the "Promised Land" are discourses specific to each transnational social field and affects the form and intensity of the transnational connections migrants cultivate with the sending country. Although migrants in both transnational social fields were performing cleaning and caring labor to the elderly, the meanings attached to this work were strikingly different. In Italy, migrants saw the knowledge that they learned from living in Italy about being "capitalist" and "European" as a gift they were able to transmit to family members in Ukraine to further Ukraine's Europeanization project. Domestic work was a vehicle for transnational nation-state building. Respondents in the United States, often hired to provide care to the elderly through a state agency, instead saw domestic work as a vehicle for integration not into American culture, but the U.S. state. Nevertheless, those with transnational families also communicated cultural knowledge about capitalism and aspirations to being "Western." Finally, the intersection between sending and receiving sites made different sets of discourses around motherhood available to migrants. Surprisingly, middle-aged women migrants to Italy, rather than celebrated as agents of nation-building, were constructed by the Ukrainian state as "prostitutes" and "bad mothers," whereas those who migrated to the United States were constructed as "good mothers" sacrificing to give their children a better life (see Chapter 1). Migrants both resisted and subjected themselves to these discourses. Comparing these two transnational social fields makes visible the structural and discursive constraints that produce gendered migrant subjects whose collective practices build nations from the outside in and also shape discourses of nationalism in receiving countries.

Metaphors of Destination

"Gulag" and "Promised Land" are metaphors of destination (see Conclusion). My Italian colleagues and the many dedicated Italians I met working to improve the lives of migrant careworkers may take offense at the term "gulag" to describe Italy as a receiving country. Others may feel the metaphor belittles the horrors and loss of life experienced in Soviet-era gulags. Much of the time, the daily challenges for migrants in Italy was not like being in a Soviet gulag. Similarly, given the struggles migrants to the United States described, nor was the United States much like the "Promised Land." Nevertheless, "gulag" and "Promised Land" are the destinations attached to exile and exodus. These are culturally and historically specific metaphors that were both available and deployed by the migrants in this study. As we will see, these metaphors are powerful not because they are true, but because they shaped how migrants framed their relationship to Ukraine as the sending country as well as how they constructed meaning and engaged with institutions in the receiving countries.

Exile to Italy: The "Gulag"

The experiences of Soviet exile were vivid for many of my participants in Rome. Alla, 54, was not unusual in answering my first interview question, "Where are you from?" with her own family's experiences in the Soviet Gulag system. As we sipped tea at a quiet bar in Rome, Alla explained that both her parents were Ukrainian and lived outside L'viv, but her family was exiled to a labor camp in Kazakhstan in 1947. Three years into their exile, Alla was born. Alla recounted:

> One day Ukrainian partisans [freedom fighters seeking independence from the Soviet Union] held a gun to my young brother's head. They told my father either you join us or we kill him. So this was the excuse. We were sent to the gulags [by the Soviet state] because my father was supposedly helping the partisans who wanted a free Ukraine.

When Alla was a young adult, she and her family were able to come out of exile and returned to Ukraine. Alla graduated from L'viv University in chemistry. I was struck by the pain and emotion in her stories about her time in exile. She recounted her family's experiences in the harsh labor camps as if they had occurred yesterday.

In *The Gulag Archipelago,* Alexander Solzhenitsyn argued that the Soviet government could not govern without the threat of exile and that the Soviet economy depended on millions of exiled laborers, like Alla's family, to push policies of rapid industrialization.[45] The Soviet Union was, according to Solzhenitsyn, built on forced exiled labor. Solzhenitsyn further explained that, in an attempt to make sense of exile, these laborers had to come to terms with the moral implications of the gulags for the entire Soviet system and for themselves as Soviet citizens. There are striking similarities between Soviet exile and today's post-Soviet exile to Italy. The new Ukraine is being built, in part, on the labor of exiled migrants and this has similarly produced a moral crisis between Soviet and capitalist systems of honor, rewards, and punishments with which all Ukrainian citizens, and exiled migrants in particular, must come to terms.

Unlike Soviet exile, the current Ukrainian state is not using violence to deport women to Italy. Nevertheless, gendered state-driven processes are pushing middle-aged women out of Ukraine. Alla noted that her daughter finished university when higher education was still free and subsidized by the state. Alla's youngest son was not so fortunate. After his first year, L'viv University instituted tuition, and Alla could not afford to pay. With deep sadness Alla said, "I got down on my knees in front of the director and begged him to keep my son, but in the end he had to drop out." Eventually Alla's husband turned to her and said, "Everyone else is in Italy, why not you?" Alla continued, "Cinzia, I was thinking the same thing. Why them and not me? But I hadn't yet dared to say it out loud." Alla loved her small village outside L'viv, and exclaimed, "I am a Capricorn. I need green! I suffer living in the city." Moreover, like many respondents, she simply never imagined that she would leave her home, children, and grandchildren. Alla said, "I have only left our Ukraine twice: once when my family was sent to Kazakhstan and once when I was sent here [to Rome]. Cinzia, which was worse? I don't know …" One reason why Alla compared Italy with her family's experience of Soviet exile was that, without documents, Alla felt "stuck" in Italy. She was caught between a desire to return home and the knowledge that she would not be able to re-enter Italy where she felt she had no choice but to labor to support her family.

Participants like Alla experienced their migration to Italy as a painful expulsion. Precisely because exile to Italy is constitutive of Ukrainian nation-state building, migrant women in Rome are pulled into a constant and intimate engagement with the gendered meanings and moralities of the "new" Ukraine. Ukrainian migrants in exile to Italy, even those who deviate from the dominant structural position of exile such as men or those who manage to bring their families to Italy, are nonetheless constrained by the structural and discursive realities of this transnational social field.

Exodus to the United States: The "Promised Land"

The narratives of migrants in California suggested experiences of "voluntary" exodus reminiscent of the biblical story of exodus in which Moses led the Israelites, entire families with their livestock, out of bondage in Egypt to the Promised Land. However, in order to settle the Promised Land, the Israelites had to enter into a covenant with God and pledge their faithfulness. This biblical story of exodus resonated with the Ukrainian migrants I spoke with, in part because exodus was the dominant migration narrative of the previous waves of Ukrainian migrants to the United States, making California a significantly different receiving site from Italy.

Two waves of Ukrainians, "Diaspora Ukrainians," who came to the United States in 1940–1956 fleeing the Soviet Union before it solidified during and after WWII, and Soviet Jews, who arrived after 1975, pushed for the liberation of Ukraine and other republics from the Soviet Union. Both groups were important in shaping California's context of reception. WWII Diaspora Ukrainians and their descendants founded organizations whose primary goal was an independent Ukraine and they actively compared the organized Ukrainian Diaspora to the Jewish Diaspora arguing that Ukrainians are an ethnic group that experienced its own Holocaust, a famine-genocide known as the *Holodomor*, under Stalin.[46] Both Diaspora Ukrainians and their descendants, as well as Soviet Jews understood the situation of their compatriots toiling behind the Soviet Union's Iron Curtain as bondage similar to the captivity experienced by the Israelites. Although only two respondents from the San Francisco site identified as Jews (see Chapter 4), this context nevertheless made exodus a framing that resonated with participants in California.

Many countries, including the United States, put up walls to keep people out, but the Soviet Union put up walls to keep people in. By the time the Soviet Union collapsed, the U.S. Immigration and Nationality Act of 1965 had already created a preference system for family members of U.S. citizens. As a result, the visa requests from family members in California to sponsor relatives in Ukraine soared. Post-1991 migrants reported that they were "lucky" to find a relative among the Diaspora Ukrainians and their descendants to sponsor their migration. Often migrants were unable to communicate with these relatives during 40–50 years of Soviet rule. Or they felt "lucky" to have Jewish family members who arrived as refugees but were now able to sponsor non-Jewish family members.

This was how Elena came to San Francisco. Drawing on Soviet-era nationality politics where "Jew" was considered a nationality, Elena explained that she was Ukrainian, but her husband, Dmitri, was a Jew.[47] Dmitri's parents were already in California and able to sponsor him and his family. Elena, a 55-year-old woman with broad shoulders and bright make-up, scowled as she explained how disastrous those years after Soviet collapse were for young children who did not have access to milk or medicine. Elena felt helpless and useless as a medical doctor. "I didn't have enough clothes and food for myself and my children. How could I help my patients?" Buying goods and then selling them at a higher price for profit was a rare and morally reprehensible practice in the Soviet Union. After its collapse, many people in dire economic straits bought items in nearby Turkey or Poland and then sold them for profit in Ukraine in what was called the "shuttle trade."[48] Elena shook her head in disgust as she explained these practices she considered beneath her as a member of the *intelligentsia* (intellectual class) and which were "immoral" under socialism. Elena said:

> Shuttle traders voyaged between countries to buy chewing gum, clothes, or something. And they even earned more money than me, a doctor! … I am not a salesperson. I cannot change my profession and buy something in Turkey and then come back to sell it in Ukraine or Russia. It is too difficult for educated people to make such a moral compromise. And then, as they say, we had a "ticket," a "Jewish ticket" to the land of milk and honey! And we left, all of us who could left.

The very process of exodus, collecting family members in California through the family reunification allotment of U.S. immigration law, requires U.S. citizenship and therefore some identification with the U.S. state. For this cohort of Ukrainian migrants, I discovered that their integration strategy involved creating connections with the U.S. state. This inclusion by the U.S. state through naturalization and homecare work was in direct contrast with the exclusion of Ukrainian migrants by the Italian state. However migrants in California were excluded from the organizations, many with transnational ties to Ukraine, founded by Diaspora Ukrainians who ultimately felt they had little in common with

"Soviet," post-1991 migrants (see Chapter 4). This made it rare for post-1991 migrants to foster transnational connections beyond those with immediate family still in Ukraine. Whereas the transnational social field of exile to Italy was constitutive of Ukrainian nation-state building, the exodus to California had important but less salient effects.

Gendered Global Ethnography

In his call for a "global ethnography," Michael Burawoy argues global processes are necessarily produced in local contexts by specific agencies, institutions, and individuals and therefore, ethnographers can and must study "globalization from below."[49] Global capitalism creates macro-level links between systems of gender inequality that span from receiving to sending countries. Therefore, a global and transnational approach, grounded in feminist ethnography, reveals that people in their everyday negotiations with nationalisms, markets, and moralities are driving Ukrainian nation-state building, economic transformation, and the spread of neoliberalism. *On the Shoulders of Grandmothers* illustrates that global processes are produced in specific locales by the collective practices of individuals who act, think, and construct meaning locally.

Studying Ukrainian Migrants and Their Families

On the Shoulders of Grandmothers is based on extensive ethnographic work and 160 in-depth interviews conducted over two years, 2004–2006, in Rome, Italy; L'viv, Ukraine; and San Francisco, California. I spent six months in Italy and conducted 61 in-depth interviews (51 women and 10 men) with Ukrainian migrants who provided care to the elderly as well as 16 other formal interviews with community leaders including religious leaders and labor organizers. Domestic work was almost exclusively the only work available to middle-aged Ukrainian migrants in Italy. I also spent seven months intensively immersed in the San Francisco field sites. I conducted 41 interviews (34 women and 7 men) with domestic workers from Ukraine providing in-home cleaning and caring services to the elderly as well as two more interviews with local religious leaders. I attended Russian-language union meetings for homecare workers, participated in the parishes of two Ukrainian churches, and attended countless community cultural events.

I kept certain characteristics of my sample of migrant workers in Rome and San Francisco constant. They all left Ukraine after 1991 and, with the exception of a handful of interviews, were between 40–65 years old. This is in line with the overall population of Ukrainian migrants to Italy. Although not every Ukrainian migrant domestic worker in Italy was a grandmother, most were. Ukrainian women migrants in Italy were "predominantly over 50 years of age" and the largest age bracket of Ukrainian migrants to Italy is 50–54 while those over 65 represent 20 percent of the total.[50] There was more age variation in the migration to California because entire families migrated. However, migrant-receiving institutions in San Francisco channeled middle-aged migrants into jobs caring for the elderly, making the San Francisco sample comparable in age and occupation to those interviewed in Rome.[51] All interviewees had some higher education and nearly all had technical or advanced degrees as well as professional work histories. The most common pre-migration professions reported by participants were high school teacher, accountant, and engineer.

Interviews with migrants in Rome and San Francisco were snowball samples and referrals by key informants I gathered following a reflexive model of sociology and with attention to feminist methodologies.[52] Therefore, my samples are not representative of all Ukrainian migrants in these locations, rather they are representative of the two transnational social fields of exile to Italy and exodus to California. I conducted and recorded the interviews, and then had the interviews transcribed in the language of the interview, most often Russian but occasionally Italian. I then translated the interview texts into English myself. The primary language of communication was my American-accented Russian. As a result of Soviet-era Russianization policies that forced non-Russian communities to give up their language in favor of Russian, a considerable proportion of ethnic Ukrainians speak Russian as their main language.[53] I was most concerned that language might be an issue during fieldwork in L'viv, the only region in Ukraine that is predominantly Ukrainian-speaking and in interviews with young people who grew up with Ukrainian as the official language. Yet young people were also fluent in Russian, noting that Russian was the language of television and social media. Several young men noted that Russian and English were the languages of business and of capitalism.[54]

As the U.S.-born daughter of Italian migrant parents, my fluency in Italian also proved vital to the project. My own family's migration story helped me gain access and establish rapport with participants. My mother's jobs included seamstress in Boston's sweatshops, homecare worker, childcare worker, and hairdresser in nursing homes. My father, an agricultural worker and manual laborer in Italy, worked as a landscaper after arriving in the United States. Sharing my parents' labor history reassured participants that I would not disparage their current work, which most experienced as downward social mobility. Fluency in both Russian and Italian allowed me to conduct participant observation in the Italian organizations that represented and provided social services to domestic workers as well as the Ukrainian workers union and the offices of Rome's Russian and Ukrainian language newspaper. I conducted ethnographic work in several Ukrainian Greek Catholic parishes and Rome's Russian Orthodox Church where I attended weekly services, meals, and activities. Three months into my fieldwork, a contested presidential election in Ukraine sparked the Orange Revolution (see Chapter 1). I spent countless hours observing Ukrainians demonstrating in solidarity with the mass protests in Ukraine in addition to attending cultural events and informal gatherings.

Italy and Ukraine were physically connected by a fleet of Soviet-era courier vans and buses that carried goods and workers back and forth. I rode the "migration bus," a three-day ride from Rome to L'viv in Western Ukraine, the region the majority of my respondents were from. I stayed in L'viv for three months and conducted 39 interviews with teenagers and young adults who had one or both parents working abroad as well as with other family members left behind. While in Ukraine, I followed political and media representations of emigration. I completed the migration circuit by taking the three-day bus ride back from L'viv to Rome with Ukrainians heading to Italy to work.

Why Italy and California?

It might seem like a strange choice to compare Italy and California. After all, following Soviet collapse, Ukrainians migrated not only to Italy and the United States, but also to many other countries including Greece, Spain, Portugal, Poland, Russia, and Israel. Excluding Israel which received Ukrainian Jews who are beyond the scope of this project, Italy and the United States were the two top receiving countries of Ukrainian migrants.[55] If Italy is the immigration country in the European Union, then California is the immigration state in the United States. California experienced a large increase in immigration in the decades following Ukrainian independence because larger economic trends such as the privatization of public goods, explosive growth in service-sector jobs, increased workforce casualization, and declines in unionization are changes that came sooner and were more extreme in California than elsewhere in the United States and created a greater demand for cheap, migrant labor.[56] This means that if you are interested in post-1991 Ukrainian migrants, Italy and California are the places to be. The Appendix provides more details regarding the site-selection and the demographics of the two migrations as well as the Ukrainian communities in both receiving sites. As in Italy, Ukrainians and other migrants from the former Soviet Union are filling domestic work positions in numbers disproportionate to their population in California.[57]

Perhaps even more importantly, however, the migrations to Italy and California are the most qualitatively significant inside Ukraine. The migrations to Italy and California are critical to our understanding of Ukrainian emigration because they occupy two different structural positions both historically and vis-à-vis Ukrainian nation-state building.[58] Discussions and debates about these two migrations were central to political discussions inside Ukraine. How the Ukrainian state differently addressed these two migrations (see Chapter 1), highlights the role of migration in the Ukrainian state's attempt to break with its Soviet past and constitute the New Ukraine.

Reframing Migration in a Globalized World

On the Shoulders of Grandmothers makes three key contributions to how we understand the nexus of gender, migration, nation-state building, and globalization. First, although it seems logical to study migration from the vantage point of the places where migrants arrive, this book illustrates that dynamics within the sending country stratify migrants in surprising ways, because not all migrations are treated equally by the sending state. Ignoring the important role that sending countries play, obscures the cultural practices, values, and convictions that animate migrant lives.

Second, this book shines a light on the analytical terrain of transnationalism to show how migrants build nation-states from the outside in. Looking for nation-building processes solely inside the country at the national level, or how nation-states might be constructed between countries at the international level – especially tempting in the Ukrainian case with Russia as such a close and foreboding neighbor – ignores where I suggest most of the action is. The fundamental restructuring of Ukraine's institutions of family, labor market, economy, and even political structures are largely produced at the transnational level. Furthermore, the insight from feminist literatures about intersectionality infuses this discussion of transnational nation-state building. Intersectional approaches to social research suggest that systems of oppression such as race/ethnicity, class, gender, age, and sexuality interlock to shape the experiences of individuals. In this book, I take this intersectional approach to gendered migrant subjectivities and apply it not only to individuals, but to relations between national institutions inside Ukraine, transnationally between nations, and in relation to global processes.

Finally, by applying the methods of gendered global ethnography, which takes for granted the centrality of historically marginalized groups in the making of global processes, *On the Shoulders of Grandmothers* allows us to see how globalization is produced from the bottom up. Globalization can seem like a disembodied force in which we as individuals have no part.[59] The social inequality produced by these processes is indeed complex. Yet the approach of gendered global ethnography helps us see that the inequities created by globalization are made by individuals and therefore, through the collective actions of individuals, can be undone or redone to decrease social inequality.

Overview of Book

Part 1 of the book, Genesis, includes Chapter 1 with a close look at post-Soviet Ukraine and its new nationalisms. I show that Ukraine's opening up to neoliberal market reforms is a gendered process that has implications for how the institutions of work and family are organized and for a "capitalist" (as opposed to "Soviet") moral order. These large-scale national, transnational, and global processes become understandable to individuals through a gendered language of motherhood and result in the marginalization of middle-aged women, most *babushki*, who lead the migrations to both Italy and the United States.

Part II of the book focuses on "forced" exile to Italy. In Chapter 2, I describe Italy's context of reception with a focus on immigration laws, the position of domestic work in the Italian labor market given the "care crisis" for the elderly, and the local organizational landscape that shaped migrants' experiences in Rome. The Italian state's policies of exclusion contributed to making transnationalism a salient characteristic of exile. In order to uncover the gendered migrant subjectivities produced in exile and how these migrants were building the new Ukraine transnationally, I provide five ethnographic narratives in Chapter 3. Each narrates the experiences of a migrant in exile to Italy and that of their family. Together these narratives highlight three key themes. First, migrants actively attempted to learn to be "capitalist" and "European" subjects and transmitted this knowledge to their children in Ukraine. Second, both migrants and the Ukrainian state articulated the struggle around migration and nation-state building on the gendered discursive terrain of reified motherhood and failed masculinities with consequences for both migrants and their children in Ukraine. Finally, exile contributes to the ongoing production of a "traditional" nuclear family in Ukraine – a stark contrast to the extended Soviet family. Gendered discourses about appropriate behaviors for women and men in nuclear families become the "building block" of ethnicity and nation and the basis for a reorganization of the labor market. As a result of these shifts in work and family structures, many middle-aged women were painfully pushed out of their families as well as their country to labor abroad.

Part III, Exodus, begins with Chapter 4 on the context of reception in California. I present U.S. federal immigration laws, the role of the state of California in organizing carework, and the community organizations that affected the experiences of Ukrainian migrants in California. I show that U.S. policies of inclusion encouraged a discourse of "luck." Migrants attempted to collect family members in California in a context where anyone could "win" the Green Card Lottery or be next in line for family reunification. For middle-aged women migrants, this produced a state-based integration strategy. To explain both the gendered migrant subjectivities and practices produced in exodus and their relationship to transnational nation-state building, I provide five narratives of migrants and their families that highlight three dimensions of exodus to California in Chapter 5. First, middle-aged women migrants rejected the Ukrainian state as a "bad provider" and cultivated a personal connection to the U.S. state as their new "husband-provider." Those who had children in Ukraine sent back both monetary and social remittances about capitalist subjectivities and aspirations. Next, the adult children of these migrants in the United States learned to be "capitalists" through market-based integration into American life. This, coupled with a politics of exclusion practiced by the previous wave of Ukrainian migrants and their descendants, led the adult children of migrants to disassociate from other migrants from the region. Third, even the few undocumented individual migrants in exodus whose families are in Ukraine were shaped by the dominant discourse of "luck" and family reunification in exodus.

In the Conclusion I highlight women's contributions to Ukrainian nation-state building, both during the Euromaidan protests of 2013–2014 inside Ukraine and as migrants building Ukraine from the outside in. Women's contributions to nation-state building are made visible though the "bottom up" approach of gendered global ethnography, which takes gendered migrant subjectivities as its starting point. I also describe the painful implications of the intersection of gendered neoliberalism and nationalism for men across generations both inside Ukraine and as migrants. The stakes for accurately understanding Ukrainian emigration, nation-state building, and post-Soviet economic transformation are higher than ever. In the current context of a Ukrainian–Russian war, these stakes include the redrawing of the map of Europe.

PART I

Genesis: Ukraine

FIGURE I.1 L'viv's city center.
Photograph by the author.

FIGURE I.2 Just outside the center square, women and some men come from the
surrounding villages to sell fruits and vegetables on the sidewalks
Photograph by the author.

1

MARKETS, MORALITIES, AND MOTHERHOOD IN TRANSITION

Yulia Tymoshenko, a co-leader with Viktor Yushchenko of the Orange Revolution and Prime Minister of Ukraine from January to September 2005 and again from December 2007 to March 2010, is a key figure in Ukrainian politics. As part of her second bid for prime minister in 2007, Tymoshenko made a documentary titled *Mother and Step-Mother* which was widely viewed inside Ukraine. In it Tymoshenko argues that Ukraine has been a "bad mother" to its people who have had to seek nurturing and sustenance in the arms of "step-mother" Italy. Walking through the streets of Naples, Italy, Tymoshenko speaks with Ukrainian domestic workers about their lives and informs viewers that 5–7 million Ukrainians are forced to search for work abroad and 3–4 million Ukrainians are working in Italy.[1]

The documentary opens with Tymoshenko, dressed in a flowing white dress, standing on a windy hilltop overlooking the Ukrainian countryside and leaning on a large white cross, a burial marker. The scene recalls a famous Ukrainian short story, *The Stone Cross* (1900) by Vasyl' Stefanyk, detailing a father's tortured decision to immigrate to North America with his wife and adult children. The father leaves a white stone cross for his fellow villagers to remember him and his family by. Staring poignantly into the camera, Tymoshenko says, "If every person who has left for a foreign country set a stone cross today, all of Ukraine would look like a cemetery." In a symbolically powerful move, Tymoshenko revives the image of the stone cross from Ukraine's Great Migrations of the 1880s and applies it to the mass emigration of the current post-Soviet period. It is no coincidence that Tymoshenko's focus is on Ukrainian migration to Italy which came to include what my participants call "the masses" in the mid to late 1990s. In the post-Soviet era, women who migrate without their families to Italy and to a lesser extent migrant women who take their families with them to California, are Ukraine's "cross to bear."

When families migrate, scholars and policymakers tend to consider men the "migrants." Women and children in the family are labeled "dependents" and garner less attention. However, much negative attention is paid to the individual migration of women, especially mothers who leave children behind. In public and even academic discourse, explaining the migration of mothers without their children is fraught with moralism. There are many reasons considered sensible for why men might migrate and leave children behind, but for many of us in wealthy countries, abject poverty seems to be the most frequently offered explanation for why mothers would "abandon" their children.[2] Looking closely at the socio-economic changes occurring in Ukraine since the collapse of the Soviet Union and the connections between Ukraine and its receiving countries challenges some of the basic assumptions we have about why women migrate and further explains how migrants construct narratives to make sense of their lives and those of their children and grandchildren.

Notions of motherhood and grandmotherhood are intimately connected to the gendered subjectivities of individuals and are often used in public discourse as a language for making national and international relations understandable.[3] In her documentary, Tymoshenko uses the language of motherhood to explain why people are migrating: the Ukrainian motherland is unable to care for her children. It also explains Italy's relationship to Ukraine: a wealthy "step-mother" can provide money to its Ukranian step-children but cannot nourish the soul as only a "true mother" can. The economics of creating post-Soviet markets is also made palatable through changes in gender expectations for men and women but most significantly for mothers and grandmothers. Market changes in Ukraine also signify a change in the moral order. What one does to gain honor and success is different in a socialist versus a market-based economy.[4] One of the legacies of Soviet socialism in Ukraine is a "moralizing lens" through which to evaluate wealth and consumption practices.[5] After a Soviet state-driven ideology that celebrated unity and collectivism, Ukraine now wrestles with competing notions of morality concerned with balancing individual and collective interests in the pursuit of wealth. The participants in this study struggled with whether the increasing economic and social inequality was a morally justifiable price to pay for the "bright future" market capitalism claims to offer. Therefore, changes in markets, moralities, and motherhood are closely intertwined in Ukraine. The language of motherhood is used by the state and individual actors to articulate what these changes mean for the everyday practices of persons seeking an honorable livelihood in a context of mass emigration and a post-colonial struggle for independence through nation-state building.

When Ukraine gained its independence in 1991, it faced many challenges. Perhaps the most salient was first, constructing a national identity that constituted Ukrainians as a people separate from Russians and gave them legitimate claims to a territory governed by Ukrainians. The second was opening to world markets and the imperative for economic transformation. Nation-state building and the move toward market capitalism in Ukraine were gendered processes with different effects across generations.[6] I found that Ukrainian nation-state building hinges on a particular construction of Ukrainian femininity that reifies young mothers and devalues middle-aged, "Soviet" women. The intersection of neoliberalism, capitalism, and Ukrainian nationalism discredited the Soviet gender order in which an extended family with mother-workers, peripheral fathers, strong *babushki*, and the Soviet State at its head supported a labor-intensive, manufacturing-heavy socialist economy. The post-Soviet gender order, characterized by a neoliberal retreat of the state, asserts that a nuclear family with mother-housewives, father-breadwinners, and a much truncated role for *babushki* is necessary for the economic transition to capitalism and for Ukraine's eventual entrance into the European Union. However, low wages for men and limited opportunities for women's employment means that many *babushki*, doubly marginalized from the labor market and their position in the family, are "forced" out of Ukraine to help their families and their country. The monetary and social remittances sent by middle-aged women laboring abroad makes possible the nuclear family, the transformation of the labor market, and the withdrawal of state services that together form the bedrock of Ukrainian nation-state building.

In this chapter I take an in-depth look at Ukraine's nation-state building and economic transformations since Ukraine's independence, as well as the resulting double marginalization of middle-aged women that is the genesis of exile and exodus. I first explain the emigration context in Ukraine where the three rings of the nation-state[7] – people, government, and territory – are all in dramatic flux even as processes of nation-state building attempt to fuse them together. Next I turn to the rise of neofamilialism in post-colonial Ukraine embodied in the rise of *Berehynia*, a symbol of ethnically pure, family-centered, Ukrainian womanhood. I show that the accompanying new expectations for mothers and grandmothers as well as fathers creates a painful gap between new gender ideals tied to social rewards and the material realities of most individuals' lives that prevent them from attaining those ideals. Finally, I ground the intersections of markets, moralities, and motherhood in the experiences of three individuals located in Ukraine, but who are also part of the transnational social fields of exile and exodus.

Contested Nationalisms: One People, one Government, one Territory

The dissolution of the Soviet Union in 1989 left Ukraine suddenly independent in 1991 and in a state of economic collapse. The decline in gross domestic product over the 1990s was calculated at 54 percent, worse than Russia at 40 percent, and twice as severe as the general estimate for economic decline in the United States during the Great Depression of the 1930s; not until 2000 did Ukraine experience positive economic growth.[8] However of equal if not more pressing urgency was that Ukraine became a political entity without a unified nation in a fraught post-colonial context.[9]

One People: Eastern versus Western Ukrainians

Forging a single people with a national identity has been highly contentious in Ukraine. Even while nearly 80 percent of the population identifies itself as Ukrainian, a substantial 17 percent identify as Russians.[10] Yet there is great regional, ethnic, religious, and historical diversity within the category "Ukrainian." Although an oversimplification, we can think of Ukraine as bifurcated between "Ukrainianized" Ukrainians in Western Ukraine and "Russified" Ukrainians in Eastern Ukraine.[11] I saw animosity between Eastern and Western Ukrainians over questions of culture, language, and religion play out in my fieldwork. I often heard Western Ukrainian participants dismiss Easterners as "lost Ivans," more Russian than Ukrainian, who had to be taught their own forgotten Ukrainian language and culture. Eastern Ukrainians I met in my fieldwork retorted that Russian *is* a language of Ukraine and were insulted by accusations that they were not "real" Ukrainians.[12] Some Eastern Ukrainian participants argued that Western Ukrainians were "more like Poles" than Ukrainians and dismissed Westerners as "radical nationalists." They explained their preference for the Russian language by noting that Ukrainian was a "peasant" language for uneducated and uncultured people, and many noted they had never bothered to learn it.[13]

Western Ukraine did not become part of the Soviet Union until 1936 and possessed a well-developed Ukrainian ethnic identity, whereas ethnic Ukrainians in the East and South, part of the Russian empire for 300 years, did not develop the same "sense of ethnic and national identity anchored in culture, language, religion, and historical memories."[14] Once Western Ukraine became part of the Soviet Union, it was subjected to an often violent Russianization campaign, but a struggle for an independent Ukraine was maintained abroad and underground in the region. One of the organizations driven underground was the Ukrainian Greek Catholic Church (UGCC).[15] Under Polish rule, the UGCC became a stronghold of Ukrainian religious and cultural identity and has long championed the creation of an independent Ukrainian state.[16] Today the UGCC continues to be an important player in Ukrainian nation-state building and is a significant presence in both Rome and San Francisco.[17]

It comes then as no surprise that Western Ukraine overwhelmingly supports distancing Ukraine from Russian power and champions becoming part of Europe by joining the European Union and NATO (North Atlantic Treaty Organization). By contrast Eastern and Southern Ukraine emphasizes Ukraine's cultural and historical affinity with Russia and favors maintaining close political ties to Russia. Although a majority of citizens in all regions of Ukraine, including those in the East, voted for independence in 1991, Western Ukrainians together with elements of the elite in Kyiv, have been the architects of Ukrainian independence and seek to create unity around a singular national narrative about Ukraine's ancient origins, linear historical trajectory, and distinct cultural characteristics that justify claims to independent statehood. There are proponents for a Ukraine that is multi-ethnic and multi-lingual, but these discussions also include the idea of an "ethnic core."[18] Galician nationalism with its stronghold in Western Ukraine suggests that a Ukrainian nation unified by a Ukrainian ethnicity, language, and religion was torn from its European roots by Russian imperialism.[19] This ethnonationalist version of Ukrainian nationhood is not universally accepted in Ukraine where there are competing nationalisms. However, Galician nationalism has been adopted by the organized Ukrainian Diaspora and by many political elites within Ukraine perhaps because this ethnonational imagining makes the strongest claim to Ukrainian independence.[20] In order to acquire international recognition for Ukrainian statehood, Ukraine had to establish its separateness from Russia and embarked on an uneven process of Ukrainianization after independence.[21] This involved promoting the Ukrainian language, replacing Russian narratives about Ukraine's history in textbooks, and constructing Ukraine's national symbols.[22]

One Government and One Territory: Pro-Europe versus Pro-Russia

These divisions about what policies Ukraine should have toward Russia and toward Europe have resulted in highly fragmented and weak governments.[23] Ukraine's internal divisions fuel the Russian state's claims that Ukrainians and Russians are in fact one people and should therefore be one territory.[24] The contested presidential election of 2004 that led to the Orange Revolution and President Viktor Yushchenko's government is a premier example. The two leading presidential contenders were Viktor Yushchenko, who campaigned on a "pro-West" platform, and the "pro-Russia" Viktor Yanukovych backed by Russian president Vladimir Putin and Ukraine's incumbent president Leonid Kuchma. November election results declared Yanukovych the winner; however, evidence of fraud led to mass protests in Kyiv's Independence Square where orange-clad protesters (Yushchenko's campaign color) camped out in the snow. A new round of voting was ordered in January 2005. Yushchenko, with the support of Yulia Tymoshenko and her political party, won the majority vote with just 52 percent. Yushchenko declared that the peaceful Orange Revolution showed the world a "genuinely different Ukraine ... a noble European nation, one that embraces democratic values."[25] On the other hand, the Orange Revolution also revealed a deeply divided population with Yushchenko winning overwhelmingly in Western Ukraine and in most of Central Ukraine and Yanukovych winning in the heavily Russified eastern and southern regions.[26]

The Orange government with Yushchenko as president and Tymoshenko, "Goddess of the Revolution," as prime minister proved too weak to realize many of the expectations of the revolution. The following Ukrainian presidential election of 2010 saw a runoff between Tymoshenko and the pro-Russia Yanukovych and highlighted once again the divide between East and West.[27] The result was a Yanukovych victory. Yet, popular protests called *Euromaidan*, with thousands of demonstrators calling for closer relations with Europe and the European Union, ousted Yanukovych in February 2014.[28] The promise of Europe – economic stability, political accountability, and a capitalist moral order – looms large in Ukrainian nation-state building. "European" also offers a supranational identity, much the way "Soviet" did in the past, to a diverse population struggling to find unity and protect their geographic boundaries under threat from Russia.[29]

Russian elites continue to deny Ukrainian independence and instead argue that Ukraine is part of Russia.[30] In April 2008, Putin described Ukraine as an "artificial" entity with lands given to it by Russia and the USSR and a "failed state" that needs Russian oversight.[31] Ukraine's former ambassador to the United States, Yuriy Shcherbak, responded by stating that Russia's state-orchestrated ideological campaign against Ukraine is "ideological-propaganda preparation of a future operation for the seizure of the territory of a sovereign state."[32] Nevertheless, Western powers were taken by surprise when Russia annexed the Southern Ukrainian territory of Crimea in March 2014.

We cannot understand why Soviet legacies have left Ukrainian national identity, its government, and even the country's borders ill-defined when such entities are traditionally both more clearly established and fused together in modern nation-states without examining the gender relations that underlie Ukraine's post-Soviet transformation. A fuller account of the transition from the Soviet gender order to the post-Soviet gender order allows us to see how nation-state building occurs from the bottom up, enacted by the collective decisions of individuals living inside Ukraine, and from the outside in, by the collective decisions of Ukraine's post-1991 migrants abroad.

The Gendered Economics of Socialism in the Soviet Union

The Soviet state needed full employment to meet production quotas in a labor-intensive, production-based socialist economy. To facilitate the employment of women and "liberate" women from the "triple burden" of housework, mothering, and wage work, the Soviet state socialized aspects of reproductive labor and provided maternity benefits, state-run childcare facilities, and collective dining halls.[33] As a result, the state made a direct alliance with women as primary beneficiaries of these state services, and motherhood was constructed as a public service.[34] Therefore, mothers had a direct relationship through subsidies to the Soviet state. The Soviet state found traditional patriarchy, the idea that every man was a "little tsar" in his own home, as a barrier to the state's influence on individual family members.[35] Therefore the state usurped certain patriarchal functions and responsibilities and eliminated men's legal authority over wives and children. With the exception of offering a paycheck, men were relegated to the periphery of family life.[36] Therefore, women became dependent, not on individual men, but on the state; indeed women were "married to the state."[37] Wives were supposed to control their husbands because, according to the state, men were "weak."

Men, deprived of patriarchal authority, were supposed to find self-realization in work linked to the development of the Soviet state.

True gender equality was never achieved in the Soviet labor market. Women rarely achieved top level jobs, were channeled into sex-segregated occupations, and earned lower wages than men.[38] Nevertheless, work was also important to women's identities. Women achieved near full participation rates in the labor force, but, although the Soviet state did take on some of the burdens of reproductive labor, women continued to take primary responsibility for the home as well as perform wage labor.[39] The Soviet state relied on youthful retirement ages so that middle-aged and older citizens, especially grandmothers, became responsible for rearing their grandchildren and performing other unpaid household labor, thus creating an extended family household.[40] As a result, a particular gendered understanding of the relationship between men and women and women and the state, driven by the economic need for women's employment, not only made "mother-workers" a structural reality, but was accompanied by state discourses that exalted gender egalitarianism and mother-workers as Soviet "heroes."[41] However, with the collapse of the Soviet Union, the socialist economy was dismantled and with it this Soviet gender order.

The Gendered Economics of Capitalism in the New Ukraine

The opening to capitalist markets in Ukraine in the 1990s resulted in widespread unemployment estimated at over 9 percent in 2003.[42] This number is likely an underestimate because of large numbers of unregistered or underemployed workers. For that same year, 38 percent of Ukraine's population was living below the poverty line.[43] Not only was this a shock for a people used to full employment during the Soviet era, but unemployment is now understood as a gendered issue. Since Ukrainian independence, gender inequality has increased. Top management and executive positions are overwhelmingly male-dominated, sex segregation of the labor market has increased, and women currently earn wages 30 percent lower than men.[44] Women face considerable gender discrimination in Ukraine's expanding free market: job advertisements that ask only young, attractive women apply, sexual harassment at work, and discrimination in hiring have been well documented.[45]

According to the 2013 World Development report, women's labor market participation rates in Ukraine are 63.5 percent of working-age women compared to 69.3 percent of working-age men; this is higher than the European average of working-age women which is 58.5 percent.[46] Nevertheless, in Ukraine, women have fewer working hours than men even when employed, less access to better paying jobs, a significant motherhood penalty, and lower quality of life after retirement.[47] The report concludes that young women in particular have become less active in their job search efforts due to household and care responsibilities and state policies and discourses that encourage women to stay home.[48]

The neoliberal project of divesting from state services and benefits has resulted in the privatization of motherhood and the transfer of responsibility for reproductive labor, once shared with the state, to individual women.[49] For example, the number of state-subsidized childcare facilities has drastically declined due to budget cuts and they have not been replaced with private sector options.[50] The transformation of the workplace from state-run to private industry has forced women who can no longer rely on the state for childrearing support to take substantial time out of the labor market.[51] In an economic system based on competition, women assigned extra familial responsibilities by dominant gender discourses seem both unreliable and too expensive to employ by private companies.[52]

In the current era of global capitalism, the Ukrainian state concluded that it could not be competitive and continue to provide the level of social services made available by the Soviet state, especially when that same labor is called "housework" and provided for free by women in most capitalist countries.[53] It is then not surprising that the ideal of the private, patriarchal family with women economically dependent on husbands and primarily responsible for raising children is being rehabilitated in Ukraine and across the post-Soviet region.

The Rise of Neofamilialism: An Imagined "Return" to a Traditional Family Structure

The consensus in the region is that women have been "too empowered" by Soviet policies, and that they occurred at the expense of men.[54] General Secretary Mikhail Gorbachev famously argued, shortly before Soviet collapse, that many of the Soviet Union's problems could be attributed to women's employment, which resulted in "weak families." He called for women to recommit themselves to their duties as wives and mothers and "return to their purely womanly mission." Gorbachev wrote:

> Many of our problems … are partially caused by the weakening of family ties and a slack attitude to family responsibilities. This is a paradoxical result of our sincere and politically justified desire to make women equal with men in everything.[55]

In post-Soviet discourse, gender relations are one of the fundamentals Soviet thinkers "got wrong."[56] In post-Soviet discourse, the way to deal with Ukraine's unemployment problem is to send women "back to the home where they belong."[57] It suggests that Soviets were "enemies of nature" by trying to force humans to act contrary to their biologically determined, gendered nature, and thus created "weak" men and "masculine" women. Socialist paternalism and women are now jointly accused of having destroyed the Ukrainian ethnonation (almost extinct due to low birth rates), the national character, and "traditional" national values.[58] The Ukrainian state criticizes "Soviet" one-child families for causing "egocentrism and communication problems" and instead encourages two-parent families with three or four children by suggesting that large families are an ethnically Ukrainian trait.[59]

According to survey data, most Ukrainian respondents believe 18–21 years old is the ideal time for women to marry, and most expect women to have their first child between 18–22 years old.[60] Although the already low fertility rate declined in the first decade after independence from 1.8 in 1991 to 1.1 in 1999, the decline was due to a drop in second births and not a reduction in the number of women becoming mothers (and grandmothers) because almost all Ukrainian women have a child in their early 20s.[61] The low fertility rate led the Ukrainian state to launch a campaign to increase birth rates and glorify motherhood to "save the ethnonation" through population growth among ethnic Ukrainians. They have focused on rural areas where the state believes traditional culture has been better preserved, and therefore women are more likely to produce children who are "bearers of authentic Ukrainian identity."[62]

While women are to focus on being mother-housewives, young men are expected to fill the void left by the state and become patriarchal heads of family as well as breadwinners. Women also seek to re-engage men in family life, although for women the return to patriarchy means men taking responsibility for the home and not necessarily men's interpretation of men as breadwinners whose word is law.[63] With the construction of market capitalism as "masculine," and the exclusion of women who were no longer seen as an essential part of the work-force, market reforms were supposed to raise the economic welfare of families by making possible the one-earner family where the earner was a man.[64] In post-Soviet discourse, this ideal Ukrainian family with a mother-housewife and a father-breadwinner as exemplary of the "natural" order between the sexes would be the basis of the "modern" and "Western" Ukrainian nation. In popular discourse this is framed as a "return" to the housewife–breadwinner family structure of Ukraine's pre-Soviet past. However, in reality, the family structure of man as provider and woman as homemaker never existed in Ukraine in the first place.[65] Ukraine was an agricultural society and women largely worked alongside men in the fields until the communist push for industrialization where women performed wage work. Nevertheless, this imagined "return" to a traditional patriarchal family structure and the rise of neofamilialism have become part of nationalist and religious discourses in Ukraine.[66]

The Other "Post": Post-Colonialism

A focus on family structure and the social position of women in particular as tied to ethnonational identity is due in part to Ukraine's post-colonial context.[67] The post-colonial condition heightens the necessity of the nation-state construct for political and cultural survival, and thus makes the terrain of culture and national identity a privileged terrain of struggle.[68] In other instances of colonialism such as India or Africa, post-colonial countries often have clear ethnic/racial lines dividing colonizer and colonized around which to forge identities and resistance. This is not the case in Ukraine. Not all Ukrainian citizens can passionately agree that Ukraine is radically separate or culturally distinct from Russia. However, all can emphatically agree that Ukraine is NOT Soviet. As a result, Ukrainianess is defined against all things Soviet and the Soviet gender order is perhaps what is most reviled. Just as Ukraine struggles to find a unifying rhetoric of what it is *not*, so too does it seek for a unifying rhetoric of what Ukraine *is*. I assert that this nation-affirming rhetoric of nationalism and economic transformation is expressed in gendered terms.

Gendered Nationalism: Berehynia *Symbol of Family and Nation*

Women's organizations multiplied in Ukraine during the early 1990s. Activist women were divided between those who promoted maternalist activism drawing on pre-existing Soviet discourses and those advocating for the kind of "Western" feminist activism supported by international women's groups that were well represented in Ukraine.[69] Those who drew on Soviet maternalist discourse and made it "Ukrainian" sought to engage women as "activist mothers" in politics by drawing on the imagery of *Berehynia*, an ancient pagan goddess associated with the idea that Ukraine was and is matriarchal.[70] In present discourse, *Berehynia* was retooled and women as *Berehyni* (plural of *Berehynia*) became guardians of both the Ukrainian family and nation.[71] *Berehynia* is the "perfect Ukrainian woman" and "ideal mother" and is also credited with preserving the Ukrainian language and national identity despite Soviet rule.[72] Like ordinary Ukrainian women, *Berehynia* is strong but committed to maternal duties, independent but family-oriented and respectful of husbands. She symbolizes a pre-Soviet and distinctly Ukrainian national culture in which Ukrainian men and women had separate responsibilities but were equally respected. In nationalism discourse, it is this respect accorded to women for their "separate responsibilities" that makes women as *Berehyni* "matriarchs." This is important because, despite the privatization of patriarchal nuclear families, the Ukrainian state must be "progressive" on gender issues in order to be considered "modern" and "European" in the international arena.

Under Ukraine's President Leonid Kuchma (1994–2005), politicians borrowed from the *Berehynia* discourse, praising women as guardians of the Ukrainian nation while ignoring their policy demands.[73] This wave of women's rights organizations was unable to develop enough political leverage to push forward either a Western-inspired or a maternalist rights agenda. In fact, many activists, especially in university-rich Western Ukraine, believed that the struggle for women's rights should be put on hold while they joined forces with other political groups to first fight for Galician nationalism and stabilize Ukrainian independence, and only then attend to social justice issues for women.[74] The belief that constructing institutions such as family, labor markets, and the post-Soviet economy are gender neutral and women's rights could be fought for at a later date was perhaps a lost chance for instilling gender equality as part of Ukrainian institution-building. Gender, nationalism, and economic transformation in Ukraine have nonetheless become inextricably linked, but gender inequality was embedded in the structure of key social institutions and the national definition of authentic Ukrainianess.

It is not only Ukrainian women who were called to embrace new ethnically "Ukrainian" norms. Men had new moral rules as well. The state asked young Ukrainian men to reject the "weak" and "effeminate" position of their Soviet fathers, reclaim their masculinity through breadwinning, and take back from the state their rightful place as patriarchal heads of family. Middle-aged working-class men struggled to come to grips with the declining prestige of old-style male jobs, especially the disappearance of manufacturing work. The more lucrative post-Soviet jobs are now connected with trade or computer programming, which are not seen by Soviet-generation men as "worthy of 'real men'."[75] One migrant respondent in Italy showed me his callused hands saying, "These hands have worked! My son [in Ukraine] sits in front of a computer all day. How can that be work? How can he earn that way? I do not understand." These men grew up believing that work in heavy industry was a "noble calling." Soviet morality which disparaged trade as a capitalistic, parasitic venture was deep-rooted for middle-aged men. For professional men, the declining value of scientists or academics in favor of being a business man was also difficult to accept. Masculine professional identities developed under communism, which included being professional, noble, and honest, "have become an obstacle to success in the transition period."[76] Since men's status at work was key to their overall identity at home and among peers, a fall in work status was a severe blow to individual men.

Although post-Soviet gender discourses for men are important and affect young men and middle-aged men differently (see Conclusion), in the gendered narrative about Ukraine's national identity, it is "our women" that make Ukrainians *Ukrainian*. *Berehynia*'s image is ubiquitous from her statue atop a 40-foot-tall column that has replaced the statue of Lenin in Kyiv's Independence Square – the events of the Orange Revolution unfolded under her outstretched arms – to Tymoshenko's peasant plait which none too subtly associates her with Ukraine's national goddess.[77] The particular iteration of maternal femininity embodied by *Berehynia* bridges the divide between Eastern and Western Ukrainians. *Berehynia*'s power as a discourse of gendered nationalism lies in part in her repudiation of the Soviet gender order and its "unnatural" gender relations. She is mother of all Ukrainians and a symbol of an independent Ukraine that Ukrainians from east to west can embrace. *Berehynia* unites Ukrainian citizens who perhaps cannot agree on Russia as "Other" but can agree that Ukraine is *not* "Soviet."

Babushka's Double Marginalization

Despite Ukrainian policymakers' belief that transportable nuclear families with a single male wage-earner are required by a capitalist economy, the new Ukrainian family formation embodied by *Berehynia* did not happen spontaneously with capitalism. Men were left with the expectation by both the state and individual women that they will retake their place as the heads of family and breadwinners. Yet men found their wages were simply not high enough to support their families on their own.[78] In order to produce Ukrainian women as *Berehyni* and Ukrainian men as breadwinners, the money to supplement men's incomes had to come from somewhere else. Young women saw their wage-earning potential decline and opportunities on the labor market contract, while their value for their role in nurturing children and husbands as *Berehyni* expanded. Middle-aged, highly educated women, many *babushki*, who contributed wages to the family in the past, were especially hard hit by state collapse, because they were clustered in state-run enterprises such as education, healthcare, and scientific research and, once they lost these jobs found they were marginalized from the labor market.[79] Middle-aged women watched their sons and sons-in-law struggle to support their families and their daughters and daughters-in-law increasingly become under-employed or stay home to care for children full-time. *Babushki* were therefore marginalized from both their work and their expected role of providing primary care to their grandchildren. Participants reported that this *double marginalization* made them "feel useless at home." They explained that they still felt they must contribute to their families and the most helpful thing they could do was to migrate and send back money from their labor abroad.

Nearly all of the Ukrainian migrants I spoke with in Rome and California were university-educated professionals who asserted that they never imagined they would go abroad to work. Rather, they expected to finish careers, retire, and raise their grandchildren. In Soviet Ukraine, women with young children were expected to be students or workers while their mothers as *babushki* cared for their grandchildren, did the housework, and stood in bread lines, thus freeing their daughters and daughters-in-law for the labor market.[80] The migrant women I met in Rome and San Francisco, raised in the Soviet Union, expressed deep ambivalence both about Ukraine's new gender order and about the kind of lives their migration and remittances made possible for their daughters and sons in Ukraine aspiring to be housewives and patriarchs.[81] Migrants identified deeply as mothers and *babushki* and told their migration stories through this idiom.

Roxalana, a migrant woman I met in Rome, expected to do for her daughter what her mother had done for her. She said: "I am a *babushka* and I thought I would be with my grandson during the day and take care of the house while my daughter worked." Roxalana's daughter, despite her university degree, was unable to find work in her field and was "sitting at home." In the former Soviet Union where women were expected to work in the labor market, there was no commonly used term for "stay-at-home-mother."[82] Participants instead used the phrase "sitting at home," which implied wasting time and potential. Roxalana explained:

> I felt useless at home. All I was doing was fighting with my daughter over, you know, what to feed my grandson, how to dress him and how to discipline him. And with just my son-in-law working and my small pension, there was not enough money. So I came here [to Rome].

In the Soviet Union, the State supported young retirement ages so that grandparents were still physically able to perform childcare and other reproductive labor. The official retirement age was 55 for women and 60 for men.[83] Many of the migrant women I met in Rome were high school teachers like Roxalana, who retired even younger, in their early 40s, after 20 years of service. This was not by choice. Rather, the Ukrainian state was simply unable to pay its teachers and solved this problem with early retirements. Roxalana felt she was forced to retire and give up her salary for a much smaller pension. Roxalana, like many other women of her generation, was doubly marginalized from both the labor market and from her expected role as primary caregiver to her grandchildren.

Women migrants I spoke with in California also experienced this double marginalization. In fact, just the anticipation of double marginalization was enough to convince Vlada, a 45-year-old physician, to seize an opportunity to migrate to California with her husband and two daughters and join her husband's extended family in San Francisco. Vlada explained:

> You know, I thought like everybody did in the Soviet Union: Ok at 55 I'm going to retire and I am going to help my daughters raise my grandchildren. It was a set plan, everybody's plan! And now what do I see? No future for me [as a doctor] and my daughters sitting at home! I made up my mind to leave.

The migration from the former Soviet Union to the United States is significantly older than other migrations. While this is often explained by noting that adult migrants bring their parents with them,[84] my fieldwork revealed that it was in fact the older generation – specifically middle-aged women squeezed out of Ukraine – who motivated the family's decision to migrate.

The Migration of Women: An Affront to National Dignity

Although the articulation of *Berehynia* as the essence of a nation is specific to Ukraine, Anne McClintock notes that studies of colonialism reveal that the "cult of domesticity" and biological determinism have historically been produced by Europeans as central to the idea of progress and the "natural" gendered division of labor.[85] In nationalism discourse, women are often constructed as the symbolic bearers of the nation and therefore responsible for both its biological and cultural reproduction.[86]

Large-scale emigration poses a challenge to nations and nationalism. Nana Oishi writes, "Women are not a value-neutral workforce: they symbolize a nation's dignity and constitute the foundations of nationalism and national identity."[87] Therefore, Oishi asserts that the kind of emigration policy a state has toward its women and whether or not the state is "protecting" their women, is understood as an expression of the kind of values that nation possesses, a reflection of the national identity, as well as an indicator of where the nation-state lies with respect to the accepted global markers of development: democracy, human rights, and gender equality. Simultaneously, women are seen as male property and symbolic property of the nation, therefore their sexual abuse and labor exploitation by foreigners abroad is experienced as a humiliation for the state and nation.[88] This is heightened in Ukraine where one of the few claims to national identity that the bifurcated population can all agree on hangs on a particular idealized conception of an authentic Ukrainian family with a Ukrainian woman as *Berehynia* at its center. Mass emigration also challenges Ukraine's international prestige. While Ukraine is making claims to Europe and the "First World," nothing signals "Third World" in the international arena quite like the mass emigration of a country's women to perform domestic labor abroad.[89] Ukraine and its emigrants are acutely aware of Ukraine's position in the global hierarchy of nations. Ukraine is struggling to join the First World even as slipping into the Third World is a plausible and feared outcome of post-Soviet transformation.

Negotiating the Gap: Gendered Ideals versus Material Realities

Berehynia, an expression of the high level of respect given to women for their "separate responsibilities" and therefore symbolic of Ukraine's "First World" standing, is a dominant discourse that shapes the behaviors and aspirations of both Ukrainian women and men. Although *Berehynia* bundles together statements about ethnicity, religion, nation, and "middle-class" mothering practices that are specific to Ukraine, there is a similar dominant mothering discourse in the United States that sociologist Sharon Hays calls "intensive mothering."[90] In the United States, intensive mothering suggests mothers (assumed to be white, married, and middle-class) should engage in child-centered, time-consuming, labor-intensive mothering practices. Women should dedicate themselves to these practices 24/7, which therefore precludes the possibility of wage labor for mothers.[91] Although only a small percentage of women in the United States are stay-at-home mothers (23 percent in 2000 and 29 percent in 2012), research shows that all mothers are nevertheless held to the intensive mothering standard by others and themselves.[92] This results in discrimination against mothers in the U.S. labor market and shapes the behaviors and aspirations of men and women both in families and at work.[93] The discourse of intensive mothering powerfully shapes aspirations and practices of individuals in the United States even when women are the primary breadwinners and when men are stay-at-home fathers.[94] Therefore, although migrant women in Italy and the United States certainly saw native women in the paid labor market, they also learned a dominant gender discourse that prescribed how families *should* be structured – with a breadwinning husband and a stay-at-home wife – even if few families actually conformed to this ideal. In fact, many of the daughters of migrant women in my sample were not stay-at-home mothers in Ukraine. But they were nonetheless caught in the painful gap between their material reality, which required them to earn money even as gender discrimination in the labor market increased, and the post-Soviet *Berehynia* ideal of women as dedicated homemakers against which their status as good mothers and good Ukrainians was measured.

Stigmatization, Migration, and Nation-state Building

This gap between the possibilities available to individuals and the *Berehynia* ideal was even more pronounced for migrant women who were often both mothers and grandmothers. Emigration is a transgression of the Ukrainian nation in two fundamental ways. First, women who migrate seem to flout the practices associated with *Berehynia*, and therefore the behaviors that are now considered indicative of true, ethnic Ukrainian womanhood. Second, the emigration of women in particular is governed by global level discourses that suggest that mothers who leave their family behind would only do so to "escape poverty." This is the only reason that is considered acceptable for the migration of mothers and is the only reason that allows migrant women to make credible claims to being "good mothers." Yet, this global discourse is at odds with national level discourses about Ukraine's glorious forward journey into Europe and the First World. Therefore, the Ukrainian state attempts to deter migration and, in the process, stigmatizes its emigrants. Inside Ukraine, women migrants are blamed for a range of social ills including the "degradation of the family," "orphaned" children, men's alcoholism, and even men's moral debasement by driving men into the arms of mistresses.[95] However, exile to Italy and exodus to California, the two most salient migrations in Ukrainian public discourse, are not stigmatized in the same way or to the same degree.

Exile and exodus are differentially implicated in Ukraine's nation-state building project. The exile of *babushki* to Italy is productive of Ukrainian nation-state building and part of a large-scale reorganization of gender relations. As we have seen, this gender reorganization has a structural dimension which consists of a shift from an extended to a nuclear family with new gendered moralities for men and women as well as a changing labor market that includes men as breadwinners while excluding more and more women as mothers or potential mothers. The post-Soviet gender reorganization also has a discursive dimension that constructs this particular family formation as "modern," "capitalist," and "European" as well as ethnically and culturally Ukrainian.

One might assume that the Ukrainian state would view exile to Italy favorably. After all, the physical removal of these women as grandmothers and the monetary remittances earned through their labor power abroad helps to build this new Ukraine. And yet, whereas the migration to California is benignly tolerated by the Ukrainian state, those who leave to work in Italy are negatively stigmatized by the Ukrainian state as "prostitutes" and "betrayers" of the Ukrainian nation.[96] In fact, although former Ukrainian President Leonid Kuchma famously addressed Ukrainian women inside Ukraine as the "*Berehyni* of our people," every respondent in Italy repeated with indignation that Kuchma also called all Ukrainian women abroad "prostitutes."[97]

The women who led their families to California are also stigmatized by the Ukrainian state as "defectors" and are accused of abandoning their country. However, this label was not deeply felt nor usually mentioned by respondents in San Francisco and it did not have political bite inside Ukraine. One might think that mothers who migrate to the United States and leave behind children whom they may not see for many years would be more heavily stigmatized as "bad mothers" than those who go to Italy and, once they receive papers, visit regularly. I found that those in exodus, even those who have a child left in Ukraine, tend to stop sending remittances as they attempt to improve their living standards in California and have car payments, high rents, or home mortgages. Once again, we might expect that those in exodus would be more vulnerable to accusations of "bad mothering." But the migration to the United States, while noted, was not actively stigmatized by the Ukrainian state. This may be because in today's Ukraine, the cultural project of forging a Ukrainian nation is of utmost concern. Exodus is a migration associated with Ukraine's Soviet past, a continuation of the migrations to flee the Soviet Union. Exile, however, is central to the current nation-state building project and therefore constitutive of Ukraine's capitalist future.

Post-Soviet Mothering: When the World Has Been Turned Upside Down

For migrant women, motherhood was one of the terrains on which battles for honor and status were fought. In Italy, participants wrestled with the connections between poverty, migration, and nation. They placed remittances at the center of their narratives as proof of being a "good mother." They lived on a bare-bones budget, denying themselves basic needs or small comforts in order to send most of their wages to their family, usually adult children, in Ukraine. There is popular and media recognition within Ukraine that monetary remittances from temporary labor migrants abroad (*zarobitchany*), including those in Italy, have a significant impact on the Ukrainian economy. According to World Bank data, in 2012 these remittances totaled 4 percent of Ukraine's GDP. However, given the substantial amount of remittances transferred through informal channels, researchers suggest they are even more significant and estimate the number closer to 20 percent of Ukraine's GDP.[98]

In the context of post-Soviet transformation, participants exclaimed that it seemed all the rules governing what one does to be a successful or honorable woman or man have been "turned upside down." Exactly what one should do to be a "good" mother in this time of cultural flux and uncertainty was unclear. Confusion about which moral teachings and behaviors the Soviet generation should pass on to their children now that the Soviet moral system they came of age in had been discredited, gave questions of morality tied to capitalist markets, mothering norms, nationhood, and their migration experience abroad heightened meaning. How migrant women resolved this had consequences not only for their children back in Ukraine, but for how they negotiated how they should be perceived and treated by Italian employers.

Questions about what values and lessons a parent should pass on about how to be "successful" in the unfamiliar landscape of capitalist markets with its own set of moral codes was salient in exodus as well as exile. However, struggles over motherhood in exodus took a significantly different form than struggles over motherhood in exile. Once in California, migrants who arrived with their families or with the expectation that their families would soon follow were spared the painful negotiations of determining who was or was not a "good" mother. Good mother/bad mother discourses were not as salient among Ukrainians in San Francisco as among those in Rome. Mothers in California were considered "good" mothers by default. The underlying assumption was that they had made great sacrifices to bring (or were in the process of bringing) their children to a place with "more opportunities." However, Ukrainians in exodus had a different iteration of markets, moralities, and motherhood with which to struggle. As the adult children of my respondents integrated into American culture through market mechanisms, respondents in California, like those in Italy, also came to realize that markets were attached to moralities. For example, the adult children of respondents in California delayed having babies in order to attain certain labor market goals. They were not only upwardly mobile through markets in terms of living standards and status, but they were geographically mobile and often moved away for jobs and brought respondents' grandchildren with them. Finally participants complained that their adult children's parenting style became "too American." These developments placed the moralities and familial practices of adult children at odds with my respondents' "Soviet" desires for their role as *babushki* within a particular organization of family life.

Motherhood discourses in Ukraine, such as those embodied by *Berehynia*, bundled together conceptions of nation, development, economics, and ethnic identity. Although rooted in Ukraine, motherhood discourses shaped the terrain of possible actions for those in both sending and receiving countries. But they did not do so uniformly. Despite sharing a sending country, motherhood discourses were differently embedded in the transnational social fields of exile and exodus and contributed to the production of contrasting migrant subjects.

Motherhood Discourses and Transnational Social Fields

When women migrate, everyone has an opinion about who is a "good" and "bad" mother including the migrants themselves. In order to understand how motherhood and migration are constructed in Ukraine, I draw on three exemplary interviews I conducted in L'viv: the experiences of a mother who was a return migrant; a daughter whose mother was in Italy; and a son whose family was in California. These narratives illustrate the differing motherhood discourses available to participants in the transnational social fields of exile and exodus.

Zoya: Should a Good Mother Stay or Go?

During my time in Ukraine, I rented a room in a convent for Ukrainian Greek Catholic nuns. Sister Mariya, a tall woman with large brown eyes who radiated kindness was in charge of bringing me meals, which I took alone every day since the Sisters were cloistered. I grew to look forward to her visits every evening where she checked to make sure I had made it back by the 10 p.m. curfew and we shared stories about our day. Today, Sister Mariya had a visitor, Zoya, from her home town outside L'viv and sat her down to lunch with me. Sister Mariya suggested Zoya and I talk about life in Ukraine and left us to go about her work much to Zoya's displeasure. Zoya scowled at me over the small plates that held canned sardines, boiled potatoes, cabbage topped with a swirl of mayonnaise, and black bread. Zoya began by explaining in Ukrainian that, even though her husband is Russian, they are patriots and speak only Ukrainian at home. She scoffed, "I don't even remember Russian!" I apologized profusely for my limited Ukrainian and noted that there was no access to Ukrainian language study at my university. Zoya softened and sighed, "Well not all Ukrainians speak Ukrainian. I suppose we can't expect more from you." In flawless Russian, Zoya began explaining that she took a trip to Italy the year before with her UGCC parish and was hosted by a Catholic Italian family. Once there Zoya decided she would overstay her tourist visa and look for work. Zoya, 38, lived outside of L'viv in a one-room apartment with her parents, her husband, and her 13-year-old son. Zoya said of the tight living quarters:

> You just don't feel like a normal person like this. You can't have a normal sex life; you can't have a fight because your son is there and understands everything. We expect that by 40 you should have your own home. My husband is reaching 40 and despite the fact that he works 12 hours a day, we don't have anything and he doesn't feel like a man and I, as a woman and wife, can do nothing about this.

Zoya was the director of a rural school, and she earned $10 a month. She said that enrollment was low because there were always fewer children, and she was afraid they may close the school entirely. She suggested that the low birth rate was part of a Russian plot to "eliminate the Ukrainian population." Russians were also responsible, according to Zoya, for the lack of jobs, the low wages, and the cramped living spaces. Zoya reasoned that long work hours, constant worry, and no outlet to express frustrations at home would turn the population "into zombies" that would be unable to stand up against Russian aggression.

Zoya decided she would work in Italy and earn money, like so many women do, and save enough to live separate from her parents. However, she only stayed in Italy one month. Zoya explained that she made the "ultimate sacrifice as a mother" by going abroad to work, but it turned out she was "too good" a mother to stay abroad. Zoya explained:

> My son cried for me and asked why I abandoned him. I called home every day. My husband explained to him that I hadn't left them, that I was working for our bread. But it didn't work. And then I realized that I could not live without my family. What kind of a mother can live without her child?

Zoya expressed discomfort that she was not able to "make it" in Italy. She was unable to find steady work and found the experience "stressful" and "grueling." Women who migrate to Italy are labeled as "bad mothers" and denigrated as "prostitutes" in public discourse. Zoya tapped into these motherhood discourses to justify what she called her "failed migration." Zoya reveals that for individuals negotiating the mass emigration they see around them, it was not clear if "good" mothers were those who migrated or those who remained. What was clear was that motherhood was the language of migration.

Olha: You'll be a Prostitute like your Mother

Olha, 17, was a journalism student at L'viv University. Her red hair and freckles would have given her a girlish appearance, but her eyes were intelligent and she had the poise of a young woman. Olha explained that in her hometown, a small village an hour outside of L'viv, there were "no women left. They are all in Italy." Her mother had been working in Italy for three years. At first Olha cried and asked her mother not to go. I asked Olha how her mother responded. Olha replied, "Mama looked at me and said: Someday you will want to study and then you will look at me and say Mama, why didn't you go?"

Olha was left in the care of her stepfather and her stepfather's mother. Olha said that her step-grandmother "hated her" and her sister. Olha's mother had been sending remittances to Olha's stepfather who in turn gave the money to his mother to run the house. They did not buy Olha clothes, the things she needed for school, or even nourishing food. Olha's step-grandmother would not let Olha speak with her mother on the phone for fear that she would tell her how she was being treated. Olha's eyes smoldered with quiet rage:

> It was bad enough that they said my mother was a bad mother for leaving, but my step-grandmother would call my mother a prostitute. When I protested she said she knew it was true, even President Kuchma had said that our women in Italy were prostitutes and my mother was no different. She would tell me that I would never go to university; that I was not smart enough; and I'd just end up going abroad and being a prostitute like my mother.

Olha shook her head. She said that her mother was a school teacher and earned 80 *hryvni* ($16) a month. Her first husband told her she was "nothing," because she did not earn enough money. Now, Olha explained, she is in Italy where she earned 20 to 30 times that, but this was also "not good enough for her second husband," because she worked abroad.

Olha's mother now sends her remittances directly to Olha. Olha rents a room in L'viv and goes back to her village every weekend to monitor the renovation on their home. Olha's mother is still married to her second husband and allows him to live in her house "because she feels sorry for him," but Olha said there are "no longer feelings between them." I asked Olha how she felt about her mother's migration now. She replied:

> Mama calls herself a feminist, and I am the daughter of a feminist. Both mama and I are stronger for what we have lived through. Mama made the absolute right decision to go. She did what she needed to do for her kids. What choice did she have, really? If mama was not in Italy, I would not be in University. I am grateful to her.

Most of the young adults I spoke with in L'viv expressed gratitude and pride in their mothers who went abroad. This does not mean it was easy for Olha or any of the young adults I spoke with to have a parent abroad. No one I interviewed was happy to have a parent leave and many cried and expressed great pain at their separation. However, in sharp contrast to the children of Filipina migrants who refused their migrant mothers' attempts to expand the meaning of mothering to include being a provider,[99] Ukrainian children, because of Ukraine's Soviet past, saw earning money as part of mothering. Nearly all of the children of migrants I interviewed recognized and valued their mothers for providing. Olha, however, was the only Ukrainian I met who used the word "feminist."[100] For Olha, being a "feminist" meant finding a man who would be "her partner." Olha's mother had recently visited from Italy and Olha explained with tears in her eyes all the wonderful things they did together and all the nights they had stayed up talking. Olha explained, "Some say that feminists cannot be good mothers, but I say my Mama is the best mother I know."

Kolya: It's been 10 Years since I saw my Mother

Kolya arrived to our interview with the air of someone who was busy. He kissed his pregnant wife, who waved to me and walked off to run her own errands. The nerves on one side of Kolya's face had collapsed due to stress. His inability to move one side of his face, his tired eyes, stocky build, and short cropped blond hair made him look much older than his 24 years. He was distracted as he spoke. Kolya was in medical school studying to be a family practitioner but, he explained, doctors do not make enough money, just $100 a month. Therefore – after asking me to momentarily turn off the recorder – he explained that he had many "businesses" on the side. He took a call from an "associate" with whom he owned a billiard club, while I sipped my tea. As he put his cell phone away he huffed that there were a series of problems and he believed it was "time to sell." Kolya's wife worked for an international company earning $700 a month which, combined with Kolya's "businesses," meant a combined earnings of $1,000 a month. Kolya noted that with this income, "we can live well in L'viv." He had plans of opening another business. "Maybe cosmetics this time." He mused, "I have a lot of friends in dermatology." Kolya gave me the impression that many of his ventures were not exactly legal and the anxiety of managing corruption, he said, had taken a toll on his health and his nerve-damaged face. For the older, Soviet generation, calling someone a "businessman" is considered an insult. It implies a dishonest person who profits from exploiting others. As endearing as I found Kolya personally, I did not think he was helping the "shady" businessman stereotype.

Kolya's parents left for California in 1995 when he was 14 years old. They had an aunt and uncle who went first to Chicago and then California in the upheaval around WWII. After the Soviet Union collapsed, Kolya's parents started to correspond with a cousin who was born in the United States and who eventually sponsored them. I asked Kolya what it was like when his parents first left:

> It wasn't hard. My mom was 19 when she had me and she was in medical school and my father was also studying engineering at university, so I was raised by my grandparents. This is normal. We all lived together in a two story house. My parents were on the first floor and my grandparents were on the second floor. My bedroom was on the second floor so really my grandmother did everything for me. Of course I was sad to see my parents go, but it didn't really change my daily routine.

Kolya's parents have not returned to Ukraine since emigrating. He noted that this too was "normal for those that went to the United States. It isn't like going to Italy and being able to come back by bus." After four years, Kolya's parents brought his younger sister, Lena, to California. I asked why Lena but not him?:

KOLYA: Many reasons. First I didn't want to go. I was 18 already and wanted to go to medical school. I knew I could not do this if I went to California. Then my mother, she thought it was more important for Lena, because she is a girl.

CINZIA: Why is it important that she is a girl?

KOLYA: I don't know … I think my mom was afraid that she would marry the wrong man or that she would go to university and then sit at home … I don't know. It is hard to find work that pays well and it is harder for a woman to find business opportunities.

I pointed out that his wife was earning the highest salary of anyone I had met in L'viv. He gave me a half smile and noted she was an exception and that she would not have the job much longer now that they were having a baby. Regardless, Kolya explained that he thought it was too late now for him to leave Ukraine: "My life is here."

In the beginning, Kolya said that his parents sent money, about $100 every month and this was "good money." But now they only sent money on birthdays and holidays. Kolya explained:

> They have everything on credit over there. They bought a house and two cars all on credit. They work, and they don't even see their money! My sister is attending university and that is on credit too. Before my uncle, my mother's brother, used to ask for money from her. You know $1,000 to do a little business here, $1,000 to do a little remodeling there, but he doesn't ask anymore. He knows that they have everything on credit plus their second child to support over there.

Kolya was able to visit his parents for the first time in 10 years just two months earlier. He had tried to go to the U.S. consulate in Kyiv once before. He told them he wanted to visit an uncle rather than his parents, but they still determined that he was at risk of becoming a "potential immigrant" and would not give him a visa. He noted that it was not fair that "Ukrainians are not allowed to go to the United States and look around the way Americans can come here and look around." On his last visit to the consulate, Kolya had a pregnant wife in Ukraine, and he was deemed unlikely to remain in the United States. They gave him a visa. Kolya had recently returned from spending three weeks with his parents in California:

> I didn't recognize them. They were both older and fatter. [laughing] I think they did the right thing. They made the right decision to leave when they did just after the Soviet Union collapsed. They have realized themselves in the States, and I wouldn't have been able to go to medical school … My sister and I wouldn't have had all that we do if they didn't leave. They want

me to join them there and my friends think I am crazy not to take this opportunity … But, my parents, they think about how everything was better [in Ukraine] before the Soviet Union collapsed. They don't know Ukraine anymore. In 10 years it has changed, and it is still changing. We won't join Europe tomorrow, but we will someday soon. I think we can live in Ukraine.

Kolya's parents received their U.S. citizenship the previous year, making them eligible to sponsor Kolya. Kolya is married and over 21 years old and therefore low priority for family reunification according to U.S. immigration laws. The wait time would be many years. As of yet, however, his parents have not started the paperwork. "What for?" Kolya insisted. "I am not going anywhere."

The Children of Exile and Exodus

Markets, moralities, and motherhood are bundled together in Ukraine's nation-state building process. Zoya, living in rural Ukraine, experienced the economic devastation of Ukraine's opening to global markets. The decline in the birth rate, a result of economic uncertainty and the withdrawal of state services that supported mothers, left Zoya's school on the verge of closing due to lack of students. Zoya's broken heart went out to her husband who, now expected to provide for the family, experienced a "crisis of masculinity" created in the painful gap between his economic reality and the gender expectations of post-Soviet manhood. In the Soviet Union, Zoya and her family might have been on a housing list, in post-Soviet Ukraine money to buy housing and to care for her son could only be earned by working abroad. However Zoya was confronted with both the structural and discursive elements of exile. Structurally, exile encouraged separation from family and performing cleaning and caring labor that in the Soviet Union was considered so lowly that it turned workers into "slaves." Discursively, Zoya struggled with her stigmatization as "bad" mother for leaving her family and her son's longing for his mother's presence. If Zoya ultimately concluded that a "good mother" stays, many other women rejected the state-sponsored stigmatization and believed instead that being a "good" mother or grandmother meant they had no choice but to migrate.

Olha resisted those who called her migrant mother a "prostitute" or a "bad" mother. Instead, she valued her mother for providing her with the possibility of an education through remittances from Italy. This did not mean Olha was happy to have her mother leave, but rather she understood the changing socioeconomic conditions and believed her mother had no choice. Individuals embedded in the transnational field of exile struggled with the connections between markets, moralities, and motherhood, but Tymoshenko, in her documentary that opened this chapter, noted that states also struggled with this migration. Tymoshenko explained the inequality between nations by deploying motherhood discourses and critiquing Ukraine as a "bad" mother because it forced her children to seek comfort in the arms of "step-mother" Italy.

Kolya did not have to struggle with the stigmatization of his mother and father who left Ukraine for the United States. He did, however, have to grapple with the central project embedded in the transnational social field of exodus: family reunification. Although his sister left for the United States and Kolya believed his parents made possible his education through migration, the United States is an "adoptive" mother. Kolya's family will not return and Kolya will not leave Ukraine.

National and transnational processes of post-Soviet transformation impacted not only how migrant women and men understood their migration experience, but what kind of person, parent, and national subject they were or were becoming. They also impacted how children and families left in Ukraine experienced the transnational social fields in which they participated. Gendered migrant subjectivities is a key vantage point from which we can excavate larger global and transnational processes. However, the effects of these changes in Ukraine are not uniformly experienced in Italy and California, and therefore the migrant subjectivities produced also differ. The varied effects of the sending country in the contexts of reception can only be understood by analyzing the transnational social fields of exile and exodus produced through the intersection of sending and receiving contexts.

PART II

Exile: Italy

FIGURE II.1 The Garbatella outside Rome's city center
Photograph by the author.

FIGURE II.2 On Sunday mornings 5,000 Ukrainians come to send goods and money to family in Ukraine, collect letters, photographs, and foodstuff sent from home, and meet friends
Photograph by the author.

2

ITALY'S CONTEXT OF RECEPTION AND CONNECTIONS TO UKRAINE

Italy was historically a sending country with substantial emigration and little immigration until recently. Beginning in the 1970s, Southern Europe has been receiving migrants, especially those without documents.[1] Western Europe has had decades to create immigration laws limiting those trying to enter creating "fortress Europe."[2] Instead countries in Southern Europe – Portugal, Spain, Italy, and Greece – are just beginning to see immigration as a social problem that needs regulation. Many migrants understand that entering Southern Europe is both easier and entails less risk of deportation than Western Europe.[3] There are a number of reasons that Southern Europe and Italy in particular saw a dramatic increase in immigration.[4] Since the 1970s the "developmental divide" between countries in Northern and Southern Europe closed. However Southern European expansion was not based on the expansion of industrial employment as in Northern Europe, but rather tertiary employment in tourism, which requires greater seasonal and temporary labor in the form of cleaners and kitchen staff as well as personal services including domestic work and carework.[5] This form of economic expansion occurred at the same time that Italian internal migration from Southern to Northern Italy all but came to a halt, creating a demand for migrant labor. Migrants from the former Soviet Union, especially women from Ukraine and Moldova, have entered Italy in astounding numbers since the collapse of the Soviet Union and have become the largest group providing paid domestic labor there.[6]

In this chapter, I will first explain the organization of the domestic work sector, tracing its workforce from Italian men, to unmarried Italian women from Southern Italy, to today's migrant labor force of caregivers. I will link migrant domestic workers to Italy's "care crisis" for its aging population and the limitations of its welfare state. Next I will show how Italy's immigration laws trap migrants in Italy, bolstering the "gulag" metaphor. Finally, I turn to the institutions that organize collective life for Ukrainian migrants in Rome, especially post-Soviet churches and an organized meeting space called the "Garbatella." I also foreshadow the discourses and practices that produce the particular gendered migrant subjectivities of exile.

Catholics versus Communists: The Creation of Italy's Domestic Service Sector

In the 1700s, domestic servants in Italy were mostly men and organized in guilds with a measure of social status.[7] In the 1800s, men began to be absorbed into factory work and domestic service was taken up by unmarried, rural, and Southern Italian women. The Italian communist party and its trade unions attempted to organize domestic workers, but it was the Catholic Church through an organization called ACLI-COLF (*Associazione Cattolica dei Lavoratori Italiani-Collaboratrice familiare* or Association of Italian Catholic Workers-Family Collaborators) that after a series of labor struggles succeeded in organizing these workers. ACLI is still the national representative of domestic workers in Italy today. Domestic workers in Italy are referred to as *colf*, derived from the Italian for "family collaborators." This reflects the Catholic understanding of these young, unmarried women from economically depressed regions of Italy as joining the employer's family in order to support the Italian family unit through their labor.[8] The employer had a responsibility to treat this worker as a member of the family and make sure that she did not fall into sexual transgression. *Colf* in turn were asked to see this role as an extension of their maternal role as future mothers and accept subservience.

This familial construction of domestic workers was challenged in the late 1960s and early 1970s. ACLI-COLF adopted a more radical approach influenced by changes in the trade union movement, a growing Italian feminist consciousness, and a leftward shift in Catholic activism. Although there was emphasis on the inequality between men and women and concerns about "women exploiting other women," ACLI-COLF also offered a class-based analysis, noting that it was almost exclusively elite Italian families who could afford to hire poor Italians as domestics.[9] Class-based social injustice was a more palatable framing for the Catholic Church than a gendered analysis which was seen as breeding discord within couples and destabilizing families. Yet, this class-based understanding of domestic work was a double-edged sword for those interested in protecting the rights of domestic workers. On the one hand, it laid the ground work for *colf* to be seen as workers. Until then, the domestic work sector in the Italian civil code was atypical in that individual employers, operating according to paternalist family norms, rather than the state, were expected to protect the rights of domestic workers.[10] In 1969, this article was abolished and this paved the way for national collective bargaining agreements that would eventually provide more legal protections for domestic workers. On the other hand, while job participation rates for Italian women are still low compared to other countries in the European Union (it was 13 percentage points below the EU-15 average in 2015), job participation rates for women have increased within the Italian context.[11] As opportunities for Italian women in the labor force expanded, they moved out of low-status domestic work jobs leading to a strong demand for foreign workers. With more Italian women in the labor force, not only elite families but also middle-class families began hiring *colf*, and today it is a widespread practice in Italy.[12] With middle-class Italians joining the ranks of employers of domestic workers, ACLI-COLF was no longer able to claim that the rich were exploiting the poor and found its class-based perspective unsustainable.

In the 1990s ACLI-COLF commissioned a series of articles to create a new theoretical framework with which to analyze domestic work.[13] Italian feminism never left academia to become a movement, and discussions about Italian men sharing in domestic work were no longer on the table. Instead, the debate centered on the *need* of Italian women for domestics and obscured issues of gender, class, migration, and race/ethnicity. The analysis focused on the lack of early childcare options, schools that only operated for half the day, and the increased number of elderly who also needed time-consuming assistance. According to the ACLI-COLF reports, more women in the labor force meant that women had "no option" but to hire domestics. The mantra of "women exploiting other women" fell to the sideline just as foreign women replaced Italian women as domestic workers. Although ACLI-COLF recognized that for Italian women, live-in work was anachronistic, they did not extend this same recognition to the migrant women coming to Italy from Ethiopia, the Philippines, South America, and most recently Eastern Europe.

Italy's "Care Crisis" and the Italian Welfare State

Demographics as well as economic restructuring has been driving the demand for domestic workers. Italy has an aging population, the oldest population in Europe, and the lowest fertility rate in the European Union, indeed one of the lowest fertility rates ever recorded in work population history.[14] The Italian state recognizes there is a "care crisis" and sees immigration as the solution to providing care to the elderly.[15] The Italian welfare state is dependent on the household as provider of personal services and relies on money transfers to households rather than the provision of services.[16] Sociologist Giuseppe Sciortino argues that migrant domestic workers are the "pillar of the Italian welfare regime." Sciortino notes that, given Italy's demographics and labor market imperatives, not only do migrants in Italy have a strong incentive to do domestic work because they have few other work options available, but also the Italian welfare state depends on migrants to provide these services.[17] Seven percent of households used state cash benefits to pay migrant careworkers in 2005–2008.[18] Scholars suggest that this number is significantly larger when considering Italian families who pay out of pocket for migrant caregivers, the reality that the Italian population keeps aging whereas population growth has been stagnant, and that the number of migrants arriving in Italy to work as caregivers to the elderly keeps increasing.[19]

Ukrainians in Italy are defined by carework, and the majority are *badanti* (*badante* in the singular), a term that refers specifically to those providing care to the elderly.[20] With limited exceptions, the only option for someone who needs round-the-clock-care in Italy is either a family member willing to take this responsibility or a hired live-in domestic.[21] Most immigration services and academic research is sponsored by the Catholic Church, which has a liberal view of the rights of people to migrate. Catholic organizations such as the Community of Sant'Egidio, which provided many important services to participants I spoke with in Rome, advocated for fewer restrictions on migration and even publicly thanked Ukrainian migrants in Rome for "caring for Italy's grandparents" at a gathering I attended. However, when it came to individual negotiations between *badanti* and those for whom they cared, the moral waters were murky.

Migration and end-of-life care are closely connected in Italian public discourse and often place the needs of migrants and elderly Italian clients in opposition to each other. I was invited to a conference in Trento to present my U.S.-based research as part of a panel of researchers who had funded a series of studies using EU grant money to study domestic workers and the eldercare sector. In Italian, I presented interview data that suggested migrants often found providing bodily care to an elderly person difficult and, at times, found the emotional labor required both draining and requiring great patience. I was surprised to find myself publicly attacked by the other panelists as "un-Christian" and was lectured that providing care to the elderly was morally just, honorable, and fulfilling work. Panelists also expressed indignation that, in their perception, I had sided with foreign workers over "my own people" given my Italian heritage. Afterwards, I was quickly surrounded by domestic workers, many Ukrainian, who had been trying to found their own organization in Trento and had hopes of accessing some of the EU funds used to sponsor the conference. One women quickly huffed in Russian, "If this is such great work, why don't Italians do it?!" In fact, 72 percent of *colf* and *badanti* in Italy are foreign migrants.[22] Another continued, "Italians, they think their mother always smells pretty. Well, they stink like everyone else when they go to the bathroom! Why can't they understand this work is hard?" Although there was variation in how personally fulfilling those I interviewed experienced eldercare, these workers reiterated that all careworkers must negotiate difficult personalities, bodily care, and emotions that can range from love to disgust. Compared to the United States, the moral terrain for discussing carework and migration, both in public and academic circles, was more fraught in Italy where Catholic values of love and care co-existed uneasily with the performance of that work by migrants often precariously positioned by vectors of power that included race/ethnicity, class, gender, age, and citizenship status.

Nowhere were these tensions between foreign careworkers and Italian clients more evident to me than in the ACLI offices where, according to Catholic ideals of labor, ACLI workers represented both employers and workers. I conducted two months of participant observation in ACLI placement offices where they helped match migrant domestic workers in search of work and Italian families searching for a *colf* or *badante* as well as mediated conflicts that arose between migrant domestic workers and their Italian employers. Although ACLI workers were supposed to be impartial, they sometimes contributed to unequal power dynamics. ACLI workers always called migrants by their first names but Italians with the term of respect, *Signora* or *Signore*. I observed workers side with Italian employers with negative consequences for migrants in disputes I believed were based on differences in cultural practices or understandings. However, I also witnessed ACLI employees help employers and workers complete the paperwork detailing back wages in vacation days, overtime, and liquidation payments, and side forcefully with migrants when it came to issues of wages. Nevertheless, after attending a three-day yearly conference for ACLI management in Rome, it became clear that ACLI, the only organization charged with protecting the rights of domestic workers, had an identity crisis. The members of ACLI's management attending the meeting were torn between protecting Italian families who are left in dire straits by the weak Italian welfare system and protecting the rights of foreign careworkers. One attendee, a woman from Latin America who had been in Italy for over 25 years became frustrated with the indecision about "whose side we are on" and pointed out that it was not difficult for them to choose sides in the days when both workers and clients were Italian. She exclaimed, "Our job has always been to protect the workers. Just because those workers are no longer Italian, does not mean we stop protecting them!" Another attendee, an Italian woman, explained that the migrant women, especially those from the Philippines and from Ukraine did not seem "poor" and this made her less sympathetic. She continued:

> I just don't know anymore … I don't know who the weak subject is. Is it the migrant woman who is here to work so she can send her children to private school or build a big house back home or the elderly Italian who needs care? Who is the weak subject? The migrant woman who only makes €400 euros a month or the elderly Italian whose pension is €600 a month and is living on just €200 because he's giving €400 to the careworker?[23]

In fact, some in the ACLI management felt that perhaps ACLI had been "too" successful in negotiating on behalf of workers. They argued that domestic work had improved with the adoption of the national contract for domestic workers in 1986 to such an extent that the power balance had shifted, and it is now Italy's elderly that needed protecting.

ACLI and the National Contract for Domestic Workers

My fieldwork in Rome revealed many abuses of migrant domestic workers: sexual harassment and abuse, confiscation of passports, verbal and emotional abuse, and unlawful withholding of wages. Without diminishing these hardships, careworkers in Italy are provided with many more protections than in the United States where no federal laws governed carework during my time in the field. In Italy, the National Contract for Domestic Workers sets a minimum hourly wage for live-out hourly work and a minimum monthly wage for live-in work.[24] It requires that live-in workers receive Thursday afternoons and Sundays off, and, should workers agree to work those days, they are entitled to an hourly wage in addition to their monthly salary. Domestic workers are also entitled to a paid month of vacation for every year they work. Like other Italian workers, they are entitled to the *tredicesima* or the "thirteenth month," which is an extra month's salary often paid at Christmas time. They are also entitled to liquidation pay should their employment be terminated. Liquidation pay amounts to one month's salary for every year of employment. Legally, even undocumented workers are covered by the terms of the national contract negotiated by ACLI but the undocumented are less able and willing to hold employers accountable due to fears of deportation.

Much of the demand for domestic work in Italy is for live-ins who are willing to provide care to the elderly around the clock. In fact, all but a handful of respondents in Rome were doing live-in work. Migrants tend to move toward live-out work when at all possible. This is the case with Filipina domestic workers in Rome for example and was a complaint I heard among Italian employers at the ACLI offices. Filipinas, employers complained, were no longer willing to do live-in work and had learned to "game the system." They also were more highly paid than other migrant groups doing domestic work in Italy and middle-class Italian employers argued they could not afford "a Filipina." Women and some men from Eastern Europe, particularly Ukrainians, have filled this labor gap.

All Roads Lead to Rome … and Most of Them Start in Ukraine

Respondents told me remarkably uniform accounts about how they arrived in Italy from Ukraine. They reported going to "travel agencies" in Ukraine where they put in a request to purchase a 10-day tourist visa. They explained that they could not choose the country or the timing of the visa. There were some visas, especially in the early 1990s, for Greece, but by 1994 and 1995, participants explained, visas were granted increasingly exclusively for Italy with 1998 and 1999 being the years of the "masses." As one participant put it, "They say all roads lead to Rome – it's just that most of them start in Ukraine!" The Ukrainian migrants who were among the first to enter Italy reported paying several hundred euros for the entry visa. By 2004 and 2005, participants were reporting prices at

$3,110. Those who generally reported salaries between $50–80 per month in Ukraine, received help from family members and often had to borrow money at high interest rates in order to purchase the entry visa.

I heard only two minor exceptions to this pattern in my interviews. Two participants entered Italy in 2000 as part of a van sponsored by the Ukrainian Greek Catholic Church (UGCC) for the Catholic Church's Jubilee celebrations. When it was time to return, only the director of the program and Lesia, who was her assistant, turned up at the designated meeting spot. The other 30 women had disappeared into Rome. I interviewed Lesia in Rome and also spent time with her and her husband in L'viv. Lesia said that she stayed in Rome because she feared that the Ukrainian border guards might think that she had purposely smuggled people into Italy. Ukrainian Greek Catholic priests in Rome also advised her to stay and provided her with temporary housing until she found work. Lesia mused that with barely an overnight bag of clothes, she had been in Rome five years.

The second exception included several men I interviewed who came to Italy by way of Portugal or Spain. Ukrainian men are also migrating to Europe although in smaller numbers than women. In fact, anthropologist Diana Blank similarly found in her ethnographic study of a South Eastern Ukrainian city that participants repeated that Ukraine had "dumped its women into Italy" and that the post-Soviet migration had the opposite demographic effect than war leaving only "men and children in the villages."[25] Migration from Ukraine to Italy is approximately 80 percent women, and 20 percent men, with the largest age bracket among the women being 50–55 and over half of the men following a woman migrant to Italy.[26] Additionally, I found that men in Italy often had gone first to Portugal or Spain which were experiencing a boom in the construction industry in the early 1990s.[27] They too entered those countries by overstaying entry visas. As those construction jobs disappeared, Ukrainian men reported traveling to Italy where they knew there were large numbers of Ukrainian women. Italian employers understood domestic work as "women's work" and when I asked women why they migrated rather than their husband (if they had one), the answer was always that it was easier for women to find work abroad. Frequently, this was accompanied by a gender discourse about "weak," "irresponsible," and "ineffective" men that is a dominant discourse in Ukraine and the former Soviet Union.[28] Ukrainian men in Rome do perform domestic labor, often caring for elderly Italian men. Men also had more opportunities as domestic workers in the outskirts of Rome where a villa required gardening or maintenance and where driving was more likely to be part of the job.[29] Many men, however, continued to look for work in construction and reported being dependent on Ukrainian women who were working inside Italian families for help finding construction jobs. I also met men who worked as *badanti* just long enough to get their papers and then moved on to other work.

For both men and women, acquiring documents was the only way to be able to return to Ukraine and then re-enter Italy without once again having to pay the large sum for the 10-day tourist visa. This was why acquiring an Italian *permesso di soggiorno* or a "permit to stay" was so important for migrants. Ukrainian men doing construction work were severely disadvantaged in the acquisition of a *permesso di soggiorno*, because the Italian government singled out domestic work for special treatment and created limited but important paths to legalization for *colf* and especially *badanti*.

Italy's "Immigration" Laws and Routes to Legalization

The most common explanation of increased migration into Italy beginning in the 1970s is that Western Europe closed its borders and created a "fortress Europe" that made Italy an easier country of entry for migrants. However, Asher Colombo and Giuseppe Sciortino argue that increased immigration to Italy can best be explained by looking internally to Italian law.[30] They note that it was not legal immigration but illegal immigration that increased in the 1970s and these migrants were not regularized until Italy's first immigration law in 1986. Although this law regularized undocumented migrants already residing in Italy, it did not limit or regulate the entry of new migrants. The first piece of immigration legislation that attempted to do so was the Martelli law of 1990. It set up requirements for entry visas as well as launched a general amnesty for all those who could demonstrate they entered Italy before 1990, regardless of their labor market status. Regularizations and amnesties, occurring every few years (1986, 1990, 1995, 1998, 2002, 2007, 2009, and 2012), have become Italy's main instrument of migration policy.[31]

During my time in the field, some participants had acquired papers through the amnesty law of 1998, and others were still involved in the legalization process authorized in June 2002. This law, attacked by Italy's political left and the Catholic Church as racist and anti-immigrant, was called the Bossi-Fini Bill after its sponsors at the time: Deputy Prime Minister Gianfranco Fini, leader of the post-Fascist National Alliance political party, and Reform Minister Umberto Bossi of the anti-immigration party the Northern League. The bill made it easier to deport illegal migrants and made staying in Italy contingent on proof of a labor contract. Although this bill was detrimental to some migrant groups, especially those from North Africa, the bill had some positive effects for migrants from the former Soviet Union. Migrants from the former Soviet Union accounted for 53 percent of the requests for resident visas under the Bossi-Fini law.[32] The number of legalized Moldovans increased five times, while the number of legalized Ukrainians increased eight times jumping from 14,808 registered Ukrainians in Italy in 2002 to 127,000 in 2003, which made them the fourth-largest migrant group in Italy and migrants from the former Soviet Union the largest migrant group overall.[33] This dramatic jump in the number of legalized migrants from the former Soviet Union suggested that many were already in Italy illegally.[34] The Bossi-Fini Bill made domestic workers and care providers to the elderly privileged job categories and facilitated their legalization process. Precisely because migrants from the former Soviet Union were mostly women, recently arrived to Italy, and already present in large numbers, these workers benefited more dramatically from the amnesty program than other migrant groups.[35]

Despite demonstrations and activism from the political left that aimed at repealing the Bossi-Fini Bill, an even more restrictive version of the bill was passed in 2009. Again this law pertained specifically to *colf* and *badanti*, although there were restrictions that made the number of foreign domestic workers regularized smaller than expected. The restrictions included a €500 fee to be paid before filing papers for legalization and requirements that the worker earn €20,000 per year. Most interviewees in Italy earned €600–800 per month which, if their employer respected the thirteenth month payment (*tredicesima*), meant earnings of €7,800–10,400 per year. The highest paid migrant in my Italy-based sample earned €1,000 per month. Therefore, although the amnesty law did regularize *colf* and *badanti*, only wealthy Italian employers were able to meet the requirements.

Italian immigration laws recognize migrants solely in their capacity as workers. Therefore, few opportunities exist for migrants to bring their families with them or even for the migrant herself to stay permanently in Italy. I met participants who fell and broke limbs or otherwise became ill and could not work shortly before their *permesso di soggiorno* expired or whose elderly employer died just as their *permesso di soggiorno* was up for renewal. They had to quickly find a new employer willing to deal with the renewal paperwork and take on the responsibilities of hiring a documented worker or else lose their legal status. The majority of Ukrainians I met in Rome, however, were undocumented. Although those who were able to regularize their status worked hard to maintain their legal status, migrants frequently moved between documented and undocumented status.

Italy is still adapting to its status as a receiving country. Colombo and Sciortino argue that the Italian State's preference for "backdoor illegal migration" and then "mass amnesty" have "weakened the regulatory function of [migrant] networks and paradoxically made it easier to arrive in the country without having to count on help from fellow countrymen, friends, or relatives" and has led to an increase in migrant flows into Italy.[36] In conjunction with Italy's long coastline and mountainous borders that are difficult to secure, this may also explain other particularities of Italian immigration. For example, fourteen nationalities must be added together in order to reach 50 percent of the total migrant population in Italy; this is in sharp contrast to the immigration into Northern Europe where labor migrants are drawn from a more or less homogeneous set of Mediterranean Basin countries.[37]

The Italian state has made it easy to legalize domestic workers compared to migrants in other occupational categories. Legalizing domestic workers was attractive to a certain subset of Italians employing domestic workers, particularly government workers, for whom hiring an undocumented worker could cause problems. However, many employers resisted legalization for several reasons. First, once a foreign domestic worker has a *permesso di soggiorno*, they are free to switch employers and searching for work with a *permesso di soggiorno* already in hand could yield higher wages for migrant workers. In order to successfully renew their *permesso di soggiorno* when it expired, the worker must have proof of employment; it does not have to be the employer who originally sponsored the paperwork. Therefore, many employers feared that a worker would leave once they received their documents for a better paid position. A second concern of employers was that once a worker had a *permesso di soggiorno*, the employer must begin paying social security benefits for retirement called *contributi* to the Italian state. For migrants, however, once they stopped working for any reason, including illness or old age, there was no way for them to remain in Italy legally. Therefore most participants planned an eventual return to Ukraine. In light of this, none of my respondents – workers, community leaders, and union representatives – believed that workers would have access to these retirement funds from the Italian state, and migrant workers worried about low pensions (most reported $60 per month) from the Ukrainian state. Furthermore, *contributi* were the most cited obstacle to legalization by participants. Although the law maintains that *contributi* are to be paid by the employer in addition to the workers' wages, many participants reported agreeing to pay their own *contributi* by suggesting to employers that the fees be deducted from their salary in the hopes of attaining their legal documents. Many respondents thought of this as a "tax" for the benefits of having a *permesso di soggiorno*.

The quest for legal documents was pervasive among Ukrainian migrants because, without a *permesso di soggiorno*, they could not visit family in Ukraine without forfeiting re-entry to Italy. Concerns about one's *permesso di soggiorno*, problems with renewing this paperwork, and attempts to convince employers to legalize them in the first place were constant topics of discussion. Those without documents told heart-wrenching stories through tears of missing children's weddings, parents' funerals, and holidays with their families back in Ukraine. Especially bitter were migrants with legal documents who still could not return to Ukraine while they waited, sometimes for a full year, for the Italian state to renew a *permesso di soggiorno* they already had. With requirements that migrants renew their *permesso di soggiorno* every one to two years, the renewal process for those with legal rights to work in Italy as documented migrants and the undocumented alike found themselves trapped in Italy and forced to work making Italy, in the narrative of Ukrainian migrants, a "gulag."

Rome's Ukrainian Community

The Ukrainian community in Rome was highly visible. On Thursday afternoons and Sundays, when most *badanti* have time off, Ukrainians walked through the streets of Rome in large groups or congregated in public parks or squares. Ukrainian migrants, in Rome without family and often restricted inside the home of the elderly person they cared for all week, met for picnics, explored the city, and attended church in large numbers. They also wrote for local Ukrainian newspapers, sang in choirs, rehearsed in folk troupes, organized and performed talent shows, and taught classes in Ukrainian language and history to the few children migrants succeeded in bringing with them. Ukrainians in Italy participated in a collective life that simply did not exist in California. For more on the demographics of the Ukrainian community in Rome and Italy see the Appendix.

Rome's Post-Soviet Churches

There are three UGCCs and one Russian Orthodox Church (ROC) in Rome. On Sundays, the UGCC on Rome's Aventine regularly welcomed 400 to 500 Ukrainians who came for mass, to meet with friends, and ask the priests for help in various work-related and personal matters. During inclement weather, Ukrainian live-ins often had nowhere else to go to be indoors except church halls. Churches served meals at a nominal fee after mass and allowed migrants to use church spaces to meet, play cards, and socialize. There are many interesting comparisons to be made between Rome's ROC and UGCC parishes,[38] but it was the UGCC, with its strong transnational ties to Ukraine, that helped shape the way Ukrainians in Rome, regardless of whether or not they attended religious services, understood their migration.

Bishop Simenovych, during an interview in his office, explained to me that in 2000, the UGCC had two "communities" in Italy, both located in Rome. In 2004, there were over 90 Ukrainian Greek Catholic communities throughout Italy with new ones being founded regularly. Communities are formed through UGCC outreach or Ukrainian migrants who self-organize and call the UGCC office in Rome stating they have a group who would like to celebrate the liturgy. A priest is then sent from Rome to meet with the group and work with local Roman Catholic priests to find a church facility able to host them.[39] During my fieldwork, there were a total of 35 UGCC priests actively involved in pastoral work in Italy. Twenty of them were stationed in larger cities throughout Italy. The remaining 15 priests, many of whom were pursuing graduate-level studies, were stationed in Rome and traveled to smaller cities to celebrate the liturgy every week or every other week, depending on the size and needs of the community and the available resources.

Ukrainian Greek Catholic priests I interviewed in Rome saw providing social services, what they called *carità* in the Italian context, as an integral part of their work in Rome. *Carità* drew potential converts to the Church, and this type of active engagement with parishioners was also a way for priests to realize a political vision. Greek Catholic priests saw settlement practices as a vehicle for fostering a

Ukrainian national consciousness among migrant Ukrainians that they believed would eventually return to Ukraine and constitute an activist or at least a sympathetic base for the creation of a Ukrainian nation tied to Ukrainian ethnicity (not Russian), a national language (Ukrainian rather than Russian), and a national church (the UGCC not the ROC). The UGCC, after seeing much of its clergy perish in the Soviet gulags, emerged from the underground to continue its fight for Ukrainian independence. Many Ukranian Greek Catholic priests have lived or were educated in Europe. The UGCC is part of the Universal Catholic Church and recognizes the Pope in Rome as its head. It sees itself as a "European" church and therefore more "modern" than the ROC. The UGCC in Rome was engaged in an ethnonationalist project and its priests reported providing services to Ukrainian migrants in Rome as an opportunity to instill national and religious consciousness in fellow Ukrainians as well as an obligation of faith. The importance of the UGCCs in the collective life of Rome's Ukrainian community and the deep connections it fostered between Italy and Ukraine was thrown into sharp relief during the contested presidential election that sparked the Orange Revolution in November 2004.

During one of the first Sundays after the protests began, I walked into the UGCC I had been attending regularly for several months and was stunned as I looked out into a sea of orange. There were more than 400 Ukrainian migrants, mostly women, wearing orange scarves and other orange paraphernalia to show solidarity with Yushchenko (see Chapter 1). I saw a respondent, Oresta, near the back of the church and went over to say hello. She introduced me to her friends, switching from Ukrainian to Russian for my benefit. Oresta picked up her story, telling the group that I was there with her in St. Peter's Square this week when Pope John Paul II acknowledged the events in Ukraine saying, "Beloved, I assure you and all the Ukrainian people that I am praying these days in a special way for your dear homeland," a phrase I heard repeated by Ukrainians all week.[40] Just then my attention was diverted to the priests who solemnly processed into the church carrying an orange flag that read *Tak* Yushchenko! (*Yes* Yushchenko!) in large block letters and began the liturgy.

Rome's UGCC clergy were tireless supporters of the Orange Revolution. They worked relentlessly to mobilize Ukrainians to vote in Rome's Ukrainian consulate in both the presidential election and the presidential re-vote. UGCC clergy and church volunteers organized demonstrations, including the release of hundreds of orange balloons in Piazza Venezia. They sponsored a Ukrainian school to teach Ukrainian history and culture according to nationalist historiography and hosted countless cultural events such as a night dedicated to reading the poetry of Taras Shevchenko. Finally, the UGCC ran a Ukrainian-language newspaper called *Into the Light*. The UGCC in Rome acted as migration brokers, helping Ukrainians enter and negotiate life in Italy while simultaneously suggesting that these same migrants, armed with their new-found understanding of Ukrainian culture and history, return home to build the new Ukraine.

The Garbatella: Ukraine is only a Bus-ride Away

Like the post-Soviet churches, the Garbatella was also a site of collective meaning-making for Ukrainian migrants in Rome. Every Sunday between 8 a.m. and noon approximately 5,000 Ukrainians passed through a large parking lot behind Rome's Garbatella metro station. Fifty white courier vans, most appearing several decades old, lined the perimeter of the rectangular lot. The vans carried workers with documents between Rome and what seemed like most cities and even villages in Ukraine. Drivers, however, earned the bulk of their money carrying packages back and forth. Most Ukrainians in Rome passed through the Garbatella intermittently and many came every Sunday to send packages and money back to their families in Ukraine. They built relationships with specific drivers they trusted to personally hand money or packages to their loved ones. Loved ones in Ukraine often sent with this same driver letters, photographs, medicine, mayonnaise, or Ukrainian sausage to their family member working in Rome, nostalgic for anything from home. On the Garbatella, all the vans had their double back doors thrown wide open in front of mountains of plastic bags stuffed to capacity. Women stood in small groups fussing over whether the breakables were well packed, sharing the latest pictures of their grandchildren, and comparing notes about employers. In the center of the rectangular space lined with courier vans on all sides was a row of tented booths selling newspapers, magazines, and books in Russian and Ukrainian. Thousands of people browsed the books, chatted with long-lost friends, or hurried to find their courier van with arms weighted down with bulky plastic bags.

I spent many Sundays at the Garbatella before church services where conversations included discussions of children and grandchildren back home, the desire to go home, and relationships with their Italian employers. Those without documents looked longingly at the courier vans that would drive for three to four days and be in their home villages, while those with documents were constantly planning their next visit home. For those with documents, migration had a circulatory feel with migrants going home regularly for both quick visits and for extended stays, taking great care to re-enter Italy before their *permesso di soggiorno* expired. However it was questions of gender, migration, and nation that dominated Ukrainian spaces in Rome. Migrant women in exile were implicated in Ukraine's nation-state building project and bore its painful contradictions.

One of these contradictions was expressed in a question that was always hanging in the air at the Garbatella: "Is Ukraine 'Europe' or 'Africa?'" I found that Italians often presumed that Ukraine was "like Africa." Many Italians assumed that Ukrainians, and all migrants *dell'Est* (from Eastern Europe), came from a "Third World country" that was undeveloped and lacked running water, electricity, proper housing, or an education system – a place that in their imaginations was "like Africa." Italians assumed such abject poverty was the only reason why all these women would come to Italy to do low-status cleaning and caring labor. This metaphorical "Africa" was an imagined one. It was not based on data that described continental Africa as it actually exists nor did it address the great diversity within and between African countries.

Ukrainians in Italy fought against this characterization, because it was their greatest fear that Ukraine might indeed go the way of "Africa." This was a see-mingly plausible outcome of economic transformation. But also because they believed it led Italians to treat them with less respect. Klara, a 52-year-old violi-nist explained, "We are of different nationalities and Italians do not think highly of us. They say we are people from the Third World! Yes, this is how they translate us – Third World women – and it isn't true at all!" For migrant women, the nation-state building project was not just about what was happening in Ukraine, but also about how they were being treated in Italy. Migrants often showed me pictures or postcards of Ukraine and pointing at the architecture exclaimed that Ukraine is "not Africa" or said indignantly, "Italians think we live in mud huts like in Africa!" For Ukrainians in Rome, "Europe" referred to an ideal of plentiful consumer goods and democratic freedom, whereas "Africa" symbolized abject poverty, starving children, and stunted human potential. Yet, Ukraine's claim to Europe was tenuous and the fear that Ukraine might become "like Africa" was real.

The "Second World?": Between "Europe" and "Africa"

Ukraine is caught somewhere between "Europe" and "Africa." Neither First World discourses of "Europe" connected to developed capitalist markets, nor Third World discourses of "Africa" isolated from global markets capture the complexity of Ukraine in transition. Neither discourse illuminates Ukraine's relation to migration, and, more specifically, to exile. The transnational social field of exile required migrants to engage with Ukraine's nation-state building process in both very personal but also abstract ways. This engagement with Ukrainian nation-state building was concretely about their children's future, but participants also connected their own migration to global questions such as con-cerns about what this "new" Ukraine would look like and where this "new" Ukraine might fall in the global hierarchy of nations. Exile produced a migrant subject that was obligated to engage in a deep and painful interrogation into the meaning of Ukrainianess, gendered personhood, and Soviet versus capitalist moralities.

Whether participants embraced the view that they were agents in "building the new Ukraine" or not, the "new" Ukraine, defined through an idiom of gender and nation, was being built, in part, on the shoulders of these migrant grand-mothers. The removal of *babushki* from Ukraine through migration and the remittances they sent back to their families made possible the shift in workforce composition and family structure the Ukrainian state understood as fundamental to the creation of the new European and capitalist Ukraine. This involved a replacement of the Soviet extended family comprised of mother-workers, grandmother-childcare providers, and peripheral men with a nuclear family comprised of men as breadwinners, women as housewives, and peripheral grandmothers. The conditions of exile were not produced by processes inside Ukraine alone but through an intersection with Italy as a receiving country, which made permanent, family migration in Italy difficult to achieve. In addition, the organization of the domestic work sector in Italy produced a collective life that fostered transnational practices. This stands in contrast to California where domestic workers tended to be more isolated from one another. The intersection between sending and receiving contexts, Ukraine and Italy, produced a transnational social field that limited the terrain of possible actions. Although there were variations within exile, the structural and experiential reality was fairly homogeneous both in terms of who migrated and why, as well as what the possible discursive frames were that influenced both migrant subjectivities and practices.

One of the key characteristics of exile was that migrant women inhabited a space of painful contradictions. They were school teachers, economists, and engineers doing paid domestic work abroad, a job category considered so lowly it did not even exist in the Soviet Union. They did paid domestic work abroad so that their university-educated daughters could do unpaid domestic work back in Ukraine. Through remittances, these women were making economically possible a nuclear, European family that had no place for them as Soviet *babushki*. They were agents in building the "new" Ukraine, one that scorns the "old" Soviet Ukraine and the moral system that shaped participants' understandings of the world. These *Soviet* women were building *European* Ukraine. While the nation-state building work middle-aged women did through migration was unrecognized in public discourse or denigrated by the label "prostitute," these women were conflicted and excruciatingly cognizant of their sacrifices. Indeed, as Tanya said standing on the cement platform looking down at the expanse of middle-aged women at the Garbatella: "They carry Ukraine on their shoulders and don't think they don't know it." Yet, these women worried that Ukraine's European future was not guaranteed. Despite all their efforts, they feared their children might end up living in "Africa" – understood as an economically depressed country populated by "broken" families and racked with corruption.

Riding the migration circuit between L'viv and Rome, I met Slava. She was easily the youngest migrant woman on the bus and the only woman willing to sit next to me. Other women changed seats when they registered my foreignness. As the bus moved us closer to Ukraine's border, Slava began sobbing as she kissed a wallet-sized picture of her 11-year-old son. Slava's husband had left for Poland two years earlier. He had been working off and on and sending back what money he could, but it was not enough to send their son to university one day. Slava had an older sister already in Italy and was on her way to join her in the hopes of finding work as a live-in. Slava's sister gave her half of the €2,200 it cost to buy a 10-day tourist visa, and Slava borrowed the rest with an interest rate of 12 percent. Slava expected that her husband would come home and take care of their son while she was in Italy. But one never knew when the visa would come through, and Slava had to leave today, the day before her husband was supposed to return. Slava shook her head and said, "Already I have not seen my husband for two years and now I don't know when I will see him again. When will I be able to go home?" Her question hung answerless between us.

At the Austrian border, also the border with the European Union and therefore the border that mattered most, guards collected our passports. I handed over my Italian passport and Slava her Ukrainian passport with the 10-day tourist visa. I was terrified for Slava. Nothing about her looked like a tourist, and I was afraid they might not let her through. Slava was too preoccupied with wondering if she would find work right away, if her husband would really make it home from Poland, and if her aging mother could keep up with her active son to worry about crossing the border. I sighed with relief as the bus pulled into Austria. Slava's tear-filled eyes met mine as she offered me a piece of fried fish. Slava explained, "You see, when my son is grown he will either say to me, 'We have nothing. Why didn't you go abroad like everyone else?' Or 'Why did you abandon me?'" She did not like her "choices." If Slava stayed, she risked her son living in "Africa." In order to ensure that her son would live in a "European" Ukraine, Slava migrated to Europe, leaving Ukraine and her son behind. Slava was forced to join the other migrant women in this space of impossible contradictions that was experienced as a deep ache by the individual women and the loved ones they left behind.

3
NARRATIVES FROM THE "GULAG"

Exile, like exodus, is a transnational social field with a structural and subjective dimension. At the level of structure, gendered processes of transformation in the sending country and aspects of the receiving country's context of reception have intersected to produce a migration with a specific demographic profile. Migrants from Ukraine to Italy were predominantly middle-aged, university-educated women, who felt "forced" to leave because their structural position as workers and grandmothers in Ukraine became increasingly obsolete. Instead they became temporary labor migrants with few prospects of remaining in Italy permanently and equally few prospects for being able to return to Ukraine. Structurally, exile is productive of the new Ukraine because remittances from Italy and the absence of middle-aged women from households allowed daughters and daughters-in-law to become housewives and sons and sons-in-law to take their place at the head of the nuclear family. Exile makes economically feasible the family and work structures understood by the Ukrainian state to be both the basis of capitalist transition and of an authentically Ukrainian nation.

The subjective dimension of exile also has several characteristics. Embedded in exile is a painful and required connection to the sending country. Despite the variation in opinions about Ukraine's nation-state building process, the structural reality of exile led all migrants to have a stake in the shape of Ukraine's future. It left migrants longing to go back to Ukraine and making material preparations for their eventual return from exile. Migrants in exile had little or no identification with the receiving country and were oriented toward the sending country where they were diligently remitting their wages to family members. Migration is also a process of subject formation, and migrants deliberately attempted to cultivate "capitalist" and "European" subjectivities. Knowledge gained about navigating the social, moral, and economic orders of capitalist society were remitted to family, especially adult children in Ukraine, and contribute to the production of a capitalist Ukraine from the outside in and the bottom up.

In the following ethnographic narratives, I present the experiences of five Ukrainian migrants in exile to Italy. This exploration of gendered migrant subjectivities illustrates the characteristics that are common to exile as well as the variations. The first two narratives draw from the life experiences of Inna and Tatiana, both of whom occupy the dominant structural position of exile. They are both middle-aged *babushki* who have experienced double marginalization from work and family in Ukraine and both felt they were forced to leave Ukraine and their family to perform low-status domestic work abroad. However, their juxtaposition reveals variation along the subjective dimension of exile. Two ways of experiencing exile emerged from the data collected in Italy and Inna and Tatiana are typical of these two migrant subjectivities. Whereas Tatiana embraced the global discourse that mothers only ever leave their family due to poverty, Inna, even if originally motivated by material need, rejected poverty discourses as incompatible with the new Ukraine. Inna understood Ukraine as "Europe" and part of the First World, while simultaneously fearing that the trajectory of Ukraine's economic transformation might instead lead to Ukraine becoming like "Africa" and part of the Third World. Inna embraced her role as an agent in Ukrainian nation-state building, whereas Tatiana was unwittingly an agent of Ukraine's post-Soviet transformation, but an agent nevertheless.[1] The two migrant subjectivities collectively produced in exile resulted in different sets of discourses and practices in exile and also different practices for their children in Ukraine who were also part of this transnational social field.

Whereas Inna and Tatiana illustrate variation along the subjective dimension of exile, the experiences of Oksana, Yuriy, and Lydmyla in the final three narratives highlight variation along the structural dimension of exile. Oksana, never married and without children, nonetheless lived an anguished connection to Ukraine in exile. Oksana found great meaning in a vision of Ukrainian women as nurturing mothers and supportive wives. This version of Ukrainian womanhood was made tangible in national(ist) imagery through the goddess *Berehynia*. The *Berehynia* ideal was embodied by fellow migrants in the talent shows they produced and attended in Rome. Ukrainianess, with nurturing motherhood at its center, was meaningful to Oksana in her own construction of an ethnonational identity, and yet, as a childless woman, it simultaneously and painfully excluded her from a key component of this identity. Oksana felt she had been expelled from Ukraine to suffer downward social mobility as a "lowly" careworker in Italy. The collective pain of exile, overlaid with the aching desire for a Ukraine yet to come, and the need to show themselves and others that they were not just careworkers but *Ukrainians*, made the talent shows performed by her fellow migrants satisfying meaning-making experiences.

Women, as a result of their structural position in Ukraine's gendered economic transformation, bore the brunt of exile, but new post-Soviet gender expectations of ethnic Ukrainians necessarily affected men as well as women. In the fourth narrative, Yuriy understood that post-Soviet men were expected to move from their peripheral position in the family during Soviet times to the head of family life. And yet, Yuriy realized that men had lost a former prestige as workers and breadwinners in the Soviet Union. Yuriy, like most of the migrant men I interviewed in Rome, was fiercely nostalgic for the Soviet system in which work, and therefore his social standing, was guaranteed. Yuriy was committed to his family. However, without steady work abroad for men, he sent back little in monetary remittances and relied instead on his sister to support his family through her labor in Rome. Yuriy felt his masculinity was under siege. This pushed him ever further into the periphery of his children's lives with whom he rarely spoke. Women migrants saw social remittances as important gifts to their children, but men like Yuriy made monetary remittances a prerequisite for engaged fatherhood. Yet, the men I met in Rome were rarely able to send remittances, thus they often felt they lost the right to be fathers and lost touch with their children. In exile, Yuriy found himself in what he called a "concentration camp" where he was in a limbo of time – "waiting, waiting, waiting, waiting" – unable to find his footing at a historical moment in which neither Ukraine nor Italy offered the security he yearned for.

Whereas most Ukrainians in Italy were there without their families, Lydmyla, in the final narrative, was able to bring her family with her. She also felt the pain of exile. On the one hand she too had little choice but to be invested in Ukraine's Europeanization project, because it was not clear how long she and her family would be able to stay in Italy. On the other hand, her two children spoke fluent Italian and had adopted many attributes that were culturally Roman even if, as Lydmyla and many others pointed out, their "Slavic race" and ethnic features such as "broad faces" and "high cheekbones" would prevent them from ever becoming "Italian." Lydmyla's hope was only to make sure her children did not feel like *stranieri* (foreigners) as they negotiated the contradictions of exile where they simply did not know whether exile was a temporary or permanent condition. The following five ethnographic narratives, while attentive to variation, underline what all participants in Italy had in common: exile.

Inna: Becoming Capitalist in Europe

I had been in Rome over a month and still not a single interview. I had begun to think that I would have to abandon this research project, because I could not convince anyone to speak with me. I was doing participant observation in the ACLI (Italian Workers Catholic Association) offices, going to Ukrainian churches on Sundays, visiting the union offices, and going to every immigrant aid organization I could find.

I arrived at a meeting with Carlo, program manager at the Community of Sant'Egidio (*Comunità di Sant'Egidio*), at their offices located in a Catholic Church in Rome. The Community of Sant'Egidio is a charitable Catholic organization of lay people that began in Rome in 1968 and now has outreach in many countries throughout the world. I saw this dedicated group work tirelessly to help migrants in Rome. In his friendly manner, Carlo showed me around the church and school. He explained that they taught Italian language courses, registered undocumented children in school, held cultural festivals, and welcomed interfaith sharing for migrants of all religions. We walked into an office, and Carlo's easygoing manner became formal as he introduced Donatella with great deference, making it clear that she was in charge and the person I would have to win over if I wanted access as a researcher.

Donatella shook my hand and asked me if I had read the book *Global Woman*.[2] Thinking this was the bonding moment that would get me in the door, I answered with excitement that, not only had I read the book, but I had taken a course with one of the editors, journalist Barbara Ehrenreich, and had been a teaching assistant with the other editor, sociologist Arlie Hochschild, who was a professor in my department at UC Berkeley. She looked at me coolly and said:

> I didn't like it. I didn't like it, because it put careworkers together with exploitation and trafficking in women. Caring for the elderly is not either of those things. Carework is the best job available to migrants. It is the most regular and offers the most protections.

Donatella never did let down her guard around me. Nonetheless, Carlo continued to show me around and introduced me to Inna, who was there for an Italian language class. Inna became a key contact and eventually a dear friend.

I had already spent much time with Inna over several weeks before we sat down together with cups of tea and my digital recorder. Inna, 49, was a slender woman with a round face and energetic eyes. Her smile revealed a chipped tooth, and she curled her hair in a way that evoked 1950s America. Inna was born on the border with Poland in Western Ukraine. She later moved to L'viv where she completed a technical degree in electronics and began work in a factory. Inna did not enjoy this work and, after two years, left the factory to enroll in the department of foreign languages at L'viv University. When she graduated, she moved with her husband to a small village of 8,000 people I call Vidmovapol, an hour and a half outside L'viv. There she taught French at a high school. Inna has two sons, Ivan and Oles, now 28 and 23. Inna had one grandchild, but she would soon have two.

Inna had been in Italy for four of the past six years. Like all the women I met, Inna never expected to leave her hometown. She explained that life played "many tricks on her":

> The collapse of the Soviet Union was also an economic collapse and Western Ukraine no longer gave enough for our family to live on, so I left for

Italy. … Those who worked in administrative offices could make money through bribes. Those who had tools or property attached to their work could sell them. But what does a teacher have? Nothing. There is nothing to sell, no property to claim. Look here, this is what they gave us, [showing me a promissory note] worthless pieces of paper.

Inna came to Italy in 1998 during the early years of the migration from Ukraine to Italy and, after two years in Italy, returned to Ukraine. In 2002, Inna migrated once again to Italy and had been in Italy for two years when I met her in October 2004. Inna laughed at how little she knew about what life would be like for her in Italy when she first arrived:

> I actually thought that I would teach foreign languages here! I didn't even take the address of acquaintances I knew [who were here in Rome], because I thought I would stay at a hotel like a normal person. Now everyone comes to someone, but I came thinking I would stay in a hotel and left without even a phone number to call. And then when I got here, I realized that a hotel was 40–50 euros a night … or maybe dollars at that time. I realized that on the $500 dollars I arrived with, I would sleep one week and then be on the streets!

Inna bought her first job in Rome for $150 from an agency that she said was run by a British woman and an Italian man. The job they found her was, according to Inna, "simply an insult." Inna was to care for an elderly couple. The husband told Inna that, because his wife was too ill to have sex with him, this would be part of Inna's job. Inna quit this job after a week and went back to the agency. The agency said it was not their fault that she was unhappy with her job and would not return her money. Inna spent $200 to buy her second job from a migrant who was returning to Ukraine. The returning migrant told her Italian employer, Signora Claudia, an elderly woman with multiple sclerosis, that Inna was a life-long friend and vouched for her as a worker, even though they had only just met. Inna worked for Signora Claudia for two years as a live-in careworker. Inna said that they had a very good relationship:

> [Signora Claudia] was an intelligent woman. She understood that I − how can I say it − that I was a teacher, that I am educated … and she treated me that way. She treated me as an equal. She understood my situation that it was the [Ukrainian] government that forced me to leave, and it was not my choice. I wasn't just roaming around the world for any other reason except that the government forced me to leave. I worked for her without documents. I wasn't legal all this time because the *sanatoria* [amnesty law] was in 1998, and I had only one month to do the paperwork. But this woman wasn't able to do the paperwork, and her children didn't want to do the

> work needed. So, for this *sanatoria*, I remained without documents. But she
> always paid me even if I was working informally. We say: "working in the
> black."

Signora Claudia did not pay Inna vacation days or the other benefits to which
Inna was entitled. However, when Inna left, Signora Claudia did give her four
months liquidation pay and asked Inna to sign a document stating that she would
not sue her for any more money. "Looking back," Inna said, "she had me sign
that paper because she knew she owed me more." Nevertheless, Inna felt she was
treated fairly.

Inna left this job to return to Ukraine for a number of family reasons. Her son,
Ivan, was graduating from the institute, and Inna wanted to be there. In addition,
Ivan was getting married. Unfortunately, it was not only happy events that
brought Inna back to Ukraine. Her father was dying of cancer, and she needed to
care for him. Inna returned to her old teaching job. She shook her head sadly as
she said:

> But nothing had changed at home. I understood that if I wanted my
> youngest son to study, I would have to come back to Italy. After my father
> died, I came back. Now I am already here two years. [Oles] still has three
> years to study. I am paying for his education, so I have three more years to
> go here!

Inna often drew distinctions between herself and other Ukrainian women in
Rome for whom "money was the object of life." I had interviewed Inna's
roommate, Larisa, the week before. Larisa worked around the clock, and the
remittances she sent back to her family in Ukraine infused her migration with
meaning. Inna drew a contrast between herself and Larisa:

> It is good that you spoke with Larisa. Larisa works all the time. Sunday she
> works, and Saturday she works. This is our mentality: work until you can no
> longer stand. Work, work, and again work! I work during the week, and I
> have one job cleaning on Saturday, but it is not serious work. I always have
> my eye out for more work but, for now, I just have one job. I go to these
> courses. I go to school and am never bored. I don't have free time. If I
> have a little free time, I study Italian.

Inna has a full-time job and works Saturdays but still feels that, compared to other
migrants, she works less. In fact, two ways of living in exile emerged in Rome.
For some, like Larisa, the global script that women migrate due to poverty was
worn like a status shield,[3] justifying both their migration and their claims to being
a "good" mother. This motherhood discourse shaped the practices of Larisa and
others like her who reported feeling that they could never appear to be having

fun in Italy. Life was on hold while they sacrificed and toiled. For others, like Inna, poverty was not what gave migration meaning. Instead, Inna and others like her saw themselves building the "new" Ukraine.

Inna called herself a "patriot" and spoke passionately about Ukraine's European future. She often shared with me her worries about how Ukraine would make this so-called "transition to Europe," and what this would mean for herself, her sons, and her grandchildren. The majority of migrants in Rome, like Inna, were from Western Ukraine. Western Ukraine is the center of a Ukrainian nationalist movement that mimics what respondents called the "European model of nation-states" in which there is a single people, language, and religion bound to a national territory, even though not all European countries follow this model. In Ukraine, these elements should be *Ukrainian* and not *Soviet*. Inna poignantly asked: "How can a Soviet person teach her children what it means to be successful in a post-Soviet world?" Inna said:

> Imagine, Cinzia, that all the rules change, that all the things that you learned growing up about what you were supposed to do are gone. I am supposed to tell my children what to do to be successful, to live a normal life, and to be respected. How will I learn these new rules so that I can teach them? Some of this I learn here in Italy. My children will stay in Ukraine and help build the new Ukraine. I do not want them to have to go abroad. I must help my sons and also our Ukraine from here. This is why I study and take classes: to learn the rules, understand?

Inna used exile as a way to learn about what it meant to be European and attempted to share what she learned with her sons. She mused that her grandchildren will not need to learn a European subjectivity; they will just know it from growing up in a European Ukraine. Although Inna sent home most of her wages in remittances, she also made time in the evenings and weekends to attend language classes, take driving lessons, and explore Rome. During these activities, Inna was not earning money and, in the case of driving lessons, she was actually spending money. That made her vulnerable to accusations of being a "bad" mother by those migrants for whom "money was the object of life."

Inna pushed both her sons to learn foreign languages, because she believed that this would help them in a Ukraine destined to join the European Union. Inna often spoke of bringing back more than just money to Ukraine. During our recorded interview, she phrased it this way:

> You see now I have this … well this dream. Maybe it is not a dream because, when you are already 50 years old, it is strange to think too far ahead, yes? But even at this age, it is a bit early to retire and too early to lay in a body bag. Therefore, I thought to myself that maybe I could take another course here at an Italian university and then return to Ukraine and

be able to teach Italian when I go home. I could teach European culture. We need this in Ukraine. That is why you met me at school.

Inna hoped that she could, through social remittances, send back or bring back herself knowledge useful for Ukrainian nation-state building and the creation of a European citizenry.

Inna had material dreams as well. When she first left for Italy, she thought she would pay for Ivan's university and for her in-law's medical expenses. She also installed running water at their house, so they did not have to use the well anymore. But, the house was small. Inna and her husband, Dmytro, decided to build a larger house in Vidmovapol. Inna thought Ivan and Oles would marry, and each son would live in a section of the house with their families. Then Inna would retire to raise her grandchildren. Inna proudly showed me the pictures of her surprisingly large house under construction. Her eyes sparkled as she asked me to imagine a completed bathroom here and another bedroom there. Inna continued:

> You see? Italians, they think Ukraine is Africa. They think we live in mud huts like in Africa! Does this house look like Europe or Africa to you? … I show these pictures to my employers, so they know I am educated and not poor; so they will know how to treat me.

Sending monetary remittances home was important for Inna, but it was not the act of remitting that gave migration its meaning, but rather the symbolic value attached to what that money could buy seen through the lens of Ukrainian nation-state building. Inna saw herself as actively engaged in Ukraine's Europeanization project.

We were interrupted by Inna's roommate, Larisa, who had arrived home a few minutes earlier and paused to look at Inna's pictures. Larisa shook her head and exclaimed emphatically, "Who, Inna? Who is going to live in that big house?!" Inna collected her photos protectively and shrugged her shoulders saying, "That is all to be seen. It doesn't matter. It is my monument (*pamiatnik*)." Inna explained that life had played another "trick" on her. Her oldest son, Ivan, had a gift for languages. She had pushed him to learn English and join the military as a translator, because the military was still paying salaries. Ivan was assigned to Kyiv and was earning well but, in order to maintain his station, he had to become a resident of Kyiv. Inna spent the money she earned her first two years in Italy to buy Ivan and his family a small two-room apartment in Kyiv. Now, several years later, Ivan and his family had no intention of moving back to a small town like Vidmovapol. Her youngest son, Oles, was renting a room in L'viv while a university student and hoped to join his older brother in Kyiv when he graduated. Inna joked that after all this time in Rome, it would be hard for her to live again in the countryside, especially if her children and grandchildren were in Kyiv.

Inna continued work on the house even though she knew in her small village, no one could afford to buy such a large house or, as Larisa pointed out, "even keep it warm during the winter." Nonetheless, the house was her "monument." It was a monument to a particular understanding of a European Ukraine and her family's place in this future Ukraine. It was a rejection of the dominant narrative that all Ukrainians are "poor" and come from a place that is "like Africa." Inna, and participants like her, felt that they could not be poor *and* make claims to Europe. According to these respondents, poverty implied low education levels and a traditional society without modern values which, they reasoned, might characterize the "Third World" represented by "Africa," but not Ukraine. Ukraine experienced a Soviet modernization process and has high education levels. In fact, Italy's push to increase access to university education occurred much later than in the Soviet Union. As a result, most of Italy's elderly population had only a fifth-grade education level, while their Ukrainian caregivers had university or other advanced degrees. Interviewees often noted as scandalous the lack of books in Italian homes and complained of the "low culture" of their elderly wards.

Inna's monument did other symbolic work as well. It was "proof" that, although Inna spent some of her time taking Italian classes in Rome, she was also working and sending her money home to sustain this very visible project. This helped to shield her from accusations of being a "bad mother." Showing the pictures to Italian employers also helped to signal to them how she should be treated in Italy: not as a "poor" migrant, but as a fellow European whose country was about to arrive. Inna felt that by building her house, she was also building the new Ukraine.

I was often shown pictures of cars, furniture, computers, and other consumer items that were bought with remittances earned abroad. For some women, like Larisa, a computer was a computer with no more meaning besides tangible evidence of their self-sacrifice in exile for their children's education. Yet for Inna and participants like her, who prioritized Ukraine's nation-state building process in their migration narratives, consumer goods took on a larger meaning as evidence of Ukraine's Europeaness, which they felt was constantly under siege in Italy. Later on in my fieldwork, after many conversations about the kind of computer Ivan should buy to help him with his continued language studies in the institute, Inna showed me a picture of Ivan working on his new laptop and told me that he had an internet connection at home in his apartment. Inna nodded her head and exclaimed, "You see? Ukraine is not Africa, we're connected!" For Inna, the laptop was not simply a laptop, but a symbol of Ukraine's Europeaness and evidence of her role in shaping Ukraine's European future.

It was soon Inna's 50th birthday. As is customary in Ukraine, the birthday celebrant organizes her own party, invites guests, and provides food and drink. Given the small living spaces, Inna invited 15 friends out for dinner. Everyone brought a side-dish or a bottle of champagne to share, and we ordered the main course from the restaurant. This was a loud and celebratory gathering. Guests were on their feet making toasts, reciting poetry, and singing songs with glasses raised and swinging. As we completed the meal, the waiter walked over the black book that contained the bill, and the laughter ended as a tense silence fell over the group. It was as if the whole table was holding its collective breath.

Inna turned over the bill, and her face flushed red. She announced, "It's nothing! It's normal! I do not live for money, and it's my 50th birthday!" The guests exhaled in unison – except me. I was sitting close enough to have seen the bill when Inna turned it over and was horrified at a bill of almost €500. That was nearly a month's wages. Inna winked at me and clinked her glass with my glass still on the table. That touched off a series of orations to the birthday celebrant that I had come to expect at Ukrainian birthday parties. A dark-haired woman, a friend of Inna's I had not met before, stood and raised her glass for yet another toast. She spoke in Russian to their collective sadness about leaving families, friends, and neighbors to work in an unknown place. She continued:

> We are all stuck sitting in Italy. But, we also should remember that many Ukrainians want to come to Italy and are unable to come. We, who are here, should not forget this. Italy is a beautiful country, and we should all study its culture, history, and art. We should not complain or be sad that we are not back in Ukraine but value the gifts that Italy has to offer us.
>
> When you are away from your family you look for something else that is like a family. We have found this in each other. It is difficult to find kindred spirits here, to find people with goals more interesting than just making money. We are lucky to have found family in each other.
>
> To [Inna] and to all of us!

Among those in attendance, there was a recognition that they were more than their monetary remittances. That in fact, consumption practices, even 50th birthday parties, were infused with meanings about what kind of Ukrainian one was or aspired to be. Inna replied with a blunt toast of her own: "Tonight, comrades, we are capitalists!" The table erupted into laughter.

Over eight months after Inna's birthday party, on a Sunday in mid-August 2005, Inna and I boarded a bus in L'viv, Ukraine. We were on our way to her home in Vidmovapol. I had been unable to contact her upon arriving in L'viv. Her Italian cell phone did not work, and I had incorrectly recorded one of the numbers to her landline phone in Vidmovapol. Inna, knowing the day I was arriving, had simply gotten on a bus and come into the city to find me. It seemed a miracle that she did in fact find me wandering the streets of L'viv's city center. Inna wanted us to immediately take a bus to Vidmovapol. I had just ventured out to explore a new city, and I did not have my overnight bag with me. Inna reluctantly concluded that we had to go back to the room I was renting to collect my toothbrush and a change of clothes, even if it meant having to stay the night in L'viv. "No," Inna sighed. "You'll need your things because it's my home, but it isn't like I *live* there. I don't have more than a towel to offer you." She was back from Italy for a visit herself and laughed that she too was a visitor in her own home.

The next morning, Inna, anxious to get back, was fidgeting as we waited for the bus to depart. She explained, "When you haven't been home for so long, you have so much to do. Then, you also want to be home to cook meals for your family." She had been back in Vidmovapol for three months and had just a few weeks left before the family she worked for in Italy was expecting her back. Inna explained that her mother-in-law was ill, and she had been by her bed night and day until she passed away almost a month before. She wondered out-loud how she would get done all she needed to get done before she had to return to Italy. Inna was busy supervising the construction of the new house. She noted that her husband was unable to manage the construction project on his own. "Some things you need a woman to get done." She had contractors to meet, work to inspect, and tiles to pick out. Additionally, she was cooking, cleaning, and doing maintenance work on the house in which they were currently living. I had spent a lot of time with Inna in Rome, and I had never seen her looking so tired and stressed out.

During our time together in Ukraine, Inna was often frustrated by what she perceived as the gap between the reality of present-day Ukraine and what she saw as its glorious European future. Looking out the bus window was one of these moments. Inna sighed, "It makes me sad to see the countryside." "Why does it make you sad?" I asked. She replied:

> Because before there used to be collective farms (*kolkhozi*) that made sure that people worked the land, but now it is fallow. When people pooled resources, they could afford to buy tractors and equipment. Now that everyone has their own plot, individual farmers cannot afford this equipment on their own. They have gone back to working the land by hand. And look, [pointing to a tract of land overgrown by weeds] abandoned. In Italy you don't see a single strip of land that isn't cultivated. Ukraine used to be the bread basket of the Soviet Union. Now look …

Our rickety bus pulled into the center of Vidmovapol, a small square dominated by the statue of a woman from the sixteenth century who, born in Vidmovapol when it was part of the Kingdom of Poland, went on to influence the Ottoman Sultan to deal favorably with her homeland. This motif of women and nation was echoed in many of the city squares I visited in Ukraine. Inna's husband, Dmytro, was waiting for us in a battered and dusty 15-year-old car that he had purchased for $1,000 with remittances Inna sent back from Italy.

At 58, Dmytro still had jet back hair. He was dressed in what most men were wearing: shorts, flip flops, and an old t-shirt that covered a round belly. Outside the town's center, many of the roads were unpaved, and Dmytro was dusty. It would only be a matter of hours before I, too, would be powdered in dry earth. Dmytro used to be an engineer. He now worked as a taxi driver, using his car to drive local people to nearby cities or the train or bus station. He had kind eyes and gave me a shy smile as he drove us home. Later on, during an interview in L'viv, their eldest son Ivan would tell me how worried he was for his father. Ivan said:

> It was not traumatic for me to have my mother go abroad. I was already out of the house, living in L'viv [for university]. I am very grateful that my mother was able to send me to university. And then, you know, she bought us an apartment in Kyiv. I think going to Italy has been good for my mother, too. I mean it was hard and some of it was awful, but overall it has been good for her. It has broadened her horizons. It has been hardest on my father. He is uncommunicative. He has no friends, and now I am in Kyiv with my own family and Oles is in L'viv. These past three months that my mother has been home, he has come back to life.

Inna explained that it was hard on Dymtro to have to depend on her for money. She quickly added that now, he earned well as a driver. In fact, her remittances were no longer used for daily expenses, but for bigger projects. For a Soviet man, whose primary responsibility to his family was his paycheck and whose identity was defined by his occupation, the situation was delicate. Inna often praised Dymtro as a provider to me when he was in earshot. My fieldwork was filled with stories of "weak men" who had found other women, or gambled, or drank, or neglected the children. In comparison, Inna felt lucky. Dymtro was an involved father. Inna noted that most children became more detached from their fathers once their mothers left. She, however, watched Dymtro become increasingly close to their sons. Dymtro had become especially close with their youngest son, Oles. Oles was shy around me with his parents there, but he opened up when I met him again for a beer in L'viv and turned on the recorder. I asked if his relationship with his parents had changed since his mother went abroad. His eyes filled with tears as he explained that he was 16 when Inna left:

> She was among the first to go to Italy. Lots of people then left and came back within a few months, only the strongest or the scrappiest, like my mother, remained … No, my relationship with my mother is the same but my relationship with my father, yes it changed over time. If before I used to go to my mother for advice, now I go more to my dad. We spend more time together and we became better friends I guess. But my relationship with my mother is the same.

I noticed that Oles and Dymtro often communicated with just a glance as we moved about in their small house.

Inna and Dmytro had inherited the small house they raised two children in from Dymtro's parents. It had one bedroom, a living room, a kitchen, and an outhouse that so embarrassed Inna, I almost regretted coming and causing such discomfort. But soon I was at the site of the new house. I stood in awe in front of the "monument." It was large, even by American standards. The bottom floor was four rooms, a kitchen, and a bathroom. An elegant spiral staircase led to an equally spacious second story with another four rooms and a second bathroom. The two stories sat on a garage and full basement and gave the house an imposing height. The house was four times larger than the house Inna and Dmytro currently lived in.

Over lunch Inna asked if I had spoken with Ivan, who would host me in Kyiv later that summer and who I would meet in L'viv the following day. I replied that we had spoken on the phone, and that he was gracious in inviting me to his apartment in Kyiv where he lived with his wife and toddler. Inna exclaimed, "We paid for that apartment so he has to be gracious! You are *our* guest!" Inna wanted to know if I had spoken with him in English and what I thought of his English skills, or if he was shy and had spoken with me in Russian. "Inna," I said truthfully, "He speaks beautiful English! He even answered all my questions with our American accent!" Dmytro stood in the doorway and paused, visibly moved. Inna's eyes also welled up with tears. "See," said Inna, "Papa is happy that our money is not wasted." She turned to Dmytro, "You are head of this family, and so you should be proudest of all!"

After lunch we walked down Shevchenko Street, Vidmovapol's central street. If every U.S. city has a Main Street, then every Western Ukrainian city has a Shevchenko Street in honor of the famous poet considered to be the founder of modern Ukrainian literature. He is credited with preserving the Ukrainian language from near extinction due to Soviet Russianization policies, a form of assimilation to Russian cultural and political practices that targeted non-Russians in the Soviet Union. Inna walked me down the street, and we decided to count how many of the houses represented families with a member working abroad. Inna gave a nod to each house and explained how many people were abroad from each household while I took notes. "This house is really a sad story," Inna sighed. "They are just too poor to send anyone abroad. Lyubov is my age and willing to go to Italy to work, but they cannot afford to pay for the visa." Those going to Italy must pay a "travel agency" to buy a 10-day tourist visa. They then entered Italy and overstayed the visa to work. "People think, isn't it terrible, all of our women must travel abroad to work but, I don't know …" Inna paused as she looked out at her neighbors' houses, "Maybe what is truly terrible is not having enough money to go and being left behind." I replied that it sounded like it was hard to go and hard to stay. Inna smiled weakly, "Tough time to be Ukrainian."

By the time we had reached the end of our walk down Shevchenko Street, we had counted that 55 of the 214 houses relied on remittances from abroad: 22

households had someone in Italy, 11 had someone in the United States, seven in Spain, seven in Portugal, six in England, one in Germany, and one in the Czech Republic. Inna asked to look at my notebook for the tally. "So," she exclaimed. "That's what? More than 25 percent of the families on this one street survive on money from abroad. And Cinzia, I am surprised it isn't higher … it probably is higher. I am sure I am missing people." As we walked back to Inna's house, we shared the road with cows sauntering freely and carts of hay drawn by horses. Inna shook her head and asked, "What European country still has cows walking in the middle of the street?" Inna became quiet and withdrawn. I shared her melancholy mood as we walked back in silence looking at our dust-covered feet in sandals. "Yet another thing that doesn't happen in Italy," she said jocularly pointing at our feet. We both laughed as she put her arm through mine and we finished the stroll toward home.

Tatiana: Sacrificing for Motherhood

I was sweating despite the chilly mid-November day. There was a delay on the metro and I was racing toward Piazza Venezia to meet Inna and some of her acquaintances. These were not the women Inna usually spent time with, and I was nervous and excited to meet a new group of women. It was not difficult to spot them on the piazza huddled in conversation. Something about their winter coats and hats suggested they were from Ukraine or as Italians say, *donne dall'est* (women from Eastern Europe). Simply the fact that they were standing outside on this cold morning suggested they were likely not Italians who were hurrying to be indoors least they catch cold. These women, live-in domestic workers with Sundays off, had no other place to go. As one woman told me, "If we stay home then we have to work. Rain or shine we walk the streets outside."

I hurried toward the group of five women. Inna hugged me and introduced me as her friend, one of "ours" (*nasha*). Inna, who had taken me on as her personal project, was always on the look-out for interviewees for me. She had launched into "the hard sell," explaining my project to the group who looked at me skeptically and a bit annoyed that they were being bothered by such things on their day off. I, forever grateful to Inna for all her help, was at the same time embarrassed by her blunt and pushy introduction. I squeezed Inna's arm and announced that today we just enjoy each other's company. The group soon pulled me into their discussions with three of them speaking in Russian for my benefit and two insisting on Ukrainian for close to 15 minutes more until they too slipped into Russian in order to participate in a discussion I now was used to having: Why was I childless? The fact that I married at 25, young by the standards of my social milieu but barely finding a husband before being condemned to being an "old maid" by Ukrainian standards did not win me any points with this crowd. Everyone switched to Russian to make sure I understood: "You've been married five years almost and no baby?!" Women shook their heads, exchanged looks of pity, and debated if they should scold me or comfort me because maybe I had a "feminine problem." "Cinzia, it is time to have a baby. Your dissertation will not take care of you when you are old." In the former Soviet Union and now in Ukraine, having a child is the most important marker of adulthood and having a husband is secondary. Children and grandchildren were why these women were here in Rome at all, and this gave motherhood discourses heightened prominence. For women who had lost their jobs and professional identities as well as their role of providing daily care to grandchildren, being a mother who sacrificed for their kids was what gave their lives as migrants meaning. In fact, "mother" was one of the few identities they had left, and they held on to it tightly.

Inna announced that she was cold and that we should go inside somewhere to have coffee. The group was reluctant, but Inna insisted making a fuss as is her way and pushed us into a café. A waiter signaled a table for us. We sat down, but the group was somber. In Italy you can either have a coffee at the bar standing up, which means you only pay for the coffee, or you can sit down, which means you also pay for the table. In a tourist spot such as Piazza Venezia, that table can be expensive, and this made everyone, myself included, very nervous. Inna went on about how they work hard and can afford to have their coffee brought to them, while the other women looked as if they were being bullied and were extremely tense. Suddenly Tatiana burst into tears. Another woman promptly said, "We do not belong here," and stood up. Soon the whole group hurried out the door before the waiter could get our orders. It was Tatiana who Inna would later convince to meet me for an interview. Out on the sidewalk the women looked as if they had narrowly escaped financial ruin. Inna turned to me and said loudly, "Fine just the two of us will go in." Without so much as a goodbye to the others, she pulled me by the arm back into the café. Once inside, Inna insisted that they do belong here and that the women she was with today were not her usual company. "We are not Italian; I don't pretend we are Italian. We have Slavic features and will never be considered Italian. But we are civilized! Don't we also enjoy to sit while we drink our coffee?" My housing costs – now for a place in Berkeley *and* Rome – flashed through my mind as did the amount of my research grant, which barely covered housing not to mention plane tickets and food as I nodded feebly at Inna, feeling a bit bullied myself. Inna squared her shoulders, looked the waiter in the eye and said, "*Un caffé macchiato, per favore. Cinzia, what would you like?*"

Tatiana and Inna represent two variations of living in exile. Both women feel the pain of forced exile and are intimately connected to Ukraine through family. They both experience a deep engagement with the direction of Ukraine's post-Soviet transformation. Nonetheless, the money that was earned in Italy had different symbolic meanings. For Inna and others like her who declared they were "not poor" and Ukraine was "not Africa," being able to spend the money needed to sit at the café was a symbol of her Europeaness. For Tatiana and the others, spending the money that was destined for home caused distress and was not part of their frugal Soviet pasts or their even more frugal post-Soviet present where remittances legitimated claims to self-sacrificing motherhood. In fact, spending money on oneself was considered by many participants as the behavior of a "bad mother."

A week later I met Tatiana at the apartment Inna shared with three other women. She had a dark-colored knit hat that she kept on despite the warmth inside. Her short reddish-blond bangs and her hair just below her ears peeked out from under the cap and framed her face lined with worry. Inna prepared us tea and shook the powdered sugar over the *pandoro*, a common Italian Christmas cake, I had brought. Tatiana, 54, had been in Italy almost four years. She came to Rome in 2001 from a mid-sized city located on the Dnipro River in Central Ukraine outside Kyiv. Tatiana had worked in a pharmaceutical factory as a technician. Women retired at 55 under the Soviet system but, because Tatiana handled chemicals, her work was considered dangerous and therefore qualified her for early retirement. Tatiana had retired at 45. She explained:

> In Soviet times early retirement was a reward for doing dangerous work, but now it feels like a punishment. They push you out of your job early and give you a pension so small you cannot live … $25 a month! I couldn't live on this. I could either eat or pay for my rent. If you pay for your apartment, there isn't enough money for food. If you want to pay to eat well, then you cannot pay for your apartment. This is why I left for Italy. And there is not just me; I have a son, and I am a grandmother! Just thinking of it, ah, horrible!

Tatiana was still nervous as she tried to make sense of me and my recorder. She sipped her tea uncomfortably. Inna joined us and said:

> Tanichka, do you know Cinzia's parents are immigrants like us? Cinzia's mother left Italy to clean other people's houses in America and we left Ukraine to clean other people's houses in Italy. Tell me life isn't crazy! Italy was not so different from Ukraine 40 or 50 years ago.

Tatiana's eyes went wide as she asked me if this was true. I nodded and recounted my own family's migration story. I shared with her pictures of my family that I carried with me for this purpose. It seemed only fair that, if I was expecting participants to share of themselves, I should be prepared to do the same. Tatiana told me my husband was handsome and that I should not leave him alone for too long. I answered that I was not nervous about him. He grew up in Italy and knew Italian men so *he* was the one who was nervous. We laughed and Tatiana removed her coat and settled in visibly more comfortable:

TATIANA: Now I understand why you are interested in talking to me. Before I thought, who am I? No one important! But yes, I understand.

INNA: Understand Tanichka? Her parents didn't even go to school. Cinzia is not a big or high status person (*bol'shoi chelovek*). You tell her everything. She is writing the story of our Ukraine. We are part of the story. This is why I help her. Plus look at her Tanya; she is sweet. If we do not help her who will? Think of her poor mother. No babies until she finishes the dissertation she said!

Inna moved back into the kitchen and Tatiana went on to tell me about her son Zhenya and his family.

Zhenya was 32 and a computer programmer with a university degree. He used to work in their home city where he earned $60 a month. His wife worked in the same factory Tatiana worked in and also earned $60 a month. Tatiana explained that this was not enough to live on. It was barely enough to keep her grandson, Danya, fed. Tatiana took care of Danya while her daughter-in-law worked. Her daughter-in-law's own mother had died, and there was no one else. But then something unexpected happened: her daughter-in-law got pregnant again. Tatiana explained:

We were not expecting this. So now we have Danya who is 10 and Anuchka who is 4. My daughter-in-law lost her job when she got pregnant, so now Zhenya works in Kyiv during the week where he can earn more money and then goes home during the weekend. He earns more, but he pays $200 [a month] in rent in Kyiv! It is hard, but lots of people do this back and forth now.

I asked Tatiana what made her decide to leave for Italy. "Where did the idea even come from?" I asked. Tatiana pulled her chair in closer to the table and leaned in:

Now I'll tell you. Zhenya did not need me to stay with the children, he needed money. I wanted to help my son. But also the idea came from the fact that here you are 45 years old and you are destitute and without work! You are already destitute, but you still have to live. Even for these last years of life, you need money. They have laid us bare because even when we worked they paid us very little. I have to renovate the apartment, the television is already old, and the washing machine broken.

You see our women in Ukraine like all of our things to be clean, pretty. She might be there and she herself hasn't had enough to eat, but she will buy something or do some renovation. We have this kind of women. They will do the work themselves. They try somehow to do something by themselves, by their own strength. And so us too. The TV is broken, the washing machine doesn't work, the faucet drips, and the wallpaper has fallen off. In general, I see something must be done because it is impossible to live like that.

I asked Tatiana if she was married or had other sources of financial support. She waved her hand dismissively in the air and announced that she was divorced long ago. In Italy, she continued, men "protect their families," but in Ukraine "our men are useless. It is women who carry the family. It is women who go abroad to Italy to work, while men become alcoholics." Returning to the discussion of her apartment, Tatiana said that her apartment was small, just two rooms (bedroom, living room, and kitchen). But, she wanted it to be comfortable, so she will not be embarrassed to have friends over. Tatiana watched many of her friends leave for Italy, and she felt she had to do something too. Her sister, a structural engineer for whom Tatiana said there was no work in Ukraine, left for Italy just before Tatiana did. Tatiana sighed and wrung her hands:

> This was a very difficult decision to make. It was a heavy decision, because I am a home-body. I never went anywhere in my life, and it was very difficult to come here. I did not want to come. Life forced me to. The collapse of the Soviet Union forced me to.

When Tatiana first arrived, she stayed with her sister in Rome who was doing live-in work. The elderly Italian person she was caring for was kind and allowed Tatiana to stay with them until she found work. In 2001, when Tatiana arrived, there were many Ukrainians already in Rome looking for work. After six weeks of searching, she took a job caring for an 80-year-old man who lived in a small village six hours south of Rome. When Tatiana arrived, the man told her that not only was she to be his house cleaner, but a replacement in his bed for his wife who had died. Tatiana looked at me shaking her head and repeated that he was 80 years old! She returned to Rome the following day.

Next she took a job in the mountains outside Rome where she was in charge of cleaning a large, two-story villa and cooking for a couple in their mid-40s, who she referred to as "the Doctor and his wife." Like most of the women I met doing live-in work, Tatiana described it as "being in prison." Tatiana felt she should have been paid €1,000 a month for all that work but was being paid €516 instead. Nonetheless she stayed because: "I had debts to pay. I needed money quickly to pay for my ticket, the bus ride, and the visa." Tatiana agreed to work Sundays and holidays and worked without rest from 7 a.m. to 9 p.m. She described the wife as withdrawn and sullen, while the Doctor yelled at her all day. After a month, on her first pay-day, the Doctor told her he would only pay her €400 instead of the promised €516. Two weeks later Tatiana said she could not take it anymore, and she left.

Soon after Tatiana found the family she works for now, almost four years later. The situation with this family was more complex. Tatiana was caring for an elderly couple, a 90-year-old woman with dementia and her 82-year-old husband. The woman died a year after she began working for them and the man, who she alternately called Signor Antonio or Grandfather, treated her well. She said that she had opportunities to rest during the day and to study Italian. They gave her plenty to eat, and Tatiana had her meals at the table with Signor Antonio. When Signor Antonio's daughter, Lara, came to visit, they all ate together. At her previous employer, after cooking the meals and setting the table, the Doctor sent Tatiana to the kitchen to eat alone "like a dog," a humiliation Tatiana says she could never accept. Tatiana sighed that the problem with her current job was that the pay was too low. However, given her previous work experiences, she was afraid to change jobs, because "you never know where you might end up." Once Tatiana was sick, and Lara took her to the hospital, stayed with her for all the tests to be completed, and made sure she rested. Tatiana said:

> So in this way I feel a little bit protected, because I am in a foreign country. Others have their employer say, "You're sick? Go home [to Ukraine] and rest there. Here we need you to work." I don't have this. We have a good rapport.

After four years, Tatiana also had sincere affection for Signor Antonio. "I am used to him, and he is used to me. He doesn't want anyone else." And yet her pay was simply too low. Tatiana said she would not have accepted this position in the first place had she known her rights. Tatiana explained:

> They want me to be a domestic (*colf*), a careworker (*badante*), and a companion all in one for 500 euros [a month] with one day off [per week]. This is the difficult work we came to Italy to find. First, we do not know the language; second, we do not know our rights. If I had known the language and had known my rights I would not have accepted this job because the pay is very low and the grandmother was very sick; you had to put diapers on her and everything. And then they gave me only one day off when by law they have to give me a day and a half off. And the pay is supposed to be higher.

Domestic workers are covered by a collective bargaining contract which set the minimum wage at the time of the interview at €548 a month.

Tatiana was being paid below the legal minimum, and she was the only live-in in my sample earning less than €600 a month. The salaries for live-in work ranged from €600–€800 with most reporting a salary of €600. Tatiana was also entitled to Sundays and Thursday afternoons off and was supposed to be paid an additional hourly wage if she worked during those times. Tatiana was extremely bothered that she did not have Thursday afternoons off. However, Tatiana explained, that if she told Grandfather that it was someone's birthday and there was a celebration, he usually gave her permission to go. It was not lost on Tatiana that at 54 years of age, she must ask permission to go to a birthday party.

Tatiana also learned that her employers were supposed to pay her the *tredicesima* or the thirteenth month. All Italian workers, including domestic workers, are entitled to an extra month's salary in December as a Christmas bonus. Domestic workers are additionally entitled to a paid one month of vacation per year. Tatiana repeated several times, "I came here to work and earn money for my family, not just to look around!" As she learned about her rights, Tatiana began to ask Lara and Signor Antonio about them. First she asked to be paid the thirteenth month. Signor Antonio was not pleased, but he did pay her the thirteenth month for that current year but not for the previous years, which he was still required to pay according to Italian law.

In 2003, during the Bossi-Fini Law (Chapter 2), Signor Antonio and Lara did the paperwork required for Tatiana to receive her *permesso di soggiorno*. Tatiana's eyes filled with tears as she explained how having documents meant you could go home. You were no longer "completely stuck" in Italy, just "a bit less stuck" she said with a weak smile. Tatiana spoke of how difficult her first months in Italy were. She said that her mother often told her to go to church, and she would feel better. But Tatiana said she was from Central Ukraine and was not used to going to church like the women from Western Ukraine. Instead Tatiana told her mother, "I'll feel better when they start to pay me more!" Tatiana shrugged her shoulders:

At the same time we are here, and we have to be strong here. Some women stay 2, 3, or 5 months and then go back. They cannot overcome the nostalgia. Oh, the first year is so hard, *mamma mia*! But now, I have calmed down a bit. It is better when you know you soon will have your documents and then you can go home to visit. Before then, you see people leave for home and you think: maybe you will never be able to go back. You think that you'll be stuck in Italy forever, like in prison. But now, I have my documents, and I know I can go home – not to stay but to visit at least.

In fact soon after her *permesso di soggiorno* arrived, with Lara's approval, Tatiana decided to go home after being away almost three years. She planned to stay in Ukraine three months. Tatiana said:

And this is where the daughter [Lara] tricked me. She placed a document by the accountant in front of me literally 15 minutes before we had to leave for the airport. *She* was driving me to the airport! She placed this paper in front of me and said, here Tanya, sign that you have received everything we owe you, and I didn't even understand what it was. In that moment, I was all emotions and was already thinking about home. I wanted to go, so I signed. And now I think: What have I done? Our lawyers warned us never to sign under any circumstances, because they could put you in bondage. They could make you work for free! And I signed.

After three months home in Ukraine, Tatiana said she put those papers she signed, relinquishing all claims to back pay, out of her mind. While she was away, Signor Antonio called her incessantly to ask her when she would return and begged her to come back soon. Tatiana realized that she had a little more power in this relationship than she originally thought.

Back in Rome, she found a leaflet explaining the terms of the domestic worker contract, and she brought it to Lara. Tatiana noted that she had never had vacation pay, and it was written there that she was entitled to it. Additionally employers are supposed to pay *contributi* (social security payments) to INPS (*Istituto Nazionale della Previdenza Sociale* or National Institute of Social Security). In Tatiana's case, she paid the monthly fee herself even though payment was the employer's responsibility.

All labor unions were able to calculate, following a form, the back pay in vacation, liquidation pay, and the thirteenth month owed to workers. Lara again became worried and went to a friend who worked in a union office asking her to fill out the forms to detail the money they owed Tatiana. Lara brought Tatiana these forms and told her to sign them. Lara indicated on the form that Tatiana only worked 25 hours a week. Tatiana could not contain her indignation as she exclaimed, "I work almost 12 hours a day!" Lara also listed Tatiana's start date as a year and half after her actual start date. This would release Lara from paying back wages for that time period. This time Tatiana refused to sign:

> Now I know a bit more Italian and I could read what was written there and I said, "No. First I have been working for you since January 2001 and here it is written June 2002." She [Lara] replied, "And who knows it?"

Tatiana paused to stare at me and let Lara's response sink in. She continued:

> "And second," I said, "I have already worked for you three and a half years, and I was paid my thirteenth month for only one of those years and no vacation pay for all those years." She [Lara] replied, "All the time you have been with us since Mama died, you have been on vacation." This means don't say anything and sign. But I said no, and I didn't sign. You already know my character, Cinzia, I said no and it is no. I won't sign even if you hold a gun to my head. And so, she started to scream. Grandfather who saw all this got very nervous, because when I went home [to Ukraine], he cried all the time. He cried, because he thought I wouldn't come back. He knows very well that they do not pay me as much as they are supposed to. But he is used to me, like all elderly people who become attached. I felt sorry for him, because he is like my father. He's 85 years old, and he is good. I cannot say anything against him. And so the noise came.

Tatiana went to the Garbatella where Ukrainians who trained as lawyers but were now doing domestic work in Italy set up booths and charged a fee on Sundays to help others navigate Italian law. Tatiana asked them to calculate how much her employers owed her in back pay minus her *liquidazione*. Tatiana's employers are required to pay her what is called a "liquidation" or a severance payment which is roughly equal to one month's pay per year of employment. The employer may pay this in a lump sum when the worker is let go, but many employers paid this yearly to avoid a large sum at the termination of the work relationship. Tatiana was afraid she would be out of the job if that fee was added to the document, which already showed that she was owed a hefty payment of €2,000. Lara and Tatiana were now barely on speaking terms, so Tatiana went directly to Signor Antonio:

> So I went to this employer very calmly and I said, "Signor Antonio, look please at what you are obligated to pay me. Do you know how offended I was when I went home and all our women received pay for the full year including their vacation pay except me? Some have worked two and some four years already. I was the only one who didn't receive anything from you. Please, look at the paper." Grandfather looked at me and paid me everything that was required. And now for the liquidation. I was afraid to even talk about it. For now I will keep quiet. They haven't even mentioned this topic. Maybe they think I don't know I am owed this or maybe they are pretending that they do not know that they have to pay me this. For now I am waiting but in the end I think it will not be resolved without a lawyer.

After this, Lara refused to speak with Tatiana and what Tatiana called "the noise" or the "war" began. Tatiana asked Signor Antonio to go to INPS with her so they could see together what the minimum salary was and what the true fee was for *contributi* (social security). He finally agreed, but Tatiana now wanted to wait until next month, January, to go. She thought that the minimum wage might go up with the New Year, and she did not want to miss out on this because they went to the office the month earlier. Tatiana began to cry:

> To take even one ruble from us, one euro, is a hardship for my family. Grandfather may not be so well off, but his children are rich! They own six or seven apartments and rent them out. I don't say it to them but when they say "Oi, Tanya, you are like a member of the family," I want to scream: "You are not my family. My family is at home, and I am here to work in order to help my son and to try and support myself and that's all!"

Tatiana lived extremely frugally in Rome. Unlike Inna who attended Italian language classes, paid entrance fees to museums, and was willing to pay the table fee to be served espresso in a café, Tatiana spent as little money as possible on herself and sent every euro back home.

Tatiana was always thinking of how to earn more money. She decided to take another tactic with Signor Antonio. She explained her idea:

I told him, "If you can't pay me, let me work two hours a day cleaning for someone else to earn more money. You can help me find a job." He is the president of a sports club where many elderly men gather. Maybe one of them needs a woman to clean or just prepare lunch or iron. But he feels this is not prestigious. Then people will say that he has a woman who lives badly. Cinzia, he does have a woman who lives badly! I have two grandchildren and an apartment to fix!

Tatiana felt that things were still going badly in Ukraine, and she was desperate to earn more money to send home. She explained that from Italy it seemed things were better back home, but when she returned she found, "It was actually worse!"

During this time home, Tatiana visited her mother, who was now ill. Her sister left Italy to return to Ukraine to care for her. I asked why it was her sister who returned. Tatiana said her sister was younger, so they thought she had a better chance of finding a job in Ukraine. Tatiana explained:

You cannot abandon your own mother to care for strangers. I also care for mama. I send her money and packages. … Before [in the Soviet Union] medicine was free. Now you have to pay. It is supposed to be free, but if you don't pay bribes you will not be seen. The more serious the operation the more you have to pay. Our mama was in the hospital, and I needed to send right away €100. Some people are in the hospital a month and still haven't been seen by a doctor because they didn't pay. And you have to bring them food because the hospital only gives them tea without sugar and a piece of bread. Really, you have to bring them food to eat, and there are people who cannot do it because they have their children to feed.

Every woman and mother tries first to feed her child, this is understandable. And also children pass out if they are hungry. And these elderly people lay in the hospital, nobody needs them. They are abandoned, abandoned to God or to death. They simply do not want to live. They do not want to live, because they know they are not useful to anyone. Not only because they are no use to anybody, but because their children cannot afford to care for their parents, because they themselves are hungry. The bureaucracy is awful. There is no one to protect you [the elderly and infirm], no one to turn to for help with your problems – no one needs you.

I asked Tatiana if she ever worried that no one would need her. She was quiet for a long time. She said she supposed that was part of the reason why she left, to make sure she was needed, that she was still useful. Many women described that they had become "useless" in Ukraine and migration was the only way they found to be "useful" to their families. Tatiana was afraid of the day she would no longer be able to work, because it will mean she must go back to Ukraine where she was afraid her money would "vanish and it will be as if I never left for Italy." She asked, "And then what?" Tatiana shook her head.

Tatiana voted for Yushchenko during the presidential elections, like most migrants I spoke with in Rome, in the hopes that the economic situation in Ukraine would improve. Yet she feared that in the end, it does not matter who one votes for. "Whoever is president will become a millionaire, but Ukraine will have the same problems." Tatiana spoke about how Ukraine was a beautiful country, how Ukrainians were hard-working and resilient, and she laughed as she recounted a childhood memory:

> I never thought I would be forced out of Ukraine. I had an aunt, my father's sister, who lived in America with her husband. I grew up hearing the story about how they had not a single dollar in America but worked night and day. My aunt sent us photos and packages when I was small … I wrote letters to her and was curious because I didn't know any capitalists and hearing their struggles I thought, thank God I live in the Soviet Union, because there [in the capitalist world] everyone is so poor. [Tatiana laughed covering her face with her hands.] Then there was a long time when no letters would get through. Then, just before Gorbachev, we received letters again from them. They were 90 years old. They sent a picture of their house. They worked all their life, and they owned something. We worked all our life, and we have nothing. We are destitute. The [Ukrainian] government has stolen everything and sent us to Italy.

Tatiana alternated between the hope that the Orange Revolution would raise Ukraine's standard of living and the fear that things would get worse before they got better. Tatiana participated in some of the demonstrations in support of the Orange Revolution in Rome and twice stood in long lines to vote for Yushchenko at the Ukrainian consulate in Rome. I asked her why she voted for Yushchenko. Her answer lacked the ethnonational flourishes of Inna's response. Tatiana simply replied, "For the same reason we all voted for Yushchenko: so we can go home."

Oksana: Talent Shows Performing Family, Nation, and Ethnicity

I met Oksana in the packed auditorium of one of Rome's Basilicas. One of the particularities of migrant groups in Italy was that they were run by Italians and rarely by migrants themselves. The Association of Ukrainians in Italy was an exception. It was run by a group of Ukrainian women domestic workers who, on Thursday afternoons and on Sundays, planned cultural events, especially

Ukrainian talent shows. I was fortunate to have an interview with the group's director, Olga, a slight, dark-haired woman in her late 50s bursting with energy. She invited me to their show, a Ukrainian Festival, at the end of October. She explained that the mission of the group was to do outreach to Italians and teach them about Ukrainian culture. As I continued my fieldwork, it became clear that these talent shows were also constructing a particular version of Ukrainian culture for fellow Ukrainians.

I walked into the auditorium and introduced myself to the women selling *Mist*, meaning "bridge," a newspaper publication sponsored by the Ukrainian Greek Catholic Church (UGCC). *Mist* was a transnational project with some articles of each issue published in both Ukraine and Italy and other articles catering to the concerns of the Ukrainian community in Italy. Not knowing anyone, I was relieved to catch sight of Olga as she seated spectators. Olga came to welcome me with a large smile and hurried me to my seat. She quickly provided an introduction to the woman sitting next to me, Oksana. Oksana smiled and we continued our conversation. I explained the research I was doing. Oksana nodded enthusiastically exclaiming that she was a journalist and understood perfectly what I was up to, and she thought it interesting and important work.

The lights went dim and the Ukrainian Festival was about to begin. The mission of the group may have been to reach out to Italians, but it was clear that I was one of the few non-Ukrainian spectators in the auditorium. In fact, the show began with Italians addressing the Ukrainian audience. First the *Consigliere,* an official from the City of Rome, addressed the crowd. He stated, "Thank you for caring for our elderly. You are not only here because you need us, but because we need you." The crowd cheered. A representative from the Mayor of Rome's office spoke about the upcoming presidential election in Ukraine where she said that Ukraine would decide "whether they will join the European Union or the Russian Federation." A man's voice from the back yelled in Italian, "We are Europeans, not Russians!" The representative continued, "We Italians do not know Ukraine well. We will have to learn because Ukrainians are becoming important in the mosaic of nationalities in Rome."

Next was Donatella, the director of the Community of Sant'Egidio where I had met Inna (Chapter 2). She said, "Most of you know us, and we know most of you. We have been friends since 1994. We are now fighting the battle for dual citizenship so that Ukrainians can become Italian citizens without giving up their Ukrainian citizenship." Italy's naturalization rate was negligible and citizenship rights seemed unlikely, but her words were well-received.[4] Oksana turned to me and said, "Why shouldn't we become citizens. This is part of the goal here, to show that we are not just *badanti*, but artists, musicians, and more!" Finally a representative from *Domina* walked up to the microphone. I thought this an odd choice. In Italy, not only do domestic workers have union representation but so do the hiring Italian families and *Domina* is the employers' union. I conducted an interview in their office in Rome and was struck by the discrepancy in resources between the dingy workers' union offices I had visited and the professionally decorated offices of *Domina* where everyone was *Dottore* or *Dottoressa* so-and-so, a much used title of respect in Italy that indicated the individual in question had completed university. My Italian husband had advised me to embrace the title of *Dottoressa* myself in Italian contexts. I felt pretentious doing so although, in hindsight, there were times the ethnographic situation would have warranted it. The *Domina* representative on stage stated:

> I am a representative of the families that host you. We need to thank you. If our mothers can go to work, it is thanks to you. If our elderly are cared for, it is thanks to you. Sometimes there are misunderstandings and our families at times do not know what their responsibilities are. But, we are fighting for your *permessi di soggiorno*, because our families say I can see that the woman who lives with us cries and is not tranquil. We understand the National Contract [of Domestic Workers] is up in March and that you want to work less hours and earn more money. But our families also have monetary problems. Many are retired and share their small pensions with you. So also you, please have patience with us.

After a weak applause, Lesia came out on stage and introduced herself as mistress of ceremonies. In addition to MC, she would also be providing an Italian translation of the performances. What followed was a series of choirs dressed in Ukrainian peasant garb singing traditional folk songs that the whole audience knew and were not shy about singing along. There were songs about Ukrainian Cossacks, skilled horsemen of the seventeenth century recast as Ukrainian liberation fighters, folk songs of beautiful Ukrainian maids and fertile lands, and partisan songs about Ukrainian independence. People in the audience waved Ukrainian flags as a woman recited the poetry of Shevchenko, Ukraine's national poet. The Ukrainian Festival differed from other talent shows I would attend in Rome because the various choirs that performed came from all over Italy, not just Rome. Naples, Bologna, and Trento as well as other Italian cities sent Ukrainian folk groups. Oksana explained that they invited the representatives of Rome's government and organizations to show them that "Ukrainians are all over Italy and in every village. If there is an old person there, then there is a Ukrainian taking care of them."

The following week I met Oksana at the apartment I was renting in Rome. We agreed that I would interview Oksana first and then she would interview me for *Mist* to which she often contributed articles. Oksana, 51, had been working in Italy for almost four years. She is from a town an hour outside of L'viv, but as a young student she won a competition to enter a five-year university program in literature and writing at an institute in Moscow. She had hoped to get what she called a "literary job" in film, theater, radio, or newspaper. Yet, her religious leanings always kept her out of the *Komsomol*, the Young Communist League, and without membership, she was denied access to those jobs. Instead, she taught classes at a local university. After the collapse of the Soviet Union, Oksana landed a job at a publishing house where she translated religious texts from Russian, Polish, and Church Slavonic into Ukrainian. She also wrote for a religious newspaper. Her economic problems increased as her parents became ill and their pension barely paid for one trip to the pharmacy a month. A neighbor who had already been working in Italy suggested Oksana go to Italy with her for the Year 2000 Catholic Jubilee. Oksana agreed and overstayed her visa to work as a live-in domestic worker.

This was one of my first interviews, and I was caught off guard by Oksana's tears. I felt uncomfortable but soon discovered that at one point or another, all my interviewees in Italy would break into tears with many sobbing into my recorder for several hours at a time like Oksana. I learned when to pause and give the interviewee space, when to continue to ask questions through the tears, when a hand on an arm or shoulder was appropriate, and when declaring that we must really have more tea was the best course of action. I was usually rewarded with hugs at the end of our session and women declared that they felt better. I had assumed that migrants discussed these topics amongst themselves all the time, but many told me that they have no one to speak with about their problems. They must put on a brave face for family back home and others here are carrying around so many of their own problems that they do not want to carry someone else's as well. I was not always perfect, and I certainly made mistakes. Here, in the kitchen of my rented Roman apartment, I was still a novice with this group, and I fidgeted wondering how to react to Oksana's steady stream of tears.

Oksana had been at her current job for two and a half years, but she went through six jobs in the first year and a half. Oksana paid an Italian placement agency $350 for her first job and they "deceived" her. They said that the job was in Rome, but really it was 50 kilometers outside Rome where Oksana felt isolated. After three months the elderly woman she cared for died. Oksana found herself without a job and without a place to live. She stayed with her neighbor from Ukraine who was also working in Rome and found an elderly woman to care for in the city proper. This woman was 88 and had five children whom she felt did not visit her enough. The children hired Oksana because a short time earlier their mother had a mild heart attack and lay on the floor for three days before someone found her. Oksana said she left this job because the woman told her children that Oksana beat her and insulted her. Afterwards the woman would apologize to Oksana and say she knew it was not true and that Oksana treated her well. She thought her children would come visit her more often if they believed she was being treated badly. Oksana was not unsympathetic, but this created conflict and Oksana said that it was "too difficult on my morale" and she left. Her third job she simply called a nightmare. She stayed less than a month and did not say much more about it.

Oksana said her fourth job was the best period for her in Italy. The woman she cared for was very ill and did not speak. She no longer recognized her son and yelled a lot but, Oksana sobbed, the son was a good son and a good person. Through her tears Oksana explained:

> This was the best period when I worked for this family. The best. Because they treated me like a person, a real person. Not just like some slave. He was that kind of person. … I started on Sunday and then Monday the second day he brought me a big atlas and he said, tell me about Ukraine because I don't know anything about Ukraine. And I told him about Ukraine and about who I am. So they treated me very well.

Although Oksana had told the son that she did not have documents, he misunderstood and later became very concerned that he, as a government official, had an undocumented migrant living with him and his mother. The next *sanatoria* or amnesty was expected to come out that year, so he told Oksana not to worry and he would do all her paperwork as soon as the law was passed. Unfortunately his mother died before then, and Oksana found herself once again without work.

After two more stints in families that she said were so unbearable she had to leave, Oksana found her current position. Oksana continued to cry as she explained that the woman she cares for now is not just Roman but from an old Roman family that traces its ancestry back many generations:

> And as they explained to me here [in Italy], this is a completely different genealogy. They are very proud … in general nothing interests them besides themselves. At the beginning for me it was very difficult. I arrived there as the amnesty law came out, so I couldn't leave because I didn't know if in a new job they would do my documents, and here they said they would do my documents. And so I bore it. I suffered many things that now I do not want to remember.

Oksana explained that things have gotten better but still, "Understand, Cinzia? It is difficult for us to do this work. It is easier for a simple woman to do it." By this Oksana meant that she believed it was easier for uneducated women to do domestic work.

Oksana had two brothers in Ukraine. One was divorced and unemployed and the other was married and working. Oksana's mother had difficulty walking, but her father was still able to care for himself. Her brothers checked in on their parents, and they had a neighbor who went to Poland three months on and three months off and looked in on them when she was home. Oksana would like to pay someone to care for her parents full-time but, she said, this is work that does not exist in Ukraine. Besides, she asserted, neither her parents nor a paid caregiver would accept this arrangement. I asked if she ever thought of returning home. Oksana answered:

Every day I think about returning home. But my parents, now they don't speak about this, but I feel that they are worried that I might return. All his life my father worked as an architect and he has a normal pension, the most you can receive. Before the Soviet Union collapsed, he lived without worries and he continued to work until he could. His money was enough, and they lived well. But now on this pension he can go once or twice to the pharmacy and that's it. They still need to pay for the apartment, for food, and they are used to living well. I feel that there is this fear that all of a sudden I will return and everything will end. And again there will be the problem of money for medicine. This is what I understand. My father says on the telephone, "If it wasn't for you, I don't know what would happen to us."

I asked about her brothers and whether they were able to help. Oksana replied:

One also has the possibility to help our parents [the one with a job]. The other one says come home and I will go and do your job. [Laughing] But no. I already did the hardest part, and I tell him what kind of job could you find? Italy is not for men. It is too difficult for them to find jobs. It is very difficult for our men here. There is more work for women.

I asked Oksana if she ever thought she would go back to Ukraine, and she replied she would. Unlike most participants who had children and grandchildren back in Ukraine, Oksana had never married and had no children. She was helping her parents as well as her niece with her university fees. (In L'viv, I visited with Oksana and her niece. I noted that Oksana greatly enjoyed her role as benefactor.) However, Oksana also had no apartment for herself. In the Soviet system, you placed your name on housing lists and waited to be assigned an apartment. Oksana stated bitterly that if the Soviet Union lasted just one more year, she would have gotten her apartment. But now she needs to buy an apartment, and she was saving money to do so. "I'd like to go back but I can't," she exclaimed. "Where would I live?"

Oksana had spoken earlier about how people were not free under the Soviet system and how terrible it was not to be allowed to go to church or to display other ethnic symbols of Ukraine. She recounted some of the phrases a Ukrainian dissident who had spent 12 years in Siberia told her during an interview she conducted with him as a journalist. But here she tempered her remarks:

I cannot say that everything under the Soviet Union was bad; I can't say that. I have to speak truthfully. There were many good things: free medicine, free education, and all these things were thrown away. Why shouldn't these things stay? Why can't we throw away all the bad things and keep the good things that there were? We had a very high education system. Very high. It was said that in the whole Soviet Union, ours [in Ukraine] was the best education. And in Space, we worked in the cosmos and in medicine … and all this was thrown away.

After a long pause Oksana looked at me and wondered if the post-Soviet period really did usher in more "freedom." Her words reminded me of an interview I conducted with Larisa, Inna's roommate, where she stated that in Soviet times she was not "allowed to go abroad" but now she was "forced to, and not to look around, but to clean toilets!" Oksana continued, "I think your book on women working here in Italy should be the companion book to Solzhenitsyn's *Archipelago*." I looked at her and said laughing, "Really? You mean here people think you are in Rome the city of art and culture and you're saying 'Welcome to the gulag'?" Oksana looked at me with a straight face and said, "Very good, Cinzia. Exactly. Welcome to the gulag."

I spent time with Oksana on many occasions over the next politically charged months. Ukraine was in the midst of the Orange Revolution. We decided to go together to the next talent show organized by Olga and the Association of Ukrainians in Italy. It was the end of January and, following the Orthodox Christian Calendar, it was the Christmas Concert. Unlike the Ukrainian Festival several months earlier where I was still struggling for access to this community, I now knew many of the women performing and many in the audience. It was a wonderful opportunity to check in with participants and friends as well as a social occasion for myself. I had been missing my own family and felt like a lonely researcher during the holiday season.

Oksana and I settled into seats near the front, because I would need to slip out and help Sveta, who was performing in two pieces back-to-back, with a costume change. If I was surprised by the overt nationalism of the earlier Ukrainian Festival, having now spent more time in Rome's Ukrainian community and having observed the many demonstrations in Rome in support of the Orange Revolution, I did not even bat an eye at the stage lined in orange and yellow balloons, Yushchenko's campaign colors. The auditorium was once again packed, and Lesia once again translated the performances into Italian despite the Ukrainian audience. The show opened with a skit.

A woman came out in peasant Ukrainian garb: a white peasant shirt with colorful, embroidered flowers and a long full skirt also embroidered with flowers. She carried a loaf of bread on an embroidered cloth and a salt shaker. Lesia explained in Italian to the crowd that the bread represents hospitality and the salt friendship. It is a traditional way to welcome guests to one's home or in this case to a "feast" of Ukrainian talent. The woman then carried the bread and salt to a table where a man and two children, also dressed in traditional garb, sat at the table. Each of them gave a small speech about their role in the family. The woman declared that as a Ukrainian mother and wife she supported her husband and cared for her children who she would raise to be proud Ukrainians. The man stood up and declared that as a Ukrainian man his role was to protect the family and provide for them. The children, a boy and girl, recited in unison that their role was to obey and respect their parents and be the pride of Ukraine. Oksana felt that she needed to provide me with a running cultural commentary about what was happening on stage. She explained that the family was the foundation of the Ukrainian nation:

> Do you understand, Cinzia? This is what makes us different from Russians. Russian women are cold and selfish. Do you think a Russian woman would come to Italy and make the sacrifices that our Ukrainian mothers make for their families? Do you think they would lower themselves to do the work we do here even if there is great need? No! Ukrainian women are different. They do everything for their family, everything! Ukrainian women are nurturers. It is in our blood. That family on stage: that *is* Ukraine. Write that down, Cinzia.

I squeezed her arm in thanks and wrote down her words in my notebook. I also wrote a note to myself, "Aha, now I know why Oksana says that sometimes she does not feel she has done enough for Ukraine, perhaps because she has no children of her own." Oksana, satisfied, sat back in her seat, and I noticed she was crying. I looked up at the audience and saw that almost everyone was crying! Many people were leaning on each other's shoulders as tears streamed down their faces while others patted their neighbors' shoulder and stared off in their own thoughts. Others still waved Ukrainian flags or the *"Tak Yushchenko!"* (Yes, Yushchenko!) banners of the Orange Revolution. It occurred to me that not a single person in the audience had the ideal Ukrainian family portrayed on stage. Many were divorced and nearly everyone was separated from their family through migration.

The "degradation of the institution of the family" was a phrase I heard often in my Roman field site. Even Oksana, perhaps precisely because she did not have children and felt guilty that she had not fulfilled what is now not just a womanly but a nationalist duty, often spoke of the *Ukrainian* family. In our interview months earlier she explained:

> After the collapse of the Soviet Union, we experienced a degradation of the institution of family. All of our families fell apart. Why? Because the family cannot survive now. Who is supposed to protect the family? The man. The husband has to. The woman has to raise the children and be in charge of the family. Then if she goes to work, I don't know, she can be president of a company, but at home she must be wife and mother and support the family. But she cannot do this because she has to think about earning money because the men aren't bringing anything home. All the factories closed. And women organize the men, they organize the children, and they go abroad to work for money. She sends the money home. The men drink this money or

they find another woman. The children see all of this and start to fight with their father for the money. And if they do not succeed they threaten to tell everything to their mother. … I mean this money that was earned with much hardship, a lot of hardship on the part of their mother, then the kids buy drugs and whatever they want. So this money does not always do good. I don't want to say it is like this for all these families. There are very good, decent families where the husband waits for his wife and raises the kids well, but I am telling you what the negative is. … *And the institution of family, which is the base of the government, of the nation, falls apart.*

(emphasis in original)

This discourse of the "degradation of the family" existed alongside an alternate discourse among migrant women who had children. In their narratives, middle-aged women saved the institution of marriage by migrating themselves because if they did not go, they argued, their daughters would have to. Migrant women noted that they were divorced, widowed, or in a "mature" marriage, whereas the marriages of their children would not survive migration.

For Oksana and many I interviewed in Rome, the construction of the Ukrainian nation hung on a particular and traditional conception of the Ukrainian family. According to Oksana, Yushchenko's chances for success also depended on the construction of two-parent families that teach children Ukrainian values. She wondered how much they could really expect Yushchenko to do:

Because people during this time, these 13 years when we can say Ukraine has been free, 13 years when Ukraine does not depend on Russia, Ukraine learned many bad things. It learned to curse; it learned to steal. All the bad things. The young generation who grew up during this time learned these things. And now these people have to change because they are used to the idea that they have to swear, they have steal, they have to be dishonest. If you don't, you'll just sit at home [without work]. This is already a minus.

So even if a new, decent, smart, educated president arrives, what can he do with the past of this country and with these people who now do not believe in anything or anybody? What can he do if we do not have stable Ukrainian families where the young can learn Ukrainian values? I don't know. Then most of our *intelligentsia*, they work in America, in Canada, in Italy, in Spain, in Portugal. They are dispersed around the whole world. Their people need them now, the people who are specialists, but they are not there. We have to make it so they all return.

I am not a mother, so I can work. I want to work for Ukraine, and I help as much as I can. Yes? I can do many jobs. But now they have to also pay me so I can help my parents and live normal myself. I just need to live normal. I don't need anything more than this.

Back at the talent show a series of skits and songs took the stage. The skits were once again about Cossacks as patriotic warriors that fought against Russian tsarist rule and instilled Ukraine's democratic roots, making Ukraine more like Europe than Russia. One woman read an original poem about "the day she woke up and realized she was Ukrainian and not Russian." Another gave a speech on a similar theme of ethnic self-discovery when he realized "the milk he drank from his mother's teats was Ukrainian milk, not Russian milk." Others spoke about the new President Yushchenko and the peaceful victory of the Orange Revolution to thunderous applause. Performers invoked Yulia Tymoshenko in the presentations and often referred to her as the "*Berehynia* of our people." Oksana explained how proud they were to have their first ethnically Ukrainian president, Yushchenko, "but maybe we love Tymoshenko even more." A large picture of Yushchenko surrounded by his wife (born in Chicago of a well-connected Ukrainian family) and five children was brought on stage. It was an image I had seen many times in Rome. The audience cheered and Oksana leaned in and said, "That is a real (*nastoiashchii*) Ukrainian family and a real Ukrainian man! We have hopes that he will fix things and soon all of us can go home."

Every performance – song, dance, or poem – reminded the crowd that Ukraine was a strong and independent nation. It seemed that Ukrainian nationhood was being invented on stage before my eyes as audience and performers negotiated the content of ethnic Ukrainianess. Of course the images and themes were grounded in what was happening back in Ukraine. I wondered if, like with many ethnic folk traditions, it was only abroad that Ukrainians wore this traditional dress. For example, my mother participates in an Italian folk group in the United States, but I never saw anyone in Italy wearing the Italian peasant costumes she and her group don for performances. Yet, when I was in L'viv, I was surprised to see the streets one day filled with school children wearing the peasant garb, apparently a new tradition for the first day of school. I also attended a political rally in L'viv's city center where a folk group came and performed Ukrainian folk songs dressed in these same traditional costumes. It was a historical moment in which Ukrainianess was being constructed not only transnationally across geographic space but also across historical time as they tried to connect pre-Soviet Ukraine to post-Soviet Ukraine and somehow erase the intervening Soviet years.

The focus on the family is also part of nationalist rhetoric in Ukraine as is an emphasis on women returning to their feminine responsibilities, which is framed as a nationalist act. The notion that large families are inherently Ukrainian was supported by the government's pro-natalist policies that encouraged the birth of a second child by offering a stipend. Having a single child is now looked down on as "Soviet." The nationalist cachet of Yushchenko's five children was clearly not lost on his publicist given the ubiquity of this image of him surrounded by his wife and children.

Many of the performers I recognized from the last show. A woman, who was a professional bandura player, performed again. The bandura is a Ukrainian plucked-string folk instrument which looked to me like the lute a medieval minstrel might play. A band of young Ukrainian men, who had also played at the Ukrainian Festival, took to the stage. They sang nationalist songs set to a modern beat, and I refer to them affectionately as the "Ukrainian boy band" in my field notes. I found them remarkable because, in their early 20s, they too were in peasant garb with a rock sound singing, not about love had and love lost as we might expect, but about how much they love *nasha Ukraina* (our Ukraine). As I watched them sell CDs after the show, I thought them boys any Ukrainian mother would want for a son-in-law.

The grand finale was the church choir under Masha's direction. Masha was a classically trained chorale director. I had sat through several rehearsals in Rome's Santa Sofia UGCC and listened to Masha mercilessly extol her choir to do better. After a particularly trying rehearsal, Masha said to me:

> Every Sunday I am running around like a crazy woman trying to organize practice and pull this choir together. This church it is like our family. We could not survive here without it. My *signora* (employer) tells me that I am crazy to run around all day Sunday instead of relaxing. But I do this – we all do this – so that we feel like people and not animals. That is more important than relaxing, no?

I helped Sveta with her costume change backstage just as the group went on. They sang Ukrainian folk songs which always turned into a communal sing-a-long and was the most beloved part of any show for those watching. They also sang both popular and classical Christmas songs. The audience showed their appreciation through endless applause. At the end of the show Sveta pulled me onto the stage, perhaps the most publicly embarrassing moment of my fieldwork, as people continued to take pictures of the choir and me dressed in jeans and a green sweater. In hindsight, I could have at least worn orange (see Figure 3.1).

I lingered to speak with participants after the show and tried to make myself helpful in cleaning up. I saw Taras, a dedicated church volunteer who was a key organizer of the campaign to get Ukrainians in Italy to vote in the presidential elections. He was looking pensive and I asked him why. Taras smiled and answered:

> I don't know … You know one of the things that I like about Italy is that all Italians from the North to the South call themselves Italians. This just doesn't happen in Ukraine, and it is a strong disappointment especially when you see how beautiful Ukrainian culture is like we saw tonight. I worry for Yushchenko. My hope is that the minority that carried out the Orange Revolution will drag the rest of the country into nationhood.

He gave me a kiss on each cheek as is Italian custom and excused himself to speak with someone across the hall. I saw Nataliya and Vira at the *Mist* stand still

FIGURE 3.1 Author in jeans and sweater with Ukrainian performers at the end of the talent show

packing up newspapers on my way out of the auditorium. I yelled over to them, "You two, always working!" They smiled and Nataliya yelled back, "I work for my country, so I am happy!"

I waved to Nataliya and Vira over my shoulder but kept walking forward and straight into Olga, the director of the Association of Ukrainians in Italy and the force behind the show. She had her usual harried air about her and hugged and kissed me, asking me how I enjoyed the show. I told her she had out-done herself, but she was already moving toward the lights and threatened to leave those still there in the dark. The cold January air hit my face as the lights dimmed behind me. Taras was on the sidewalk still chatting and yelled, "What do you think, Cinzia? Lights out on a dream?" I glanced at the dark auditorium and replied, "Dreams, realities, sometimes it is hard to tell them apart." Taras laughed, "You sure you do not have any Ukrainian blood in you?" I signaled maybe with a shrug of my arms and shoulders, winked, and hurried toward the warmth of the metro.

Yuriy: Negotiating Post-Soviet Masculinities

I met Yuriy, 43, at Rome's Ottaviano metro station and we walked to a *tavola calda* (cafeteria-style eatery). Unlike cafés, the seating is free. Despite the cold winter air, we sat at the tables outside as far away from the entrance of the *tavola calda* as possible in the hopes that no one would make us buy anything. Yuriy hoped we would remain unseen, because he could not afford a meal. I hoped the same because, although the women I interviewed accepted my offers to pay for the tea or coffee on the rare occasions we met at a café, I felt it would be a trickier gender negotiation with a man. Yuriy looked distraught when, after 45 minutes, a waiter did ask us for our order. He nervously put out his cigarette. We both ordered coffee, and I paid the tab as soon as the waiter came out with them. Yuriy looked pained and said that he was "ashamed" because he was "not used to that." Without mentioning the money, just a couple of euros, I told him it was right this way. It was my way of thanking him for coming out to speak with me. He was relieved, and he spoke in a much more relaxed fashion now that we were not wondering if we would be able to finish our conversation before a waiter noticed us.

Yuriy's hair was almost all white, and he had a strong if slender build with hands that looked like they worked in construction. Yuriy, born and raised in L'viv, was an electrician by training and he described himself as having "golden hands." He had worked many years in L'viv's Kinescope factory where they made picture tubes for televisions. He said he had enjoyed this work, because it was not monotonous and every day there was something new:

> But then when these hard times came to Ukraine, I went to work as a driver. I worked at this for a little while, but then even this work disappeared. I was left without work. For a long time I didn't work at a steady job. I worked some in different places and then I realized there was no way out, I had to go abroad and start earning money. After all, staying at home and sitting on the stove [as the expression goes] doesn't accomplish anything. Because I have to provide for my family. ... I am divorced, but my children live with me. Therefore, I have to support them. It is the responsibility of parents to support their children until they are adults.

Yuriy and his wife had been divorced many years, but without an income, he was unable to buy or rent a place of his own. Therefore, he continued to live with his ex-wife and children. Several people I spoke with had a similar arrangement. It caused all the tensions one might imagine and more when the ex-wife was abroad. Her remittances, whether she liked it or not, continued to support the household in which her ex-husband lived. I asked Yuriy why he decided to go abroad. He answered:

> First many had already left. Of course it is mostly women who go. Men, if they go at all, it is usually to Russia, to Moscow. Men very rarely go abroad for many reasons. First of all, in Italy for example, there is almost no work for men. There is work only for women. This is why men sit at home and do not take the risk, because you have to lay down big money to then sit here [in Italy] without work. This is very difficult. ... Yes, usually women go

abroad because they have a more mature sense of responsibility, a more mature sense of motherhood. They are always more for the children; they sacrifice for the children, always. Men there [in Ukraine] less so. … Therefore, the decision falls onto women. She drops everything and leaves for far corners of the world to work.

A handful of the women I had interviewed reported shuttling goods back and forth across the Polish border, usually illegally, to earn money. But for most of the women in my study, Italy was the only place they had worked outside Ukraine. However for Yuriy, like most Ukrainian men I spoke with in Rome, Italy was not his first stop. In 2000, he went to Germany on a visa that allowed him to stay 90 days. He did that twice and realized that going to Germany for three months once a year was not "the way out" of his "situation" so he paid $1,700 to a "tourist agency" and left for Portugal. If Ukrainian women migrated to Greece and especially Italy, Ukrainian men who migrated west went to Spain and especially Portugal to work in the construction industry. Unfortunately, he arrived a week too late to apply for documents under Portugal's legalization act. Without documents, it was hard for Yuriy to find work. He was in Portugal for one year and two months, but he only worked six months of that time. After four months without work in Portugal, he called a friend in Italy who told him to come and they would help him get by somehow. He got on a bus headed for Italy. In France they stopped him and asked for his passport, but Yuriy guessed that he did not look threatening, because they let him go and somehow he made it to Italy.

Once in Italy he borrowed money to live on and was without work for five months. Then he found work with two men from Moldova building pools. Yuriy said that this was "very heavy work," but he did not mind. Unfortunately, after five months he was again without work. Finally he decided he would never pay off his debts if he did not have steady work, and that meant domestic work. Many Ukrainian men found themselves doing carework in Italy, and so Yuriy said he too looked for a job caring for an elderly man. He met with a family, and it seemed everyone was in agreement. However, for some reason unknown to Yuriy, they never called him back. While Yuriy was waiting to hear from this family, a construction job, this time working with Italians, came his way, and he has been working consistently with them for the past four months. I asked Yuriy how he found this job. He explained:

It is very difficult for men to look for work like I said before. There is only one way for men to find work: help from women, our women who work as live-ins. They are the ones who speak with the [Italian] families and offer our services. They say, I know a guy, if you need someone to do this, this, or this. Then slowly something might come up. This is the only way. It's the way that it happens 99% of the time and then 1% is chance.

Carework and cleaning generally paid less than working construction, but it was steady work. It was also easier, when a migrant did not have documents, to find work caring for an elderly person in their home than to find construction work, because the work site is visible and more open to regulation. Yuriy said that he was paid less than Italians but more than Romanians, who "have not made a good reputation for themselves." Given this, he felt he was paid well. He reported earning €65–70 a day. Working five days a week that comes to €1,300–1,400 a month, but when Yuriy laid out his expenses, he put his monthly income at less:

> With this money you can rent a room that is normal, the way a human lives. You can eat the way we are used to because our cuisine differs some from Italian food. We are used to eating more meat – meat is expensive. This is already a bigger help to your family. Apartments here are expensive and for our workers it is very expensive. If you earn €800 a month, one fourth you must give for your bed – not for a room for a bed – plus, for example, €100 for food. Then without a cell phone you cannot live here, and this is a minimum of €50. If you smoke you must pay €80 unless you smoke more, €150. So half [of your pay] disappears on nothing, let's put it that way.

I asked Yuriy if he sent money home and he answered, "of course!" He spoke about supporting his family and even his ex-wife, but, as the interview continued, it became clear that Yuriy actually sent very little money home. He sent home gifts on his children's birthdays and holidays, but said he was unable to send home more than that. He had been in Italy for two years and reminded me again that the first five months he lived in debt and still had to pay this debt off. Those who have steady work, Yuriy explained, were able to send money back every month. But as long as he had work two months yes, two months no, he would not be able to send money home regularly. Yuriy continued: "But what choice do I have? In Ukraine practically everything is closed, practically every enterprise is closed, especially in Western Ukraine."

Yuriy has a son, Kostya, 19, and a daughter, Olya, 15. He took out his wallet and showed me a photograph of each of them where the children looked about 14 and 10 years old. Kostya was in his third year of university where he was studying economics. It seemed many of the children of those I met in Rome, especially the sons, were studying economics or "international business." Yuriy said he was unhappy that Kostya was taking this route and noted that "everything in Ukraine has changed since the collapse of the Soviet Union." Like most others, Yuriy noted that before healthcare and education were free, apartments were affordable and, most important for Yuriy, work was "guaranteed":

> Now everyone wants to study, but you have no money; there is no money! Therefore, many women work here so they can educate their children. ... Many say that we lived badly [during Soviet times], and I am telling you

honestly, we lived well. Some doors were closed, maybe this was bad or maybe this was good, but we lived well … Now there is medical service, there is education, there is the possibility to vacation, but *only* for big money! Where will you get this money if there is no work?

I asked Yuriy if there would be work for Kostya when he finished university. Yuriy shrugged his shoulders and replied that you must give doctors "presents" if you want them to care for you, teachers "presents" if you want to pass your exams, and he was sure he would have to pay someone in order to get Kostya a job. Yuriy had hoped that Kostya would go to Germany with him and work for a bit, but Kostya refused. So Yuriy suggested that he become a lawyer, a profession that Yuriy felt would almost guarantee Kostya a job. But an economist?

Who needs an economist? Economists, now every university has an economics department, every university. How many economists do they turn out a year but again, where are the jobs for them? … I wanted him to leave with me and work a while, and then go study what he wanted. Because I agreed with the way of being in Germany. I agreed with the way of life in the West. It would be useful for Kostya to learn this. There are many pluses, there are. But, until 18 years old, yes parents help their children; after 18 you are already an adult. You already smoke, you have already met a girl or a boy, and so you are an adult. You can do as you like.

Yuriy spoke with great sadness about his daughter, who he said must be beautiful now. Since he was still without documents, he has not been home in four years. I asked him what his plans for the future were:

Plans? I no longer make plans for the future, because you just cannot know what the situation will be tomorrow or the day after. I have no plans. Today I have work, tomorrow maybe I will not. I want, of course, I want to have steady work and earn like a human being and live like a human being. Yes, I will return home, I will return home … Home is home. Probably this is so for everybody, and here I am not home. This is not my native land.

Yuriy met a woman here, Raisa. Raisa was also from L'viv and, he said, it was a serious relationship. She was the person he would spend the rest of his life with. They lived together for almost two years now. He hoped to earn enough money to buy an apartment for them to live in back in Ukraine and earn enough money "for a rainy day," because he knows there will be no work for them when they go back. They will need to earn enough money to see them through their old age. Yuriy hoped that the family Raisa worked for would sponsor his *permesso di soggiorno*, even if he was only doing odd jobs for them every once in a while. He was angry that people from the former Soviet Union were not given documents, even though they worked hard:

Yes, we live in many countries. But they push us aside. I speak truthfully, they do not accept us. This is very … it doesn't only offend, but it angers you because our people almost all have higher education. They are all specialists, because we did not sit on our hands at home. We all worked. We do not need computers or calculators. For us it is easy to carry out mathematics in our heads. We are used to this and we can do this faster than any other person, including an Italian. … And yet they do not accept us. They do not want to go to the meeting to get us our documents. They do not give us the right to live here and to work. They do not give us rights. On the television we see people on boats crossing the Mediterranean Sea to arrive here on Italy's shores, and then they all get a *permesso di soggiorno* and are their own people. But us, for us it is a concentration camp [*lager*]. We toil here. I know people who have worked here for seven years and still cannot get their documents. They would like to go home and return here without having to work in the black, but to work honestly and pay taxes and be free and not hide from the police or hide from anyone. Taxes we pay them, not just to pay them, but because from these will come our pensions. This is right, no? But they do not give this to us. So now we just wait for some change in the law, or I don't know. Wait, wait, wait, wait.

An hour and a half into our conversation, Yuriy asked me to turn off the recorder. He did not want to talk politics on record. We continued our conversation and Yuriy repeated the common refrains I had heard many times from respondents. We spoke about the Orange Revolution. He shared his skepticism that Yushchenko would be able to do much to curb corruption. Like many conversations I had with Ukrainians, Yuriy went through the list of corrupt politicians and bemoaned the extent to which corruption had become part of daily life. He felt that human relations have been lost, that people did not help each other as they once did now that the most important thing is money. "In the Soviet Union," Yuriy noted, "you needed other people to survive. Now, you only need money." When I told Yuriy I was planning to go to L'viv, he gave me the contact information for his son, Kostya. He said that he would let Kostya know that I would contact him.

Seven months later, I was standing in front of the Opera House in L'viv's city center, waiting to meet Kostya. Kostya arrived with his fiancée. I noticed that the young men tended to bring a girlfriend or wife to our interviews, whereas the young women I met with came alone. Sometimes I was introduced to the wife/girlfriend and she left, in this case, Kostya's girlfriend stayed with us and quietly sipped tea while we spoke. Kostya looked older than his 19 years. He was heavyset with angular features and white already peppered his black, short-cropped hair.

The first thing Kostya asked was if his father had shown me a picture of him and his sister. He smiled when I said yes and said he was happy to help me. He wanted to know if I had anything for him from his father. He had such pain and longing in his watery eyes that my heart skipped a beat, and I froze. I thought to myself that Yuriy did not even give me a message for him. I was under the impression that Yuriy was in regular contact with his children, and that Kostya would have been told to expect a call from me. Kostya filled my frozen silence by saying that they have barely heard from Yuriy in four years. I told Kostya that I was sorry, but I did not have anything from his father. I will forever regret not telling this boy that his father had asked me to tell him that he thought about him and missed him which, though Yuriy did not say this, I believed it to be true. This was a moment in my fieldwork when the ethics were not clear. I was thinking about me – was this interview coerced because he agreed to it thinking he would have news of his father? Was I exerting power in an inappropriate way? I was thinking about my own conscience. I made a point of always being up front and honest with participants about what I was doing and what my intensions were. I reasoned that being truthful was not only the right thing to do, but I believe people responded to that honesty by opening up and sharing the narratives that are my data. I would shed many of my own tears during my fieldwork, some for myself and some for my participants, but I do not regret any decision I made in the field like I regret the decision on this day to prioritize my sensibilities as a researcher over Kostya's needs as a son.

Kostya nodded and looked dejectedly down at his hands. He explained that Papa went abroad to work four years ago, but he had not found steady work. His aunt, his father's sister, was also working in Rome as a caregiver to an elderly person. Kostya said that she called every week, and they heard news of their father from her. Yuriy had told me that his sister, eight years his senior, was in Rome, but he did not tell me that, in addition to supporting her own son, she also supported their elderly mother and sent €100 every month to her nephew and niece, Kostya and Olya. Kostya continued:

> But Papa, he practically doesn't work over there. He works a month and for two he doesn't work. … He is often sick there, because the climate is different; he is always sick. He very rarely calls because he just doesn't. Even with money, he doesn't help because he doesn't work. On our birthdays he sends money or for New Year's, and even this with varying success. In principle, if someone asked me to go abroad, I would tell them I will never go abroad to work.

Of the 30 respondents who were the children of migrants in L'viv, six had both their mother and father abroad but Kostya was the only respondent whose father was abroad instead of his mother. Children who had mothers abroad, all wished their mother did not have to go and missed having her at home. Yet they also spoke of their mother's migration with pride and gratitude. Many noted that not everyone was able to make it abroad, but their mother, despite great difficulty, was able to adapt. Children respondents explained that they would not be able to go to university, support their own child, or start a small business without the money their mother sent back, and they were grateful. There was variation in how children respondents described the changes in their personal relationships with their mothers, but they all spoke of their mothers as "carrying the family on their neck." Without his father sending back remittances to fulfill the breadwinner ideal or remaining in regular contact, Kostya simply could not understand why his father would not return.

Kostya explained that, due to his good grades, his studies were sponsored by the state, and he received a small stipend, although it was not enough to live on. His sister, Olya, received a small pension, because she was an "invalid." I understood from our conversation that she had a mental disability. This was why Kostya's mother did not go abroad. She continued to work as an accountant and care for Olya. Kostya went through their finances and tallied up all their sources of income. He explained it fell far short of what they needed to live. They would not survive without the money his aunt sent them. Kostya looked at me earnestly:

> In principle, I don't know, maybe everything now will get better, maybe we will live normally, maybe people will even come here to work [*na zarabotki*] instead of us going somewhere. Now we need the young people to stay nearby. Soon they will be of age, and they will not only do well for their pocket, but do well for everyone, for Ukraine.

Kostya continued that he was not afraid of work. He worked in construction over summer vacation and earned €100–150. He was also looking for a job in the evenings maybe at a café. Kostya lamented the social problems that beset families who had a parent abroad. He gave examples of friends who lived with grandparents too old to control them, and friends who used the money their mother sent back for drugs. Kostya said that he remembered when the masses started to leave Ukraine five years ago. Most of his classmates had a parent abroad, and this was new. But now this situation has become "normal."

"But this is *not* normal," Kostya exclaimed. He explained forcefully that he would never even go to Kyiv to work, because no place else in Ukraine were the people as cultured as in L'viv. And he would never leave his children to work abroad. At the same time, he noted that others who had a parent abroad received €200, €300, or even €400 a month in remittances, and this was helpful. "It depends on what the elderly person pays," explained Kostya. However, Kostya underlined that his father's situation was different:

KOSTYA: My father has to rent an apartment. He said this is around €200. I do not understand who he lives with, but I understand that it costs €200 to rent a room there and live. Plus there is food. In principle if he worked, all that is left is €100–200, not more. This is why I do not know why he went there. He of course wanted to earn money; he did not think it would be so difficult.

CINZIA: How did he explain to you why he went abroad?

KOSTYA: Well, he went so that … well, in principle so that he could provide me with an education and an education to my sister and in order to collect money to buy an apartment. He thought he might buy an apartment so he could live on his own. But I do not think any of this will come to pass.

Kostya could not understand why his father did not come home. Kostya believed that things in Ukraine were a bit better, and Yuriy could find work in L'viv or even Kyiv. "At least Kyiv you sit on a train for six hours and you are there." Kostya reasoned that work in Ukraine may not pay what work does in Italy, but it would be steady and he would be home where he was needed. Kostya explained with great sadness:

There is not enough [of him], because I am alone. There is mama, my sister, and my grandmother and then even my second grandmother. There are not enough men at home. I am simply not enough. There might be something to do at home, and it happens that it simply does not get done. Sometimes I wish I could just sit with him a while in the kitchen with tea or something and simply sit a while and have a talk between men. … I have no one to talk to, no one to ask for advice. The first days that Papa left, I would forget he left. And then I'd remember he was gone, and I would sit and have such sad thoughts. I'd think, "If only he was here everything would be normal." … Papa knew exactly how to help me in any situation. If I went to Papa, he would quickly say do this, this, and this. If I went to mama, mama would tell me the opposite! It is simply like this. Papa is papa. Papa is for a son what mama is for a daughter.

Kostya said that, despite being divorced, even his mother wished Yuriy would come home. Kostya continued:

Maybe, maybe someday I will travel to him. I will look him in the eye … I want to, in principle, simply look at him in the eye and ask him why he left. Because I call him, I write, but he doesn't answer.

Kostya does not believe that his father will come back, and he wonders if Yuriy even wants to come back. Kostya asked me to describe what his father looked like. When Yuriy left, Kostya said Yuriy was "big guy," and Kostya wondered if he still was. Kostya hung on every word of my description. Kostya noted that they sent Yuriy photographs and was disappointed that Yuriy never sent a single photograph back. Kostya said, "Some say he has married another woman there." Having promised Yuriy and all my participants' confidentiality, I could not answer and remained silent. Kostya continued:

Maybe he will return, maybe not, this is his right to decide now. I will no longer ask him to return. This is up to him now. At this point … I am already an adult. Well he told me, in principal, you are an adult already. Take care of your sister; help your mother; help them all as best you can. And this is what I try to do.

But it also happens that I do not always listen. It happens that I do things that are not right, but in general I try to help. I try not to fight. But, in principle, this is difficult, and I often think of him and sometimes with anger: Why did you go? Why did you abandon everything and there you do not work? Because now I am able to find him a job for €200–300 here if he wanted. But maybe there he is well and he thinks it is better to live there without work than live here and fight with mama, and fight with me because he sits at home and doesn't do anything.

But, in principle, there he sits [without work], and it still happens that he fights with us by telephone: Why do you sit there if you could work here? There is work here; come back here. He says, "No, I just do not want to come back." He says it doesn't make sense to come back until, I don't know, maybe until everything is good. But for this we need a minimum of 10–15 years. We need to wait for us young people to start doing everything, because the old people, they all lived under the Soviet Union, under Soviet laws, and this is no longer how things work now. Us young people who were born in Ukraine, we can do things … I know that the young people can do a lot better than the old people who are now in power.

Kostya participated in the Orange Revolution and traveled to Kyiv and several other cities in Eastern Ukraine. He explained that when Ukraine joins the European Union, things will indeed be better. In fact, Kostya believed that Ukraine had such hard-working people, that Ukraine will one day save all the economies of Europe. At that point, his father will have to come home. The Ukrainian women I met at the talent show in Rome were unable to attain the "ideal family" because they were physically separated by migration. Men like Yuriy, unable to attain the breadwinner ideal, felt such gendered shame that they were both physically and emotionally marginalized from their family.

Lydmyla: A Family Aspiring to be European

Lydmyla, 42, was petite with straight, auburn hair down to her shoulders and a bounce in her step. She fussed about the kitchen as we spoke, preparing tea and cookies. It was clear that Lydmyla was not used to sitting. After a period of intense, animated talking, she bounced out of her chair to grab a picture of her family or the Italian toddler she cared for, hang a jacket that she suddenly noticed was on the floor, or get something from the kitchen. Lydmyla was younger than most participants. She was only 36 when she first arrived in Italy. In a transnational social field of mostly middle-aged women with teenage and adult children back in Ukraine, Lydmyla managed to bring her husband and two young children to Rome. She had secured an apartment and a job that was a day job (*lungo orario*) rather than the 24-hour live-in positions (*lavoro fisso*) that most women I encountered had. Lydmyla had also been in Rome longer than anyone else I had met, and she had a clear sense of how the situation had changed for Ukrainians in Italy over time.

Lydmyla's was one of the only interviews with Ukrainian migrants in Italy conducted in Italian instead of Russian. Lydmyla had been in Italy eight years and for all that time she spoke mostly Ukrainian at home and with her friends or Italian with her employers and everyone else. She said she would be happy to speak Russian, but at this point, felt more comfortable speaking Italian. She laughed as she shook her head, "Who would have thought that I'd be more fluent in Italian than Russian?!" We continued our conversation in Italian.

Lydmyla had arrived in Italy in 1997 from a small town outside L'viv. She explained that during this time Ukrainian women were migrating to Greece and few went to Italy. After four years of Ukrainian migration to Greece, Greece was "already full," according to Lydmyla, and a difficult country to enter. Lydmyla noted that there were 20 women from her home town in Italy. She and her friend Yelena, with whom I spent a day later on, had had no contact with these women. Their presence nevertheless influenced Lydmyla and Yelena's decision to come to Italy.

Lydmyla finished university with a degree in finance and worked as an accountant in a hospital. Her husband, Orest, an engineer, worked in a factory and had been going to work every day, but had not received a paycheck in two years – sugar, butter, and flour, yes, but no money. She explained:

> I earned little money. I decided to go somewhere in the world where people earn more money so that I could raise my children better. My parents were able to give me the opportunity to study, and I want to give this to my kids. Every mother wants their kids to have more than she had, not less. Can you imagine? My husband and I went to university, but my children no!? Everything in Ukraine is too expensive, and now that you have to pay for university, I knew I would not be able to send them to study. What choice did I have? No choice, Cinzia. But now I am happy. I am at peace. I did the right thing. I hope my children believe I did the right thing.

Like most women I spoke with, Lydmyla arrived with a 10-day tourist visa that she said cost $300 in 1997. In 2004, women were reporting fees as high as $3,300 for the same tourist visa. Lydmyla and Yelena got off the bus at Porta Portese in Rome:

> Most people on the bus were going south to Naples, but my husband wouldn't let me go south of Rome. He was afraid of the mafia. There were

> 50 women here in Rome, not more. This was the very beginning of
> Ukrainians arriving to Rome, before the masses arrived. Thank goodness that
> my husband was both mother and father for my kids. He cooked and
> cleaned and did everything himself. So I left knowing that I wasn't leaving
> my kids on the streets like some women do. … We knew it was harder for a
> man to find work abroad than for women. So we decided that I would go to
> work, and he would stay home with the kids.

When Lydmyla and Yelena got off the bus, they were greeted by Ukrainian
women who helped them find a place to sleep. They brought them to an apartment in Ostia, an hour's train ride from Rome. There they were asked to pay $6
a night. There were four women to a bed and two beds in each room. "And they
were our Ukrainian compatriots, not Italians," said Lydmyla shaking her head
disapprovingly. "And they earned money this way!"

Lydmyla and her friend had used up the money they came with within a
week. After two nights of sleeping on the beach, Lydmyla and Yelena met two
young men in their early twenties from Poland. The men were renting a small
apartment, and they allowed Lydmyla and Yelena to sleep there for six months
without paying rent. These young men showed them a kindness that Lydmyla
felt she could never repay. Lydmyla reflected on her current relationship with
"the boys":

> Sometimes when they need help they come to me. I tell them if they need
> help I will always help them. Sometimes they come they need €30 or €100.
> I tell them I am in debt to them, and I give it to them. One is now without
> a job. He says he'll pay me back. I say yes, if you have the money fine, if
> not fine. Do you know how many people are lost in this world? People say
> that they will help them and then they rob them or do something bad to
> them, and they are left on the streets! They ["the boys"] saw our need, and
> they helped us. We were lucky.

Lydmyla could only find occasional work when she first arrived. She was earning
$15 a week until "the boys" found her a job as a live-in, caring for a young child.
Lydmyla said that the job was fine, but her one regret was that she did not get
her *permesso di soggiorno* during the 1998 *sanatoria* (amnesty). The couple she was
working for was getting divorced. Although the woman employer took Lydmyla's
passport and said she would do the paperwork, she was preoccupied with her divorce
and never did. Lydmyla decided to go to the office on her own. Lydmyla said:

> I went to the office, but I didn't realize I was two days late. The *sanatoria* was
> over. The woman I spoke with there said, "Thank you for coming. I think
> you will have Christmas with your children this year because we are going to
> deport you."

Lydmyla laughed at my expression and nodded her head to emphasize that it really happened. She continued:

> But then the woman said, "But I know that you are going to go home all by yourself by the end of the week, right?" I said yes, and she gave me my passport back. I didn't get my *permesso* [*di soggiorno*] until the next *sanatoria* in 2002, but I decided right then to bring my kids to Rome. My kids came as tourists just like me. It was hard because I was one of the first to bring my family here.

Lydmyla explained that in order to bring her family to Italy, she could not work as a live-in. She needed to find an apartment, no small task in Rome where apartments are hard to come by even for Italians. It was even harder to convince a landlord to rent to a *straniera* (foreigner).

Yet, Lydmyla was able to pull this together. She was hired by an Italian man, Roberto, to care for his 80-year-old mother. Then in 1999, a year and a half after Lydmyla arrived in Rome, she brought her family to Italy by buying tourist visas for each of them, which they then overstayed. Lydmyla worked six days a week, and then went home to care for her family on Sundays. Two years later, her employer, Roberto, married and they soon had a daughter. Roberto asked Lydmyla to care for the baby as well and his mother. So Lydmyla now works 10 hours a day Monday through Friday. Lydmyla explained:

> Now I take care of two children, one who is 86 and one who is three. They are a wonderful family. I am a big sister [to Roberto and his wife] even though we are the same age. Because, they tell me, you know life better than us because you have passed such difficult times. So they listen to me as if I was the head of the family. I am very happy, because it is difficult to find a good family. I am sure others will tell you different stories. Some [Italian families] treat you like a slave, but I never felt this. If [Roberto and his wife] need to decide something, all three of us sit at the table and discuss it. If there is something that they don't like, no one ever raises their voice. If someone does then right away they say sorry. First they say sorry to me and then they ask it of each other.

Lydmyla repeated several times that she was very lucky to find this family. She even had an easy relationship with Roberto's elderly mother, who Lydmyla simply called *Signora*. Lydmyla said, "Many elderly folks can be hard and have old-fashioned ideas that I am in service to her. But my *Signora* isn't like that, and I am happy. I hope everyone finds a family like I did." The toddler Lydmyla cares for calls her "Nana." Lydmyla said, "I love her like my daughter. There is no difference between my kids and that girl. My kids are already grown and don't need me anymore. But that girl, she needs me. I know it. I feel it."

Lydmyla noted that, unlike now, in 1999 when her children and husband came, Italians were completely unfamiliar with Ukraine. "No one at school, not the kids and not the teachers, knew where Ukraine was on the map." Lydmyla went to the Community of Sant'Egidio, a Catholic charity which provided many services to Rome's migrants. It was the organization, with the exception of the Ukrainian churches, which Lydmyla also frequents, that came up most often in my interviews. There Lydmyla learned that school was obligatory in Italy until 14 years of age and that her children had the right and also the obligation to go to school even without documents. At the Community of Sant'Egidio, they helped Lydmyla enroll her boys in public school. I asked Lydmyla why she thought she was able to bring her family to Italy, whereas most others were not. Lydmyla explained:

> I don't know really. I guess it was a combination of things. First it was easier back then than now. The visas were less expensive to buy and my husband was willing to come even though we knew it would be harder for him than for me to find work here. My husband is sweet, but he doesn't take the initiative. If I say we should do something, he does it. But I have to propose it.
>
> I am the man at home. I have to make the decisions, because I am stronger. Maybe this is why I came to Italy instead of my husband. And I am happier here in Italy now than him, because he is closed and doesn't like to communicate. I mean, I cried every day the first year, but I did not show it to others or my employers that I was unhappy. Some women come and they cry in front of everyone for their kids and grandkids, and I don't think this is right. It may not be fair, but we are here in Italy, so you have to do well here or go home!

Lydmyla paused to wring her hands and sip some tea. She was visibly struggling with the contradictions of exile. On the one hand, she felt she was forced out of Ukraine and looking around her she realized that it was women who were forced to go abroad. The responsibility of helping their families in Ukraine falls to women, and Lydmyla felt the great weight of this responsibility. On the other hand, the process of expulsion, precisely because it was systemic with no one ordering her to go, no violent conflict driving her out, was then presented to her and others as a "choice." Lydmyla collected herself and gave me a sad smile as if apologizing for getting excited and raising her voice. She continued:

> I don't mean to be so hard on our women. I was lucky. I am sure you will hear different stories, horrible stories as you speak with more women. I was also lucky to find a good Italian family that helped me. I don't think, "Oh, I did it so other women could have done it too." No, I was determined, but at the beginning I didn't have anyone telling me it was impossible. And, I

was also lucky. Ukraine has kicked us out, Cinzia. We are all women here. Understand? But I said, fine, I will go, but I am taking my family with me!

Many times Lydmyla thought that she had made a mistake insisting on bringing her family to Italy.

They would have saved more money if Lydmyla came individually as a live-in like most women from Ukraine. Also, sometimes Lydmyla even envied those women who did not have to cook and clean for their own family after a long day of caring for others. Orest was an engineer in Ukraine, but now he was a jack of all trades: a bricklayer (*muratore*), a plumber, and an electrician. He had to learn these trades when he arrived in Italy, because, Lydmyla explained, Orest had never done manual labor before:

> For men it is very difficult. It is difficult for men to find work, because they need a *permesso* [*di soggiorno*]. Then the Poles arrived here before us in the 80s, and they have occupied all the spots for men. The first years, Orest was unemployed a lot. He stayed home more than he worked. We lived on my wages: €650 [a month] and €250 went to rent for a room. He was so unhappy. He said, "In Ukraine I couldn't help you because even if I went to work they didn't pay me. Here in Italy it is again all on you, because I can't find work." I was afraid to come home at night to see how he was doing. It was awful. Then he found six months of work and was only a couple months without. And then he found work for a year, and this really helped because he said, "I have contributed something." Now he has his documents and he is happier. Now for the next five months, until Christmas, he works Monday through Friday in Florence. It is very heavy work and he comes home tired but he earns €1,500 a month.

Lydmyla considered herself lucky that her husband did not drink. She listed a number of her friends whose husbands drank too much and then forgot their families. She explained, "This is a big problem. Ukrainians did not drink before. This is a Soviet problem." Most respondents were divorced, but of those who were widows, I was struck by how many explained their husband's death by stating that he fell down while drunk and hit his head.

Lydmyla helped her sister and her brother come to Italy as well, but neither of them stayed for long. Her brother and his wife worked in Naples for two years and then went back. Despite finding a live-in position with "a very nice Italian family," Lydmyla's sister only stayed in Rome seven months:

> My sister is a pharmacist. She said, "I can't do this service work." She lost 29 kilos in four months! There are some people who just cannot do service work. They really feel like slaves. In my opinion, my sister felt like that even if the family was nice. They treated her like a sister. But she felt bad and

> humiliated, and she said, "I can't do these tasks. I prefer to earn less money in my country with my friends around me than earn more money this way."

Lydmyla used to send back clothing, foodstuffs, and things that she knew were unavailable in Ukraine. Now, she said, you get anything you want in Ukraine if you have money.

Lydmyla sent €50 to her sister, €50 to her mother, and €50 to her mother-in-law every month. She gave the money to a van driver at the Garbatella. The same driver had been carrying her money for six years. He charged Lydmyla a fee of 4 percent of the money she sent, but only 2 percent if the total was over €1,000. Lydmyla's close friend in Ukraine has five children, and Lydmyla also sent her friend boxes of clothes and things she was able to collect. Lydmyla explained:

> I feel an obligation not just to my friends and family in Ukraine but to Ukraine as a nation. We were under Russian rule, and now we thought we had a chance to be free. We thought we would *join* Europe, not *migrate* there to do the work we do! Once I read in the newspaper about a community at home helping the poor, and I was so upset. We collected 25 kilos of stuff, and the driver took it to them for free. 25 kilos of stuff! I did it three–four times and then I said, I can't do it alone. I feel guilty, but what else can I do? My heart will always cry for Ukraine, always.

Lydmyla's guilt was not only a form of "survivor's guilt" contrived with a wish that she could single-handedly solve Ukraine's problems, but she was also torn about what living abroad meant for her children.

Italy's immigration laws made it difficult for Lydmyla to plan to stay in Italy, yet she did not see going back to Ukraine as a possibility for her – at least not for quite some time. Lydmyla still maintained her apartment in Ukraine and thought that, perhaps when she retired, she and Orest would return to Ukraine. However, Lydmyla believed there was little chance her sons would live in Ukraine again. The whole family went back to Ukraine for the first time since leaving this past Christmas. She said the trip home was both wonderful and frustrating. Lydmyla recounted:

> All this time Ukraine is supposed to be European, but unfortunately life hasn't gotten better there. This is something that makes me sad of course. Why can't I go back to my country and live there and work in the job I spent six or seven years at university to prepare for? Of course, I want to, but for now it isn't possible. Then we'll see … later on I don't know. But who will want me then at 50 with my youth all spent and my university degree? This means we need to live here, and then, when my grandchildren are born, I'll help raise them, and this is all. We will have to find a way.

Lydmyla's sons Anton, 19, and Pavlo, 13, had been in Italy almost six years. While Lydmyla and I were speaking, Anton came in the front door and sauntered into the room. He was handsome, of medium height with a slender build and long sandy blond hair. He was dressed in the style of Italian urban youth. Anton kissed his mother's cheek as he walked in and put his backpack on the floor. He flashed me a smile as his mother introduced us and told him to tell me about his visit to Ukraine while she prepared him something to eat. Anton sat down heavily on the couch. I could not help but smile when he began speaking to me in colloquial Italian with a thick Roman accent. He seemed at ease with the jocular style characteristic of Roman men that made them distinctive when compared to Italian men from other regions of Italy. Anton explained that he had wanted to go back to Ukraine for a long time because, when he left for Italy, it happened so fast that he did not have time to say goodbye to his friends. He joked, "When I left at 13, I was the tallest of my group of friends and, when I returned, I was the shortest! All my friends are a head taller than me and wanted to know why I didn't grow in Italy!" Anton continued:

> It was fun to catch up with people after five years. I asked about their life there, and they asked about my life here. My grandmother cried the whole time. I think there are good and bad things about living in Ukraine and good and bad things about living in Italy. Overall, our material life is better here. I think I will go back to Ukraine many more times, but I want to live in Italy. My parents, they may go back to live in Ukraine but, for better or worse, we [my brother and I] will stay here.

Lydmyla came out of the kitchen with hard boiled eggs and mayonnaise. She spoke at length about the different school systems. She was concerned that children in Ukraine are more disciplined, more respectful, and generally get a better education than in Italy. Lydmyla insisted that I speak with Anton in English. She said Anton had been studying English in Ukraine, but the Italian schools are "way behind" and are teaching him only the most basic things he has already studied. Anton, clearly wishing he was anywhere but here at this moment, agreed with his mother explaining that he was bored at school and so did not want to study. He said so in English. Lydmyla anxiously awaited my assessment and did not settle back down into her chair until I told her he spoke English very well. Anton winked at me and gave a quick wave as he made his escape and slipped out of the living room.

Just then the front door opened and a Ukrainian man came in. Lydmyla explained that he sleeps on a cot in the living room. Lydmyla mused:

> People think that money falls from the sky here and you don't have to work for your money. And they don't think that you have expenses. People say, you've been in Italy seven years, haven't you earned €100,000 yet? But after six years of doing *lungo orario* (day work), I spent €60,000 just in rent!

Lydmyla laid out her expenses. She now earned €900 a month, one of the highest salaries in my sample. Yet, she still needed to rent out a cot in their very small apartment to help pay the rent. When her children first arrived, they were undocumented. As a result, they could not apply for programs that assisted low-income families. Therefore, she had to pay for books and school lunches. Now they receive some help from these state programs. But, Lydmyla said, she has a different philosophy about money than most Ukrainians. She explained that for many Ukrainians in Italy, money was the "object of life"; but not for her:

> I can't say that I am saving money because with a family here you can't save. If you are here alone and work as a live-in, then you can save. You eat and sleep with them [your employers]. But I don't care about saving. I want my kids to have everything they need to live well. During the summer we go on vacation. We went to Capri, to Genoa, to Florence for a week. We went to Naples. We travel and this is expensive. With four people you spend always at least €1,000. But instead of saving, we take these trips, and I am happy.
>
> Even my husband says saving isn't important. If we need money, we will work and earn more. I love money, but just to live. I don't say today we won't eat because I have to save. If I don't feel like cooking, we go out for pizza or we buy a [precooked] chicken. I earn to live, not just to exist. Money is not the object of my life. My kids don't waste money, but they know that money isn't what is most important.
>
> These experiences will shape them, make them more open-minded. The way we grew up in the Soviet Union, we wanted always the secure way – stability – and so we saved. But I see that this is not the way here. My kids must learn to take chances, take risks, and to not be afraid. They must be everything I am not.

Lydmyla felt the generational divide acutely. The rules for success and even what constituted success had changed. Whether or not "money is the object of life" was a common phrase I heard over and over again in this community. It was a marker of how tied one was to the "old," "Soviet" ways of doing things. Interestingly, Lydmyla, who only went to church at Christmas and Easter before migrating, was now committed and involved in the UGCC in Rome. Her children attended Ukrainian school on Saturdays. Lydmyla believed that one day Ukraine will join Europe, and it will be important for her children to be connected to Ukrainian culture and language. She believed that there will be opportunities for them. In fact, Lydmyla had many questions for me as the daughter of Italian migrants to the United States. She said she hoped to "catch a glimpse of what her sons will be like and what kinds of understandings they might come to have about their move to Italy." Yet, my experience was closer to the experiences of Ukrainians in California who spoke about their children becoming "American." Lydmyla, and the others I met with children in Italy, never said they thought their children would become "Italian," but just the opposite. Lydmyla explained:

> No, I cannot save also because I have to buy clothes! All the kids at school dress well, so I can't buy cheap stuff for my kids. I buy designer clothes for them, because I don't want my kids to feel bad, to feel that they are foreigners (*stranieri*), I mean really foreigners. There shouldn't be this kind of difference between them and other kids. They were 8 and 13 when they arrived here. But also I am a patriot. It is difficult to know if I have done the right thing. Ukraine is becoming European and we must help Ukraine in this. My boys, they may not ever be Italian, but they *will* be European.

Italian citizenship was nearly impossible for Lydmyla and her children. After 10 years of living in Italy continuously with a *permesso di soggiorno*, showing that the family earned enough to live on (for a family of four that meant a yearly income of at least €13,324.56), and producing all the appropriate documentation they needed to apply for a *Permesso di Soggiorno per Soggiornanti di Lungo Periodo* (Long-term Resident Permit), Lydmyla and her family acquired a residency permit that can be renewed every five years for an indefinite number of times. However, it does not permit them to vote. Lydmyla and her family do not meet citizenship requirements. Italy had one of the lowest naturalization rates in Europe.[5] Yet, Lydmyla was not referring to citizenship when she stated that Anton and Pavlo would "never become Italian." Lydmyla and others noted that Ukrainians were part of the Slavic race, and therefore could never be Italian. Italy traces membership through blood ties, and Lydmyla and her family have "Slavic blood" not "Italian blood." However, if Ukraine becomes part of the European Union, Anton and Pavlo are no longer *extracommunitari* (people from outside our community). For Lydmyla, Ukraine's nation-state building project was not only about what happened in Ukraine, but also about her family's status in Italy. A European Ukraine would help her sons feel a little less like *stranieri* or at least not "very foreign" as they go about their daily life in Italy.

Social Patterns in Exile

Inna and Tatiana are representative of two migrant subjectivities produced in exile. Both women experienced the structural aspects of exile through a process of double marginalization, a result of a gendered adoption of neoliberalism in Ukraine. Both found themselves in early retirement with pensions too low to live on and few prospects for work as middle-aged women in Ukraine. At the same time, Inna and Tatiana's expectations of raising their grandchildren evaporated as their daughters-in-law found private businesses unwilling to bear the financial burdens of maternity leave, sick days for ill children, and other costs associated with reproductive labor. Their daughter-in-laws as young mothers became housewives if not by choice then by default. Inna and Tatiana shared a subjective experience of migration as painful expulsion.

Although Inna and Tatiana differ in whether they see themselves as active participants in Ukraine's nation-state building project, they are both inextricably linked to Ukraine's future trajectory. They recognized this through their global-level concerns for Ukraine. Whether they saw themselves as bringing about Ukraine's forward march to Europe like Inna, or simply hoped desperately for it like Tatiana, they both aspired to "Europe" all the while fearing "Africa." Whether remittances are symbolic of "Europe" for Inna or the sacrifices of a "good mother" for Tatiana, all these women sent the majority of their remittances home. With claims to identities as either professional workers in their fields or hands-on grandmothers now untenable, motherhood became the discursive terrain for drawing moral distinctions between people "like us" and people "like them" in exile. Whether migrants did or did not permit themselves the time and resources to study language or culture became evidence of "good" or "bad" mothering.

The ascendancy of ethnonationalism in Ukraine has tied the production of a European Ukraine to the production of a particular kind of Ukrainian woman and mother within a "traditional" family structure. Through the remittances Inna, Tatiana, and others sent back to Ukraine, they helped make the ideal Ukrainian family of women as "*Berehynia*" and men as "patriarchs" an economic reality. And yet there were many painful contradictions inherent to exile. Carework, by Soviet standards, was considered an exploitative occupation that turned workers into "slaves" and was so immoral, it did not exist in Soviet Ukraine. However, carework in Italy was now a production site of the new Ukraine. At the same time daughters and daughters-in-law were referred to by the Ukrainian state as the "*Berehyni* of our people," migrant grandmothers were denigrated by the label "prostitute." While migrants sought to learn about what it meant to be "European" and take or send this cultural knowledge back to Ukraine, they also aided in dismantling Soviet Ukraine and the moral system that shaped their most basic understandings of the world. Inna did not know how to advise her sons so that they would be "successful" and "respected" in a capitalist world, and Lydmyla felt her children should be "everything" she and her husband "are not" as Soviet persons. These women were building a new Ukraine that had no place for them as Soviet women, and this made toiling in the "gulag" all the more painful. Even if one day migrants are able to come out of exile and return to Ukraine, they will return to a Ukraine that, through their own labor abroad, has erased them as *babushki* and Soviet women from the social landscape.

Oksana, Yuriy, and Lydmyla are exceptions to the dominant pattern of exile as a non-mother or grandmother, a man, and a woman who brought her whole family to Rome, respectively. They illustrate the contours of exile as a transnational social field. Although they did not occupy the same structural position of expulsion in Ukraine's gendered transition to capitalism as Inna and Tatiana, they did share the subjective characteristics of exile. All three of them were linked in heartbreaking ways to Ukraine's nation-state building process. Oksana was working to build the new Ukraine where, not only were the claims of Soviet women to a European identity at times tenuous but, because of Oksana's non-mother status, even her most basic claims to Ukrainian ethnicity were challenged. Yuriy said he "agreed with the way of life in the West" and desperately wanted European living standards and cultural ways of being, but he simultaneously mourned for a Soviet cultural past where men and men's jobs were secure and considered high status. Lydmyla was also forced to maintain connections to Ukraine and participate in the construction of a European Ukraine, not only because she and her family might return to Ukraine, but because it would improve the status of her children even if they should stay in Italy. Lydmyla felt they would "never be Italian," but they could make claims to the supranational identity of European, therefore making them just a little less "foreign." Like all participants in Rome, Oksana, Yuriy, and Lydmyla also negotiated the meaning of remittances, had a limited identification with Italy as their host country, and perpetually wondered how long exile would endure as they lived lives of great uncertainty.

Exile, both its structural and subjective dimensions, was shaped by the intersection between processes unfolding inside Ukraine and the specificity of Italy as the receiving country. In Part III, I turn to exodus to California. San Francisco was a significantly different receiving site than Rome. Yet, Ukraine, as a sending country, was not a "constant." Exodus is better understood as the transnational product of an intersection between these two sites which in turn creates significantly different migrant subjects from those in exile.

PART III
Exodus: The United States

FIGURE III.1 Dancers from Canada performing for a small crowd in San Francisco's Golden Gate Park to celebrate Ukrainian Day
Photograph by the author.

FIGURE III.2 Spectators at San Francisco's Ukrainian Day celebration
Photograph by the author.

4

CALIFORNIA'S CONTEXT OF RECEPTION AND STATE-BASED INTEGRATION

California has a long history of immigration, both documented and clandestine. Migrants from the former Soviet Union make up an important but largely invisible population in California. Whereas Ukrainians in Italy were highly visible and racialized as a group, Ukrainians in California are simply understood as "white." In exile to Italy, the migration is more homogenously dominated by middle-aged women migrants with almost no employment options beyond domestic work. However, the dominance of legal migration through family reunification for Ukrainians coming to California means that this population is about evenly divided between men and women and that they filter into a variety of jobs at all skill levels. Migrants from Ukraine to the United States were not predominantly 40–65 year olds like those to Italy, nevertheless it is interesting to note that migrations from Ukraine and other former Soviet countries tend to be older on average compared to other migrations to the United States.[1]

The context of reception, especially U.S. immigration laws, certainly shapes exodus as a transnational social field. However, it cannot explain why this is a predominantly grandmother-led migration nor can it explain the unevenness of the process of stage migration to California. We must look to the particular gendered dynamics of Ukraine's economic transformation in a post-Soviet and post-colonial context in order to understand why it was middle-aged women that advocated for migration to the United States. These women might have migrated to Italy, but instead believed they were given an "opportunity" or a "lucky chance" to migrate to the United States, the "Promised Land." I was also disabused of the assumption that if someone has access to a U.S. visa, they will use it. In fact, these decisions also depended on where individuals were inserted into Ukraine's post-Soviet labor market. Although some adult children were happy to join their mothers in San Francisco, others like Kolya (Chapter 1) stayed behind, because they were able to find a place in Ukraine's changing economy. Those children who had steady professional work in Ukraine asked me in interviews, "Why would I want to go to California and have to clean houses or work construction?" Adult children of my California participants also delayed joining family in California to finish university degrees that were more affordable in Ukraine. Some specialized in areas that positioned them well in Ukraine's economy and decided not to leave at all, while others completed specializations they hoped would serve them well in California. Ukrainian migrants in the United States filtered into all levels of the U.S. economy. However, for middle-aged women and men, carework was one of the few options available.

In this chapter I explain the contours of the context of reception in the United States, California, and San Francisco more specifically. First I describe the federal immigration laws that favor family reunification. This makes the project of collecting one's family in the United States, rather than Ukraine's Europeanization project, central to exodus. Exodus to California is a transnational social field that produced different gendered migrant subjectivities than those in exile to Italy. Although migrants in California, especially those with children still in Ukraine, engaged in transnational practices, migrants in exodus had more limited effects on Ukrainian nation-state building than those in exile. Next, I show that this most recent wave of Ukrainian migrants was largely included by the U.S. state, which offered them legal status and work as caregivers, but were excluded by Ukrainian organizations run by WWII Diaspora Ukrainian migrants and their descendants, which did maintain transnational ties to Ukrainian nation-state building. This made transnational practices an individual choice without institutional support for those in exodus to California. For the demographics of the Ukrainian community in San Francisco, California, and the United States see the Appendix.

U.S. Immigration Law: Family Reunification and the Green Card Lottery

Unlike Italy where a temporary work visa, renewable yearly or biennially, was the best migrants could hope for, most Ukrainian migrants to California were applicants for "lawful permanent residence" (LPRs) and granted a permanent resident card commonly called a "green card." In 2012, California hosted the largest percentage of LPRs in the United States (19 percent followed by New York at 14 percent).[2] Family reunification accounts for approximately two-thirds of total permanent immigration to the United States every year.[3] Other channels of immigration include employment-based immigration, refugees and asylum seekers, and diversity-based immigration known as the "green card lottery." The green card lottery was established with the Immigration Act of 1990 to increase the diversity of immigrants to the United States from "under-represented countries." These four categories account for more than 99 percent of authorized immigration into the United States.[4]

The Immigration and Nationality Act of 1965 created a preference system for family reunification so that those with family already in the United States hold a significant advantage for acquiring legal immigration documents. When the Soviet Union collapsed, Ukrainians, who had fled to the United States after WWII and their U.S.-born descendants as well as Ukrainian Jews who had arrived in the 1970s and 1980s, began sponsoring their family members. The U.S. visa system gives preference to immediate family members. Therefore, embedded in exodus was the process of sponsoring family members in stages with the availability of visas following up and across family trees. This requires acquiring U.S. citizenship and relinquishing Ukrainian citizenship in order to sponsor family members from Ukraine to California.

Whereas there was little variation in how migrants arrived in Italy with most buying a work visa and then overstaying it, there was substantial variation in how Ukrainian migrants arrived in California (see Table 4.1). Studies on migrants from the former Soviet Union to the United States, tend to focus on Soviet Jews.[5] Although this study focuses on non-Jewish Ukrainians, because of high rates of intermarriage between Jews and non-Jews in the region,[6] connections with Soviet Jews already in California were important to my participants, because they were often the first link in a chain of family reunification.[7]

Twenty-three of 41 interviewees came to California as part of family reunification laws. Individuals in Ukraine who found family members to sponsor them to come to the United States felt "lucky." This feeling of luck was heightened for those who found a sponsoring-family member who had migrated in the 1940s

TABLE 4.1 List of various ways Ukrainian respondents came to California

Family Reunification: Status of Sponsor	Jewish Refugees	9
	Diaspora Ukrainians	6
	Baptist Refugees	2
	Green Card Winners	3
	Fiancée Visa	1
	Political Refugees	2
	Family Reunification Total	23
Other Channels	Religious Refugees	12
	Nanny Agencies	3
	Green Card Winners	2
	Ukrainian Organization	1
	Other Channels Total	18
	Total Interviewees	41

and 50s after decades without communication through the Iron Curtain. Of these 32, nine had a family member, usually an in-law or a spouse of a niece or nephew, whose family arrived in California as Jewish refugees and were able to act as sponsors for non-Jewish family members. Six interviewees had family who came to California after WWII. Two were sponsored by Baptist refugees; one was a friend who sponsored the interviewee's guest visa, which she overstayed and later acquired a green card, and one whose niece married a Baptist who later acquired refugee status. Three interviewees, after migrating to the United States on temporary visas, urged their children in Ukraine to fill out an application for the green card lottery and were then sponsored by children who had in fact won green cards in the lottery. Finally, one woman met her American husband at one of the many gatherings organized by agencies that match American men with Ukrainian brides and came on a fiancée visa. Two interviewees reported being sponsored by political refugees. A handful of respondents were illegal at some point, but only three did not have legal status at the time of our interview. These three were sponsored on guest visas from a family member. However, guest visas, such as the one Kolya sought at the consulate in Kyiv in order to visit his parents and sister in California (see Chapter 1), do not lead to green cards. These participants overstayed their visas and became undocumented.

Eighteen respondents arrived through channels more complex than straightforward family reunification. Twelve interviewees were religious refugees (eight Jewish and four Baptist). Although they were reuniting with family, they had access to green cards in their own right as refugees.[8] Three entered as domestic workers through a "nanny agency" that placed them with families in California as live-ins, and they then moved in and out of legal status. Two were themselves green card lottery winners but they both first came to the United States on guest visas. One was first sponsored by a Chicago-based Ukrainian organization because her daughter needed medical attention as a "Chernobyl baby" suffering medical issues from the 1986 disaster at the Chernobyl nuclear power plant located northeast of Kyiv. She was encouraged by this organization to apply for and later won a green card in the lottery. The other respondent was first sponsored by a relative on a guest visa and, after overstaying several years, went back to Ukraine and applied for and won a green card before returning to California. Finally, one individual was sponsored by a Ukrainian organization based in Chicago as a community artist. The variation in how Ukrainians came to the United States increased the sense of randomness or "luck" involved in migrating to California as did the discourse of "winning" the green card lottery. This stands in contrast to the experience of "expulsion" for those in Italy.

Once in California, all respondents had or were in the process of sponsoring family members with the exception of the three people who were without legal status at the time of the interview but nonetheless hoped to sponsor family members in the future. The U.S. legal system recognizes two broad categories within family reunification: "immediate family of a U.S. citizen" (this includes the parents, spouse, and minor, unmarried children of a U.S. citizen) and "family sponsorship according to a preference category" as outlined in Table 4.2. Green card holders are only able to sponsor a spouse and unmarried children. However, because most participants were interested in sponsoring married children, parents, or siblings, all which require U.S. citizenship, green card holders reported they needed to become citizens in order to sponsor family. After holding a green card for five years, permanent residents are eligible to become naturalized U.S. citizens.

The second category within family reunification is family sponsorship according to preference category. There are four classifications and they are ranked in order of preference with generally longer wait times as you move from the first to the fourth preference classification. First preference is given to U.S. citizens sponsoring unmarried, adult sons and daughters over the age of 21. Second preference goes to spouses and unmarried sons and daughters of U.S. permanent residents or green card holders. Third preference is given to married sons and daughters of U.S. citizens. The final classification is brothers and sisters of adult U.S. citizens.

This categorization system posed a challenge for Ukrainian families since Ukrainians tend to marry young and give birth to their first child in their early 20s. Adult children who marry are ineligible for sponsorship if their parents are only green card holders and are bumped down to the third preference classification even if their parents are U.S. citizens, leading to longer wait times. On the

TABLE 4.2 Family-based Sponsorship Preference Categories

Preference	Family category	Wait time Ukraine in years	Wait time Mexico in years	Wait time Philippines in years
First	Unmarried adult (21+ years) sons and daughters of U.S. citizens.	8	21	10
Second	Spouses of legal permanent residents (F2A), and the unmarried sons and daughters (regardless of age) of legal permanent residents and their children (F2B).	F2A: 2 F2B: 7	F2A: 2 F2B: 20	F2A: 2 F2B: 11
Third	Married sons and daughters of U.S. citizens, their spouses, and their minor children	11	21	23
Fourth	Brothers and sisters of adult U.S. citizens, their spouses, and their minor children	13	18	25

Source: U.S. Department of State. 2015. *Visa Bulletin for May 2015* (Number 10, Volume XI). Washington, DC: U.S. Department of State. Retrieved May 2, 2015 (http://travel.state.gov/content/visas/english/law-and-policy/bulletin/2015/visa-bulletin-for-may-2015.html).

other hand, as illustrated in Table 4.2, Ukrainians have much shorter wait times than other comparable migrant groups in California such as Mexicans and Filipinos who, in 2015, had wait times of 21 and 23 years respectively for sponsoring married children as opposed to 11 years for Ukrainians.[9] This made collecting family members in the United States, a central project of exodus, appear both feasible and within reach.

Homecare Workers and the State of California

Domestic workers were excluded from labor protections in the United States when workers won the right to organize in the 1930s, institutionalizing a devaluation of cleaning and caring labor. In 1974, the Federal Fair Labor Standards Act guaranteed a minimum wage to domestic workers who worked more than eight hours a week and could show that they devote at least 20 percent of their work time to housekeeping duties. Yet, careworkers such as personal attendants to the disabled, nannies/babysitters, and caregivers to the elderly and infirm continued to be excluded. Also excluded were live-in workers who had no right to overtime pay. There was limited or no enforcement of even these minimal labor laws when applied to domestic work.

Nevertheless, over the past 15 years, homecare workers have become an increasingly visible part of the U.S. direct care system. According to the U.S. Bureau of Labor Statistics, the need for personal care aids providing in-home care to elderly clients and people with disabilities will increase by 26 percent from 2014 to 2024, much faster than the average for all other occupations in the U.S. economy combined, which is only growing at a rate of 7 percent.[10] This will only compound the care crisis. Nationwide 40 percent of homecare workers are migrants.[11] It was not until 2016 that new regulations released by the Department of Labor in 2013 to extend federal minimum wage and overtime pay protections to caregivers to the elderly and disabled were finally upheld.[12]

Although Ukrainians in California certainly do perform informal cleaning and caring services, the majority of the migrants I spoke with worked through a state office called In-home Supportive Services (IHSS). Russian-speaking migrants make up 25 percent of the 8,000 homecare workers in San Francisco County despite only making up 3.4 percent of the county's population.[13] Created in 1973, IHSS is a division of the California Department of Social Services that administers public financing to the elderly and disabled who meet low-income and disability criteria. This office matches homecare workers with eligible clients, processes the workers' paychecks, and negotiates with the homecare workers' union. IHSS pays workers from government funds. Social workers from the Department of Human Services determine the number of work hours per month each client will receive and the tasks the homecare worker will provide. Individual clients do not pay the workers, nevertheless they are the actual employers with the power to hire and to fire the homecare worker. Most negotiations around tasks to be completed and how the work hours will be distributed throughout the month are ultimately conducted with the client rather than the absent social worker. Although some respondents cared for native-born clients, most of them cared for elderly migrants from the former Soviet Union. California also allows migrants to care for their own family members. Some respondents cared for an elderly parent as well as other clients found through the IHSS office. IHSS workers receive health and dental insurance if they work a minimum number of hours and this loomed large as a benefit of performing homecare work among middle-aged Ukrainian migrants. Churches and Jewish resettlement services in San Francisco especially channeled middle-aged women but also men into homecare work.[14]

Divided Communities: Pre-Soviet, Soviet, and Post-Soviet Migration Waves

Ukrainian migration to Italy is a post-Soviet phenomenon, but migration from this region to the United States is not new. The characteristics of those who migrate have, however, changed over time. Scholars report four waves of migration from the region, and I suggest there is currently a fifth wave. The first wave of migrants from the region arrived to the United States in the 1880s with the "Great Migrations" from Europe. WWI and the Russian Revolution of 1917 led to Ukraine's division into four different political units: Eastern Ukraine, part of the Russian Empire since 1600, became the Ukrainian Socialist Republic within the larger Soviet Union, whereas Western Ukraine was divided between Poland, Romania, and Czechoslovakia. Between 1917 and 1920 there were three attempts to create an independent Ukraine. Many partisans, who fought for Ukrainian independence from the Soviet Union, along with those displaced by the territorial upheavals, fled to the United States and Canada as part of a second wave of Ukrainian migration.[15] Those partisans who remained were deported to the Soviet gulags. In 1939, Western Ukraine was annexed to Eastern Ukraine as part of the Soviet Union and, during the turmoil of WWII, yet a third wave of Ukrainian migrants came to the United States. They were mostly political refugees who had participated in another failed attempt to found Ukraine as an independent country and resist communist expansion.[16] Many spent years in Displaced Persons camps in Europe during and after WWII before arriving in the United States in 1940–1955. In the camps they acquired political and organizational skills that they used to organize the Ukrainian Diaspora. Migrants from this wave and their descendants in the United States founded organizations whose primary goal was an independent Ukraine free from Soviet rule.[17] In San Francisco, where this wave has had the greatest impact on diaspora institutions, they were referred to as "Diaspora Ukrainians." From 1955 to the mid-1970s, Soviet Ukraine's borders were sealed. In the 1970s and 1980s the United States, as part of its Cold Qar policy, encouraged migration from the Soviet Union to the

United States as a way to further its ideological campaign against Communism and enhance U.S. prestige on the international stage. Inside the Soviet Union, defectors were vilified as traitors to the Motherland. This fourth wave of immigration to the United States from Ukraine was comprised mainly of Ukrainian Jews.[18]

After the collapse of the Soviet Union, there was another surge in migration from Ukraine to the United States, but it differs enough from the fourth migration wave of Soviet Jews that this post-1991 migration warrants being called the fifth wave. Although Soviet Jews continue to come to the United States, post-1991 migrants are predominantly comprised of ethnic Ukrainians and Russian citizens of Ukraine who have limited or no options for refugee status and had no ability to come to the United States until the collapse of the Soviet Union. Therefore, through family reunification programs and green card lotteries, which seem to favor this region, the religious and ethnic make-up of Ukrainian migration to the United States has diversified with Ukrainian Baptists and evangelicals, Ukrainian Greek Catholics, Ukrainian and Russian Orthodox, and religiously unaffiliated Ukrainian migrants joining relatives from both the third and fourth waves.[19]

Post-1991 migrants also differ from third-wave Diaspora Ukrainians. Unlike WWII Diaspora Ukrainians, post-1991 migrants were generally not Ukrainian partisans or political refugees nor did they leave Ukraine for ideological reasons. Rather, these grandmother-led migrations to Italy and California were a result of both demands for careworkers to the elderly in the receiving countries but also the complex intersections of gendered economic transformation and Ukrainian nation-state building (see Chapter 1). Some left for Italy because it was their only or best migration option, while others preferred Italy because it was geographically close enough for visits home to Ukraine where they hoped children would remain to have professional careers and help build the new Ukraine. Some of those who found relatives willing to sponsor them in California migrated to the United States and planned to bring their children and grandchildren with them in the hopes of a better life in "America."

WWII Diaspora Ukrainians, Soviet Jews, and post-1991 migrants were divided by migration waves, but also by divergent claims to "authentic Ukrainianess." Diaspora Ukrainians, who left Ukraine before the Soviet system took hold, think of themselves as the preservers of an authentic, pre-Soviet Ukrainian culture and language. They and their descendants form the organized Ukrainian Diaspora that worked to document Soviet atrocities, lobbied Washington on behalf of humanitarian causes, and worked tirelessly for an independent Ukraine. The Ukrainian Diaspora paid little attention to fourth-wave Ukrainian migrants, whom they identified as "Jews" rather than "Ukrainians." In fact, it was the organized American Jewish community, and not the Ukrainian Diaspora who, after receiving reports of the violent persecution of Jews, pushed for the United States to exert economic pressure on the Soviet Union to grant all Soviet Jews the right to immigrate to the United States with the passage of the Jackson–Vanik Amendment in 1975.[20]

WWII Diaspora Ukrainians had high expectations for post-1991 Ukrainian migrants. It is in part through the efforts of the organized Ukrainian Diaspora that Ukraine was able to finally declare itself an independent country and opened its borders for post-1991 migrants to leave for the United States. However, in San Francisco, Diaspora Ukrainians I met during my fieldwork were shocked and offended to hear recent Ukrainian migrants speak Russian and felt that post-1991 Ukrainian migrants were "Soviet" rather than "Ukrainian." One frustrated Ukrainian Greek Catholic priest, Father Mycola, told me that his San Francisco congregation had few "real" Ukrainians. He felt "real" Ukrainians were those who left due to Soviet discrimination against ethnic Ukrainians as partisans who fought against the spread of communism or as persecuted Christian religious minorities. Post-1991 migrants, Father Mycola noted dismissively, were "economic immigrants." They had what Father Mycola considered the lowly goal of earning money and lacked a commitment to God and nation.

Similarly, Father Jaroslav, a middle-aged man with a slight build, a moustache, and thinning hair who was a priest from a different parish, attempted to explain some of the divisions. His parents left Ukraine in the 1940s and he identified with third-wave Diaspora Ukrainians. The mainstay of his parish was about 200 families, all WWII migrants and their children. But the post-1991 migrants, Father Jaroslav explained, were different:

> The WWII immigrants are concerned with preserving Ukrainian culture and language, while the new immigrants are concerned about assimilating. WWII immigrants care about having an independent Ukraine, about Ukrainian language, and having the world recognize the atrocities committed against Ukrainians by the Russians. The recent immigrants are Soviets, not Ukrainians. They speak Russian, for example, and since we only speak Ukrainian and English in our church, they prefer to speak with me in English! The recent immigrants, well you can't mobilize them over an issue like the Great Famine. I mean this was an engineered genocide of our people and, for some reason, they can't go that far back in history. Maybe they'll go as far back as Chernobyl because they feel sorry for the kids or they may come out for a Shevchenko poetry night because the women like the poetry. But basically, they are just here to earn money.

As I made the rounds of Ukrainian organizations, I heard Diaspora Ukrainians and their descendants, who were now in charge of the churches, community centers, and charitable organizations in San Francisco, criticize post-1991 migrants for being "Soviet" and "not Ukrainian" and therefore always "looking for a handout" or "working the system" for personal gain. They felt post-1991 migrants were not appreciative of the sacrifices WWII Diaspora Ukrainians made to preserve Ukrainian language, culture, and tradition for their children. Father Jaroslav expected to teach the "Soviets," who he said had "lost their Ukrainian culture," how to be Ukrainian. He was frustrated to find they were not interested in learning because they believed they already were Ukrainian. Ironically, leaders from the Ukrainian Diaspora simultaneously complained to me that their organizations were dying out.

Whereas Ukrainians in Italy experienced a collective life that tied them at times painfully to each other and to Ukraine, recent migrants in San Francisco lived atomized lives that served to reinforce immediate family relations and the local concerns of settlement over the global and transnational concerns of Ukrainian nation-state building. Although younger Ukrainian migrants more easily integrated into American culture,[21] middle-aged post-1991 Ukrainian migrants reported that they were unable to learn English or "become American" and turned to Diaspora Ukrainians for help acclimatizing to U.S. society. Instead, they found themselves stigmatized and excluded from existing Ukrainian and Russian organizations. Many Russian-speaking, post-1991 Ukrainians found being called "Russian" even more disparaging than the term "Soviet," because it represented a complete negation of their ethnic identity. The label "Russian" came from Native-born Americans unable to distinguish between post-Soviet nationalities and therefore called everyone from the region "Russian." But it came most painfully from WWII Diaspora Ukrainians who asserted recent migrants might be from Ukraine, but they were not Ukrainian. Ukrainian respondents in California were obligated to negotiate these labels. Some struggled to construct themselves as Ukrainian "patriots" regardless of whether Ukrainian or Russian was their native language. Others mused that after a lifetime of being "Ukrainians" in Ukraine, they were resigned to the irony of becoming "Russians" in the United States.

As a result, participants reported feeling excluded from churches and other Ukrainian organizations because they were not "Ukrainian enough" and yet felt out of place at San Francisco's active Russian Community Center because, as former inhabitants of the Soviet Union's "hinterlands," they were considered lower status than ethnic Russians. This was particularly true at the Russian Orthodox Church (ROC), which held more institutional power than the Ukrainian Greek Catholic Church (UGCC) in San Francisco. The ROC had large parishes, aided recent migrants, and ran most of the organizations that provided services to the Russian-speaking community. San Francisco was recognized as an important Russian Orthodox community when the ROC in America moved its headquarters to San Francisco in 1870 and built the Holy Trinity Cathedral on Geary Boulevard, which is also where businesses that cater to the Russian-speaking community are clustered. This cathedral became the center of support for the new influx of émigrés during the 1920s, and today, the ROC continues to play an important role in settlement for migrants from the former Soviet Union.[22] However, Ukrainians, even Russophone Ukrainians, reported that they felt they were looked at suspiciously by members of the ROC who generally did not support Ukrainian independence or Ukrainian "nationalists."[23]

Marina, formally a music critic, had immigrated to San Francisco from Ukraine less than a year ago. She said:

> The Ukrainian Diaspora claims that they are preserving the "real" Ukrainian language! They look at me and say I do not speak "real" Ukrainian! I spoke Russian at home but studied Ukrainian at school and lived in Ukraine where Ukrainian is the official language! How can they think they are protecting the true Ukrainian language? They are protecting a dead Ukrainian language that peasants spoke over half a century ago! Language is a living thing! Real Ukrainian is changing everyday by people who live in Ukraine and interject new words and phrases that then become part of everyday speech! How can they believe that they are more Ukrainian than me? Let me ask you, Cinzia, are you more Ukrainian if you left Ukraine decades ago or have never even lived there at all *OR* if you spent the past 50 years of your life there. Who is more Ukrainian?

Post-1991 Ukrainian migrants found an institutional blank slate when they arrived in Italy. Therefore, they set about organizing their own institutions. Ukrainian migrants to San Francisco, however, found a fully formed institutional landscape, but were excluded by these institutions.

Post-Soviet Churches in San Francisco

Ukrainian churches, such vibrant facilitators of the Ukrainian community in Italy and its transnational connections to Ukraine, felt empty in San Francisco when compared to Rome. I regularly visited the UGCC in San Francisco. There were often no more than 20 people at Sunday services. There were usually a handful of recent migrants and the majority were second and third generation Ukrainian Americans. During a holiday or a festival more people attended, but the church was not the focal point of a dense community. During an interview with Father Lysko, the priest for the San Francisco UGCC, he expressed great frustration at his inability to mobilize the Ukrainian community. His wife and daughter were in Ukraine and Father Lysko had been in San Francisco with his son for two years and wondered what he had accomplished. Like the UGCC priests in Italy, Father Lysko said he was running a mission more than a parish. However, in contrast to the UGCC priests in Rome who took phone call after phone call from migrants seeking help – a place to sleep, a place to store suitcases, help finding a job or with legal documents, and more – Father Lysko said he rarely had recent migrants come and ask for help. If they did, he was poorly positioned to provide it. Father Lysko said he tried to organize a fund to help recent migrants, but he could not get enough support. He explained, "The WWII immigrants are American now and they have abandoned those who have come after them."

Like Father Jaroslav, Father Lysko said he wanted to teach Ukrainians about Ukrainian history and culture, but no one wanted to listen. He continued, "The recent immigrants, they are economic migrants and care only about money. I have one family that is truly Ukrainian and came as [Ukrainian Greek Catholic] refugees, but the rest are here for money." Observing Father Lysko interact with his parish, it was clear that he was well-loved by parishioners and that he was involved in the lives of this group. Ukrainians in San Francisco were well aware of the Ukrainian migration to Italy. When the topic arose, it was usually to criticize Ukrainian women in Italy for "abandoning their families" or becoming "prostitutes." I was surprised when Father Lysko spoke of the migration to Italy as being "morally superior" to the migration to the United States. In fact, he followed up a discussion about the complicated connections between the explosion of churches in Ukraine and their ties to political parties with the following sentiment:

> Do you know what political party those [Ukrainian] women in Italy belong to? Family and Church. Those women are doing everything for their families. They understand that our Church is a European Church. That we have much to teach about Ukraine's history and culture. Those that do not have documents cry for their families and for Ukraine and are unable to go home. That is what is so peculiar about the American migration is that they could go home if they wanted to, but they don't! They have abandoned Ukraine. They don't care what government Ukraine has. They're just interested in making money and living well.

Although some respondents, such as Viktoria (Chapter 5) felt they were betrayed by the collapse of the Soviet Union and wanted nothing to do with an independent Ukraine, the majority of respondents such as Dariya, Kateryna, Zhanna, and Halyna (Chapter 5) did care about what government Ukraine had and wanted to participate in transnational Ukrainian nation-state building, but felt they did not have institutional support to facilitate transnational practices. As a result, many respondents felt they had more in common with other recent migrants from the former Soviet Union despite nationality, what they called the "Russian-speaking community," than with WWII Diaspora Ukrainians and their descendants (see Chapter 5, Viktoria and Zhanna).

State-based Integration versus Transnational Practices

Whereas migrants in Italy negotiated what it meant to be "Ukrainian" vis-à-vis Ukraine's nation-state building project, migrants in California negotiated what it meant to be "Ukrainian" vis-à-vis WWII Diaspora Ukrainians and the landscape of Ukrainian organizations they had created. Simultaneously, the very process of exodus, collecting family members in California through the family reunification allotment of U.S. immigration law, required U.S. citizenship and therefore some identification with the U.S. state. For this older cohort of Ukrainian migrants, I discovered that their integration strategy involved creating connections with the U.S. state. Whereas in Italy the exclusion that migrants experienced from the Italian state all but forced them to cultivate a transnational relationship with Ukraine, migrants in California could choose to keep transnational ties beyond those with immediate family still in Ukraine, but they had to take personal initiative and work hard to do so in the absence of access to transnational institutions. Respondents like Elena (Introduction) felt included by the U.S. state because the state gave them legal documents that allowed them to reunite with family. Additionally, it was a state-funded program that gave Elena and others jobs as homecare workers and provided them with healthcare and their livelihood. Elena and the majority of women in my sample transferred their loyalty from the Soviet state, upon which their livelihood previously depended, to the U.S. state. Even participants who deviated from this dominant pattern, such as individual migrants who had left their family in Ukraine, were nonetheless constrained by the structural and subjective terrain of exodus as the following narratives from the "Promised Land" illustrate.

5

NARRATIVES FROM THE "PROMISED LAND"

Ukraine and California have intersected to produce exodus as a transnational social field with both structural and subjective dimensions that differ from exile. Although both exile to Italy and exodus to California was driven by the same generation of middle-aged Soviet women (Chapter 1), Ukraine's history of multiple immigration waves to California, and the United States more broadly, as well as the near impossibility of maintaining communication across borders during the Soviet era made finding a relative to sponsor an immigration visa feel like sheer "luck" to many participants in California. This intersected with U.S. immigration laws and the rapid growth of California's economy that increased demand for migrants (see Appendix) to create the structural characteristics of exile. These characteristics included grandmother-led family migration in stages, which migrants expected would be permanent due to U.S. state practices of inclusion through the granting of legal status for family members and the chance to win legal status through the green card lottery.

The subjective elements of exodus, despite individual migrants who may have had strong feelings about Ukrainian nationalism and nation-state building, included individual rather than collective choices to engage in transnational practices that bolstered Ukrainian nation-state building. This was due to post-1991 migrants' exclusion from the transnational organizations founded by WWII Diaspora Ukrainians (see Chapter 4) but also to the different qualitative meaning of exodus inside Ukraine. The migration of middle-aged women to Italy challenged the core gendered processes of nation-state building, something that the Ukrainian state both could not ignore and attempted to curb through stigmatization. Instead, the migration to California was largely ignored by the Ukrainian state as migrants fleeing Communism, a relic of the Soviet past. The need to search for ways to identify with the United States and the moral imperative to give family members the same opportunity they had to come to California was embedded in exodus. Surprisingly, participants in California, even the most fervent Ukrainian "patriots" who engaged in transnational practices, nevertheless prioritized strategies of integration through what they experienced as personal connections to the U.S. state over transnational connections to Ukrainian nation-state building.

The following narratives from exodus to the "Promised Land" are organized according to the structural dimension of exodus and therefore along a continuum of family reunification: family unit in the United States, transnational families where migrants have one child in the United States and one child in Ukraine, and individual migrants in California without their family. These narratives underline the characteristics of exodus in comparison to exile and highlight the role of sending countries in addition to receiving countries in understanding the migrant practices and subjectivities produced in exodus to California.

The first narrative about Viktoria highlights practices of state-based integration. While the project for migrants in exile was to find a way home to a more capitalist and European Ukraine, the project for migrants in exodus was to find a way to bring their family to them in California. Viktoria arrived in San Francisco with much of her extended family. Viktoria, like most of my California participants, performed caring labor for the elderly through IHSS, which pays workers from government funds. In the Soviet Union, women were "married to the state" (Chapter 1). Viktoria and the other women in exodus to California experienced the economic crisis that followed the dissolution of the Soviet Union as a "divorce" and the weak government of a newly independent Ukraine as a "failed provider." Viktoria and others juxtaposed the withdrawal of state services after Soviet collapse with the U.S. state which "provides" for them by giving them their paycheck and their health insurance. Migrant women like Viktoria understood these U.S. provisions as intimate and personal care for themselves as individuals and as a form of integration, not into U.S. culture, which they felt they were "too old to do," but into the U.S. state. Ukranian migrants' understanding of low-status, low-paid carework as a vehicle of integration is surprisingly different from other migrant groups who perform this labor.[1]

Most respondents in Italy hoped their children would remain in Ukraine. In contrast, Viktoria and all those in exodus not only hoped their children would join them in California, but further hoped that their children and grandchildren would become "American," not by following their strategy of state-based integration, but rather through an identification with capitalist markets and economic mobility. Whereas time was suspended for those in the Italian "gulag" who reported feeling their life was "on hold" and the collective yearning to return home was palpable,[2] in California time marched on at a fast clip. There, migrants like Viktoria worked but also helped adult children settle into American life. Many migrants in California were in contact with their grandchildren whose growth visibly marked the passing of time.

Dariya, in the following narrative, highlights the production of capitalist selves in exodus. Dariya eventually brought her three children to California. She, like Viktoria, also believed that her children's success depended on them learning how to navigate capitalist markets. Yet, unlike Viktoria, Dariya has come to identify with America and the "West" through a process of individuation, what she called discovering her "I," a personal journey to becoming a Western subject. Nevertheless, she still held on to Soviet ideals of motherhood and grandmotherhood. Dariya wanted her children to become Western subjects, but simultaneously struggled over what the adoption of American parenting norms meant for her own relationship to her daughter and grandchildren as a *babushka*.

In the third narrative, Kateryna also considered herself a Ukrainian "patriot." Her narrative illustrates the challenges of engaging in individual practices of transnationalism, including the sending of monetary and social remittances when confronted with the pull of exodus and the measurement of success for adult migrant children. With one son in the United States and one still in Ukraine, Kateryna felt personally invested in Ukrainian nationalism and politics. Despite her individual desire to maintain transnational ties with Ukraine, Kateryna found no institutional outlet or collective processes that facilitated a meaningful connection to Ukraine and its nation-state building project with the exception of voting in Ukraine's election at the consulate. Furthermore, in order to bring her youngest son to California, Kateryna must relinquish even this connection to Ukraine and trade in her Ukrainian citizenship for U.S. citizenship. Integration rather than transnationalism was structurally embedded in exodus. Whereas Viktoria was happy to sever ties with Ukraine and identify with the U.S. state through work and citizenship, Kateryna was required to do so in the hopes of reuniting her family.

In the fourth narrative, we meet Zhanna who highlights the importance of migration waves and the powerful role of *babushka* even in exodus. Zhanna also exposes a factor that was not yet considered as part of the expulsion of middle-aged women from Ukraine: corruption. Some, like Kolya's parents (Introduction) and Dariya, thought bringing their daughters to California was especially important given their increased exclusion from the labor market and simultaneous glorification as mothers. Others like Zhanna feared for their sons' safety in the highly masculinized ethos of "bandits" and "bribes" in Ukraine's unregulated free market. Like Kateryna, Zhanna had a transnational family with her daughter and granddaughters in Ukraine and her husband and son in San Francisco. In exile to Italy, where ethnonationalism was a dominant discourse, divisions between migrants from Ukraine were expressed in terms of nationality or as divisions between "Ukrainianized" and "Russified" Ukrainians. In exodus, these divisions existed but were downplayed in light of deeper divisions between migration waves. Zhanna illustrates how earlier migration waves from the region excluded post-1991 migrants from organizations that may have facilitated transnational connections. Zhanna, unable to mother her granddaughters in Ukraine, transferred this love to the children of her debilitated client from a previous migration wave. Despite her hurt feelings of rejection from this group, Zhanna ultimately used the Soviet ideal of *babushka* to bridge the divide between these two migration waves and mend her own heart.

Halyna, in the final narrative, highlights the power of the discourse of "luck" and "opportunity," so central to exodus, to shape migrant practices despite having left her family behind in Ukraine to work as an undocumented migrant in California. If the differences between exile and exodus could be reduced to differences between permanent and temporary migrants, we would expect Halyna to engage in similar practices to migrants in Italy. Yet Halyna behaved differently because the transnational social field of exodus shaped even those who were exceptions to the structural dimensions of exodus. Over time, Halyna sent fewer monetary remittances back to Ukraine, citing her own living expenses in San Francisco. This is in sharp contrast to the practices of individual migrants in Rome where remittances and the social meanings attached to them were an important part of their migration narratives and the construction of themselves as "good mothers." Halyna, despite leaving her daughter and granddaughter behind, did not have to negotiate the discourses around good and bad mothers. Instead she benefited from the assumption that all mothers in exodus were seeking a better life for their children. Despite her undocumented status, Halyna still hoped to find a way to stay in California and bring her daughter and granddaughter to San Francisco. In a transnational social field where things happened by "chance" or "luck," Halyna believed her daughter too could win the green card lottery. In the meantime, Halyna focused on learning English and settling in America, so she will be ready if and when her family arrives.

The transnational field of exodus encouraged migrants to focus on localized concerns of children's schooling and job searches. A theme that ran through all the interviews with Ukrainian women in California and Italy was the importance of being a *babushka*. Whereas migrant women in Italy were forced to leave their children and grandchildren behind, one of the promises of exodus was that, surrounded by your family, you would be able to fulfill the role of *babushka* and participate in the daily care of grandchildren. Yet, even in exodus this remained elusive for many. Some respondents waited or continued to wait years for visas for adult married children to materialize. In the meantime, respondents' grandchildren grew up in Ukraine without their *babushki*. Even participants who had their children and grandchildren with them found they could not be a *babushka* in the ways they had hoped. Ukrainian women in California must continue to work well past the retirement age in Ukraine of 55 in order to maintain healthcare benefits, qualify for state-based pensions, and out of economic need. This prevented *babushki* from being able to pick grandchildren up after school or care for grandchildren while their parents worked. Cultural integration of their adult children was a double-edged sword for participants in California. They wanted their children to integrate through the labor market. This meant finding jobs that placed them with American colleagues, taught them the capitalist "mentality," encouraged them to speak "beautiful" English, and paid them salaries that brought them social status and allowed them to participate in U.S. consumer culture. However, when children actually achieved market-based integration, there were unintended consequences. There was conflict between *babushki* and their children who became "too American" and engaged in parenting practices *babushki* made clear were "incorrect." Children found jobs in other cities or states and moved away, taking respondents' grandchildren with them. Or perhaps the worst unintended consequence as reported by participants: their children delayed childbirth to pursue education or careers until *babushki* felt they were too old to provide daily care to grandchildren. Participants wanted their children to live the "American dream;" they simply hoped that dream would include a place for *babushka*. The following five ethnographic narratives highlight the gendered migrant subjectivities produced in the transnational social field of exodus.

Viktoria: Married to the U.S. State

Every research site has gatekeepers and San Francisco was no exception. Svitlana, a gregarious and energetic woman from Ukraine, was the union organizer for the Russian-speaking members of the SEIU's homecare workers' union. Svitlana held monthly meetings in Russian. The meetings not only addressed union business, but forged a community between workers from different post-Soviet countries. Several participants said that Svitlana was their age or perhaps even younger, but that she was nonetheless "a mother to all of us." Svitlana invited me to union events, introduced me to homecare workers, and tirelessly searched for people willing to sit down to an interview with me. It was at one of Svitlana's union meetings that I met Viktoria. Viktoria was explaining to those attending the voting process for the upcoming local elections, while the union organizer explained which candidates for San Francisco's Board of Supervisors the union was supporting (Introduction). Viktoria's enthusiasm for California politics and her strong conviction that, as naturalized American citizens, they all had an obligation to vote and "engage with the U.S. state" was infectious.

After the toasts and speeches in honor of the members who had birthdays that month, I chatted about local politics with Viktoria over a plate of food and cake. She was thoughtful and articulate and interested in U.S. politics and American culture. I worked up the courage to ask Viktoria if she would be willing to sit down to an interview with me. I thought to myself that I was too shy to be an ethnographer, as the knot in my stomach tightened, and I braced myself for the usual response I received in San Francisco: Sorry, I'm too busy. But instead Viktoria smiled warmly and gave me her phone number. She told me that when the election was over, she would have more free time and would be happy to speak with me at her apartment. I exhaled in relief.

Even those who agreed to interviews often were nervous about having me at their home. For example, one respondent told me to go to the opera house in San Francisco. There I would find a pay phone. I was instructed to call her cell phone from the pay phone, and she would tell me where she was waiting for me. I sang the James Bond 007 theme song in my head as I dialed and worried that either my Russian or my notoriously bad sense of direction would keep me from finding her. When I called she told me she was sitting on a bench in a square whose name I did not recognize. I saw a police officer on foot and stopped him to ask for directions. I hoped that my respondent did not see me talking to the police, least she think her prudence justified! When I found her, we talked on a bench outside in the cold for two hours where I learned, like most of my participants, she had a green card. Despite legal status, I found migrants in San Francisco were more afraid of speaking with me then their undocumented counterparts in Rome. At the end of the interview she hugged me, apologized for not inviting me to her apartment, and asked if I was single and interested in meeting her son who was "very nice." I thought of the nasty cold I had caught outside on that bench and was thrilled to know the interview with Viktoria would be indoors in a warm place.

I ran into Viktoria again a couple of weeks later at a naturalization ceremony for New Americans. My husband, Davide, an Italian national, had just become an American citizen. I was distracted, already analyzing the ceremony sociologically in my head and was smiling at Davide who had been swept up in the fervor. He was having his picture taken with two young people in army fatigues and rifles in front of the American flag. Davide was holding open his own American flag, one with only 48 stars. It was a family heirloom brought back to Italy by a great uncle who had worked in the coal mines in Chicago in the 1930s before returning to Italy. Viktoria spotted me as she held voter registration cards over the crowd exiting the building and called out in Russian, "Register to Vote!" She was clearly enjoying herself. I was surprised to see her and squeezed her arm as she congratulated my husband on becoming an American citizen. Viktoria winked at my husband and said in English, "Don't forget to register to vote!" Turning to me she added in Russian, "I will see you next week, agreed?" As we pushed through the lobby to the exit, I looked over my shoulder and saw Viktoria, her arms outstretched toward the ceiling and the throng, like the parting of the Red Sea, continually dividing and then regrouping behind her.

As I sat in Viktoria's kitchen a week later, Viktoria explained that she had graduated university in pedagogy and was sent by the Soviet government to the Caucasus region to teach Russian language and literature. Although her grandmother worried about her safety, Viktoria called the years she spent in the Caucasuses a "golden period." She loved learning about a new people and thought she might have stayed if she had not met her future husband on a trip home. She soon married Sergei and moved back home to Kyiv. She was unable to find a teaching position, and instead found work as an administrator at what she called a "luxury hotel." She was one of the few working there who had a university degree, and she was soon made director. "There," Viktoria reminisced, "I saw a different life, a rich life – happy, interesting, wealthy – completely different ... Tourists arrived from all over the world and I really enjoyed working there, really enjoyed it." She worked there 20 years.

Viktoria's husband, Sergei, also had higher education. He worked in a factory as an engineer. They had their first son, Andrei, soon after they met and would have a second son, Igor, 18 years later. Viktoria said:

> Now I remember how funny this is! My family then was considered wealthy! We lived well. I worked at the hotel and my husband at the factory. As far as we were concerned, we were rich. Now I think, how could I have thought I was rich if I couldn't even eat bananas? Bananas were expensive, but I ate a banana once a week with a friend. We hid ourselves outside so our husbands wouldn't see that we had wasted money this way.

When the Soviet Union collapsed, Viktoria explained that everything changed and for the worse. She paused to urge me to take another *bliny*, a folded pancake in this case filled with *tvorak*. *Tvorak* is a cheese that has a pungent flavor I found difficult to enjoy. Viktoria continued:

> After the dissolution of the Soviet Union ... for me it was painful. I liked it when we were all one country. The Soviet Union was mighty, understand? When it collapsed, I, of course, felt this was bad. First, you sit on the train and they need to verify that you are from Ukraine. [Unlike the Soviet period, you now need documents to travel between former Soviet countries.] Second, they decided that it was obligatory to speak Ukrainian. I wanted to speak in my native language, Russian. But Ukraine: "We are going to speak only in Ukrainian." I did not like this. And all of a sudden there was all this nationalism in Ukraine: "This is Ukraine, and we are Ukrainian, and we want to be independent."

Viktoria did not know Ukrainian and, as a teacher of Russian language and literature, she said she "did not want to know Ukrainian." In the Soviet period, Ukrainian was considered a lowly language for uneducated "country bumpkins," not the language of the *intelligentsia* to which Viktoria felt she belonged. In addition, Viktoria was born and raised in Kyiv to a Ukrainian mother and a Russian father. She had lived in the Caucasuses "like one of them," and felt that the rise of nationalism created unnecessary divisions and tensions between peoples who had always been "friends" and had "the same mentality." Viktoria had complained about Ukrainian language requirements when we met at the union meeting for homecare workers as well. There she noted:

If I speak my native tongue, I am no longer Ukrainian, the country I grew up in? The United States government lets me speak Russian and says I am an American citizen. I feel I have more rights here than in the country I grew up in! The United States government does not say you cannot work in the elections because you prefer the Russian language.

This debate about language and the division between Ukrainophone and Russophone Ukrainians was present in Rome, but the debate took a different form in San Francisco where there were migrants from all over the former Soviet Union, not predominantly from Ukraine like in Italy. Insisting on only speaking Ukrainian meant you refused to communicate with other migrants from the region. Unlike participants in Rome, even the most patriotic respondents in San Francisco did not express qualms about speaking in Russian.

After the collapse of the Soviet Union, Viktoria continued, the economic situation in Ukraine also worsened. Viktoria's husband, Sergei, lost his factory job:

> Very bad, the 1990s were very poor. I woke up in the morning and couldn't make *blinchiki* because I didn't have any butter to fry them in; there were no eggs; there were problems getting flour. [Pointing to my plate.] Eat! Now we have no problems making *bliny*!

I lathered on the homemade jam to cancel out the *tvorak*, politely nodded my appreciation of the *bliny*, and watched her bustle around the small, cluttered kitchen. A large ball of soft *tvorak* wrapped in cheese cloth was hanging from the faucet and draining into the kitchen sink. I noticed that the wallpaper was peeling and discolored. In fact, everything in the apartment gave the impression that if you touched it or turned it, it would most certainly break. Despite what to my eyes were cramped quarters and chipping paint, Viktoria said they were lucky to have such a comfortable apartment. I put my fork down in relief. Homemade *tvorak* was not as strong tasting as store-bought and, to my surprise, I happily ate another. This time I went easier on the jam.

Whereas most Ukrainians I spoke with in Italy talked about how difficult the decision to go abroad was, Viktoria, like many participants in San Francisco, felt that having access to a green card was an opportunity. Viktoria said no one from her circle of friends left for abroad, and Viktoria's family had simply been "lucky." When I asked Viktoria if the decision to leave Ukraine was a difficult one, she replied:

VIKTORIA: You know, no. I, personally, was dying – I wanted to leave. I wanted to change something in my life … I tell you honestly, there was something psychological: America, all the time America, as so many said … How to

explain this? Propaganda: America is the best. Everything – the best in
America.

CINZIA: Where did you hear this?

VIKTORIA: Movies, radio … American radio and everywhere they showed: America, America, America. They planted this and it became like a psychological
revolution in my head. We decided to leave.

Viktoria's sister, Liya, worked as an English interpreter for a large state-run
tourist agency. Her main responsibility was to manage foreign visitors to Ukraine
and the access they had to the Soviet Union. Liya was supposed to propagandize
the foreigners, but it seems they propagandized her. She worked with Americans
and always told Viktoria that there was "no country in the world better than
America."

I asked Viktoria how she was able to come to San Francisco. Viktoria answered
as if rhyming, "My husband has a mother and his mother has a sister. This sister
pulled mama here. Then mama pulls her son [Sergei], the son is married with
kids …" She laughed, "It is a chain!" They were already so far "down the chain"
that Viktoria was not sure how her husband's aunt was able to come with refugee
status in the first place and set the family reunification process in motion. She
explained it by recounting a famous Russian children's limerick:

> Do you know the story "Turnip"? Grandfather plants a turnip and the turnip
> grew to be enormous. He pulled and he pulled, but he couldn't pull it out
> [of the ground.] So grandfather calls grandmother. Grandfather held the
> turnip and grandmother held grandfather, and they pulled and pulled but
> they couldn't pull it out. So grandmother calls granddaughter. They pulled
> and they pulled and they couldn't pull it out. So the granddaughter calls the
> dog and the dog calls the cat and the cat calls the mouse … they make a
> chain and they finally pulled the turnip out. That is how we came to
> America.

I laughed and Viktoria again repeated the last line from the story, which is a
tongue-twister in Russian.[3]

When Viktoria got on the plane for San Francisco, they had sold all the pos-
sessions they could in order to buy plane tickets. Viktoria, Sergei, Sergei's
mother, and six-year-old Igor were on the plane. Her oldest son, Andrei, 24,
stayed behind with his wife. Andrei wanted to finish his doctorate. However, a
year later, Andrei and his wife arrived just two weeks before their son – Viktoria's
grandson – was born. Viktoria's mother also arrived with Andrei and his wife.
After five years in San Francisco, Viktoria became a U.S. citizen. She "continued
the chain" and "pulled" her sister and her brother. Her sister Liya remained in
San Francisco with her son and daughter-in-law. Liya had two granddaughters.
The youngest was six months old and Liya, who Viktoria said was simply unable

to accept doing domestic work, was a full-time *babushka*. Now they are doing the paperwork to bring Liya's daughter-in-law's mother to San Francisco. "You see?" smiled Viktoria, "Turnip!"

Viktoria's brother, Petro, only stayed in San Francisco six months. He worked long hours, earned money, and returned to Ukraine. Petro's daughter had a child and was married to a man who had a "good job" in Ukraine, "an important position." Nevertheless, they did not earn enough money to move out of Petro's apartment. With the money Petro earned in San Francisco, he was able to buy his daughter and her family an apartment, so they could move out and live on their own. Viktoria explained that her niece did not want to come to the United States. There her niece was an "important person." Viktoria asked, "Here who will she be? There she goes home at 5 o'clock. Here she will have to work two jobs if not three." With the exception of her brother, Viktoria says her whole family was now in San Francisco.

Viktoria was 48 when she first arrived in San Francisco. She said that she had looked at America through "rose-colored glasses." In some ways this made the first year in San Francisco even more difficult. Viktoria said:

> I suffered from depression, without a doubt. I had no friends. I closed in on myself … Everything was just awful. America, I was in AMERICA – I had this kind of association. And then suddenly I arrived and I was unhappy.

Viktoria said that working for the U.S. state "brought her back to life." Viktoria explained that "the [U.S.] government helped us. The government gave us welfare. Of course this was a big help – we were able to pay rent for an apartment." Six months later they realized that Viktoria's mother-in-law was eligible for Supplemental Security Income (SSI) and for a state-paid homecare worker. Then the real economic relief came when they discovered Viktoria could be that state-paid homecare worker. Viktoria began working for IHSS, at first caring for her mother-in-law and then picking up other clients. When Viktoria's mother arrived, she too was eligible for a homecare worker paid for by the state so Sergei took on his mother's hours and Viktoria took on her mother's hours. In addition to providing care to the elderly through IHSS, Viktoria found work cleaning houses and was paid under the table. Viktoria explained:

> We call this "day laborer." … I never in my life, NEV-ER, worked so hard. NEVER! I worked at school, I worked in a hotel as a manager, but such physically demanding labor as I do here I had never done in my life … You know, we all came with higher education. We all completed university. And here I am doing this work. I clean toilets and I clean all kind of dirt. This is awful! But, we needed money. We needed the money, so I stepped over this line.

Sergei started working in construction, but he had never done such "heavy work" before. He left construction and joined Viktoria in caring for several elderly clients through IHSS. Viktoria said they were a team and, regardless of who was officially registered for the hours, they shared clients. For example, Sergei does not cook so Viktoria would do the cooking, while Sergei picked up extra cleaning. She joked that in Ukraine she and Sergei saw each other in the morning and then not again until evening, whereas in San Francisco, they spent much more time together and it was a "rebirth" of their relationship. She also came to see carework as important. She understood the work itself as "very humane" and as an expression of "the Russian soul." It was also as an integration strategy.

Participants in California understood that they were supposed to be "assimilating." And yet for those of Viktoria's generation, cultural assimilation was elusive even if they aspired to it, yet most did not even try. In Rome, most Ukrainian migrants who had been in Italy for some time spoke Italian, often quite well. They were, after all, working in Italian families and buying groceries daily, as is the custom, in Italian shops. In California, every homecare worker in my sample was caring for Russian speakers, either migrants who arrived in an earlier migration wave or the elderly members of this post-Soviet migration. Most spent time in Russian-speaking shops along Geary Boulevard, participated in union meetings run in Russian, and had access to social services delivered in Russian. Therefore, Viktoria, and others in California, spoke limited English. This was seen as a barrier to "assimilation," a word I never used in the field, but respondents used to indicate the "success" of their adult children who spoke "beautiful, literary English" and compared it to their own "limited success." Viktoria said, "I have not assimilated. No of course not. I think in Russian, I read Russian newspapers, and read Russian novels." She noted that her sons, Andrei and Igor, have "become American" and her grandson, born in San Francisco, just "is American." Yet, Viktoria and others I spoke with were orientated to "America." However, they felt connected not to American culture but the American government.

Viktoria received payment for the carework she performed through IHSS from the state of California as well as her health insurance. Viktoria repeated that "the U.S. government takes care of me" and she felt a deep connection to the U.S. state as a result. Another interviewee, Lidiya, put it this way:

I love America because its policy towards the elderly is very humane. Look at how much money the state spends on her [indicating the elderly woman she cares for]! They pay her SSI, they pay me to care for her, and they also pay for my benefits. I am very grateful to the U.S. government because they support me in a way the Ukrainian government never did. The Ukrainian government doesn't give you the opportunity to make money and live well.

The U.S. state was understood as a provider with whom they had a personal relationship. Viktoria, however, had yet another connection to the state. Viktoria exclaimed, "And then God sent me the City Hall Department of Elections. I was resurrected! I was so happy. How I love to work there! A fine collective – simply wonderful!"

Viktoria juxtaposed what she understood as her "limited success" in San Francisco with her oldest son Andrei's success in "becoming an American." She thanked God that he was now 34 years old and was always very smart, even as a boy. He finished school with a medal for getting highest marks and completed university with honors (*s kracnym diplomom*). He then went to graduate school in accounting but was unable to complete his dissertation because they came to the United States. Once in San Francisco, he enrolled in university courses and quickly completed an accounting certificate. He landed a job at a large accounting and consulting firm. Viktoria's whole face was radiating pride and joy. "He earns big money: $100,000!" She continued, "And he works for an American firm. He works with Americans. There are no Russian speakers there!" Andrei traveled a lot for work and had visited many countries. Viktoria said she was not sure why he must travel so much, but she noted they could "send someone who was born here" to represent the company abroad, but they send Andrei.

Children's success in becoming Americans was judged on three criteria: Speaking English not just competently but elegantly, earning a good paycheck, and not needing to rely on other migrants from Ukraine or the former Soviet Union. This was why announcing that there are no Russian speakers where your child works or in the neighborhood where they live – something I heard over and over again – was a sign that your child had made it and that your sacrifices as a mother were worth it. Viktoria explained that Andrei and those who migrated as young adults did not need other Russian speakers because there were no "connections" in the United States. In the Soviet Union, Viktoria said that she got everything through "connections" (*po blatu*). She explained:

> We had connections (*blat*). I worked in a hotel. There was never a room available at the hotel, never. In America, there is always a room available in a hotel, but in our country no, there were no rooms available. Therefore, I gave away rooms, but for this room I could gain everything I wanted. Yes, it was interesting. I could get chicken, foodstuffs, objects, or permits. We call this *blat* – connections.

In San Francisco, Viktoria noted, "There are no connections." The turnover was so high at the elections office that every election season it was all new people – "no connections," Viktoria exclaimed. "You do not need people to help you get what you need in America, just money."

Viktoria explained that, although there were people from all ethnic backgrounds working at the elections office, each targeting their own immigrant population, there were also some Americans there. Sergei has now earned his Certified Nurse Assistant (CNA). Viktoria joked that there was not a single American in his classes. CNAs were almost all immigrants, but she added, there are some Americans there too. Sergei worked nights at the hospital and cared for his mother, who was now very ill and had been assigned many daytime hours from IHSS. Viktoria repeated how hard they all had to work in America, harder than in Ukraine, and how difficult and unexpected this was especially at their age. Sergei is 60 and Viktoria 59. She reminded me that in the Soviet Union retirement ages are 55 for women and 60 for men, and "this is how it should be." Viktoria wondered, "How can you raise your grandchildren if you have to work even at our age?" Yet, she said she was happy in San Francisco. Viktoria said they sometimes bought fresh fruit and ate it by the ocean and thought: "We are living a fairy tale."

Viktoria's son, Andrei, had been upwardly mobile and successfully navigated the capitalist market. He worked in private industry, not for the state, and Viktoria had the same hope for 16-year-old Igor. However, Viktoria, like others of her generation in exodus to California, identified with the U.S. state through citizenship status and working for a government agency like IHSS. Viktoria extended this state-based integration strategy further through her work at city hall during election seasons and her commitment to convincing others to vote and participate in the U.S. political process. Viktoria was passionately interested in U.S. and California politics. We had a long discussion about American national politics and the past 2004 presidential elections. "It is not often you meet an American who speaks Russian and can give you an American perspective on these issues," Viktoria explained. I shifted the conversation to Ukrainian national politics. Viktoria exclaimed that she was not interested in Ukrainian politics at all. With the exception of three or four phone calls a year to her brother, she said she had no connection to Ukraine whatsoever. I asked her about the Orange Revolution (Chapter 1). Viktoria declared:

> I have absolutely no interest [in the Orange Revolution], absolutely none! … My brother sent me a beautiful picture of this Yulia Tymoshenko. He sent me a picture of her – I am not interested in her. I don't need her, and I am not interested … I live here now, and I work here now. This is what I am absorbed in, this is what I have in my head. [Arnold] Schwarzenegger, this is interesting to me. Learning about who the candidates on our ballots are, this is much more interesting to me! This I like.

Viktoria had never been back to Ukraine and did not want to go. She said that she was more interested in traveling in the United States. Viktoria noted that she is not able to travel as much as she did in the Soviet Union, however they did travel during her grandson's school vacations. She said her grandson is American, and therefore is much more interested in snowboarding in Tahoe than going to

Ukraine. They had been to Los Angeles, Disneyland, Calistoga, Las Vegas, and Hawaii several times. Viktoria said that, for an ESL class she took when she first arrived, they were asked to write an essay about why they came to the United States. Viktoria, leaving out that she could not afford to make *bliny*, said she wrote that she "loved adventure." "I adore traveling," Viktoria exclaimed. "This is why I came to America," she continued laughing. "Of course from Ukraine this was a one-way journey!"

Dariya: Discovering my Capitalist "I" in the United States

I drove out to a San Francisco suburb to interview Lyuba, whom I had met through a connection at San Francisco's Ukranian Greek Catholic Church (UGCC), and rang the bell of the large home. Lyuba, 63, a kind woman with straight blond hair, answered the door and welcomed me in. A group of people were still finishing up lunch, and Lyuba pulled a chair up to the table for me. I politely declined the meat and potatoes offered, but I accepted the tea and cookies and added the Ghirardelli chocolates I brought to all my San Francisco interviews to the table. Lyuba introduced me to her husband, Myron, seated at the head of the table. He was Ukrainian-American and was at least 10 years her senior by my eye. Lyuba introduced her friend, Dariya, who she said was also willing to give me an interview. There was also a young couple at the table. In my embarrassment for interrupting their Sunday lunch, I did not ask who they were, and Lyuba did not introduce me. Lyuba ate snatches of food seated at the table between trips to the kitchen to slice more meat, clear dishes, or make tea.

Myron asked me about my research. I felt I was being vetted before being given permission to speak with Lyuba. I saw that Dariya was uncomfortable at the table, and I sensed an inequality in power dynamics that made me nervous and cautious about my answers. I explained my interest in Ukrainian migration broadly and noted that I had done interviews with Ukrainians in Rome and was now interested in the experiences of Ukrainian immigrants in California. The young man at the table explained in a clear, Ukrainian-accented English that he did not like the word "immigrant," which implied "people of a lower class and culture than Ukrainians" in the United States. Dariya coughed into her napkin and, covering her face from the man's view, rolled her eyes at me. I gave her a slight nod of acknowledgment, but maintained a blank expression on my face for my interlocutor. He continued that he was well aware of the phenomenon of Ukrainian women in Italy. These women were simply "shirking their motherly and wifely duties" in order to be "prostitutes in Italy." Dariya and Lyuba's jaws hit the table in shock. The young man's wife sat quietly beside him and seemed not to hear any of the conversation. I politely replied that the women I had spoken with were working hard to support their children back home. Myron seemed intrigued and asked more about my assessment of "our women" in Italy. The young man scoffed as I spoke, but it was Myron who was in charge. Myron, a large, imposing man, stood up, said it was very nice to meet me, and retired for an afternoon nap. I was relieved at the break in tension as we all stood up and the young couple also left. Lyuba, Dariya, and I sat in the living room. It was a dark room with Ukrainian religious icons and Ukrainian folk art displayed upon an embroidered piece of cloth on the mantle.

Lyuba and Dariya both came to the United States through the same "placement agency." Lyuba said that she was a high school teacher of Ukrainian as well as Russian language and literature in L'viv. In 1996, she was 54 with "less than two years until retirement" and she thought she was a "spent woman" with no idea that a year later she would be in California. Yet, "life," she said, "gave her a surprise." Lyuba explained that many people who worked in the "budgetary sphere," such as doctors and teachers, were no longer receiving their wages. Many people, Lyuba said, had already left to work abroad. "In those days, few people went to Italy. Most went to Greece and some Turkey, but mostly Greece." At the school where she taught, Lyuba said that many of her students had a parent abroad, usually their mother, and you could tell who they were because they were "dressed better and already had jeans." But Lyuba conceded:

> I did not look at those who left with respect. I said we have to build Ukraine, an independent Ukraine! You know I was this kind of patriot – People's Movement … I came straight out of the Ukrainian Language Society – Who are you to leave? But you cannot live on that, so here I am.

Lyuba explained how she came to have a change of heart and realized that she too had leave Ukraine to work abroad.

Over the summer, Lyuba tutored students for university entrance exams. Lyuba told me that, in general, her generation was raised to be ashamed of accepting money for services. She explained, "We did everything for free, for the greater good." Dariya jumped in, "In other words she was Soviet." Lyuba smiled bashfully. Lyuba would spend hours with a child and then say, "Oh, no need to give me anything." If the mother of the child worked in a perfume factory, then she gave a bottle of perfume as payment. "It was a barter system," Lyuba stated. That summer Lyuba tutored a child whose mother, Alina, was formerly a history teacher and worked in Greece. Alina walked in and put $50 down on Lyuba's kitchen table. Lyuba exclaimed, "Who are you!? (*Vi' chto?*) I have never seen so much money!" Lyuba laughed explaining that, there they were peeling potatoes they had grown in the garden. In a small, one-bedroom apartment, Lyuba was living with her oldest daughter, a teacher, her oldest daughter's husband and their two children as well as with her youngest daughter, a doctor, and her youngest daughter's husband. Lyuba shook her head. "That is seven people in one room!" Lyuba said for emphasis. Both her daughters were no longer being paid at work and one of her sons-in-law, an engineer who had lost his job, was working "three months on, three months off" in Poland.

Alina, back on a visit from her work in Greece, watched them peel potatoes and said, "I know what your life is like, Lyuba, and there is no place for our generation here." Alina told Lyuba that she had to go abroad and should start studying Greek because when Alina went back, she would take Lyuba with her. "She even came by to make sure I was studying," exclaimed Lyuba, "And she practiced Greek with me." Lyuba thought about it and concluded that she already "did not have a penny (*kopek*) to buy bread with" so "what did she have to lose?" Plus, Lyuba said, she was single. Her husband died young, leaving her with two daughters, 14 and 10 years old, to raise on her own. She never remarried. Lyuba thought it would be much worse if her oldest daughter was forced to go leaving two small children behind, or if her youngest daughter went abroad, leaving a young husband alone to "pick up vices." Lyuba continued to study Greek.

Then her youngest daughter found an ad in a L'viv newspaper: "Looking for women between the ages of 39–54 to care for children in Ukrainian-American or Russian-speaking families." They wrote for an information packet and learned that Lyuba would earn $180 a week. Her daughters thought that they would be rich! Lyuba went to Kyiv to find the company's office. There a young woman, Nadya, in a large office with a Ukrainian and American flag in the background, brought Lyuba to a comfortable room and asked her to listen to a tape. On the tape there was a dialogue between a woman preparing to go to America asking questions and a man answering them. The man started to speak: "If you," Lyuba began, lowering her voice an octave with a serious expression on her face and then collapsed into Dariya's arms as she laughed. "This is so funny!" Lyuba muttered as she collected herself and again impersonated the man's voice on the tape:

> If you are an officer's wife, if you worked your whole life as a boss, if your character is one where you do not obey orders, you can get up from this couch and leave, because this means you should not go there [the United States].

Lyuba and Dariya collapsed into another laughing fit. It was laughter that came from nervous tension rather than joy. The tape went on to say how middle-class American families differ from Soviet ones. For example, "They pay you, and so they expect you to work." "You may not use the phone, and you may not watch TV." Lyuba became very serious and said, "I haven't even told my children the things I am saying into this recorder. To be honest, it was frightening." Nadya entered the room when the tape was done and said, "Well?" Lyuba answered, "Normal. Everything is normal." Nadya said, "Really? Maybe you didn't hear it well. You need to hear it one more time." She turned on the audio tape again and walked out of the room. Lyuba said she listened to the tape again and told Nadya when it was over, "I'm going." Nadya helped open a visa for Lyuba and then told her that they could send her to New York or San Francisco.

Lyuba asked Nadya to put herself in Lyuba's shoes: where would she want to go? Nadya replied that she would want to go to California. Lyuba asked, "Why is California better?" Nadya answered, "Have you seen the soap opera *Santa Barbara*? THAT is California." Lyuba recounted through more laughter, "So I told her: I want to go to Santa Barbara!"

Dariya had used this same agency in 1996, a year before Lyuba. Dariya nodded at Lyuba's story about how when she arrived in San Francisco, they took her passport and told her she would have to work six months for free to pay for her ticket. Dariya interjected, "The ticket was $600, and they wanted her to work six months! This is enslavement! I worked three months for free, but Lyuba is nicer than I am, so they made her work six months." Lyuba explained that the family she was working for were Russian-speaking Jews. There she cared for two children. After six months, the agency told Lyuba that her visa had expired, and she was now illegal. Dariya shook her head, "Same with me! This is good for them because if you are illegal, you have no rights here, and you are in their hands!" Dariya says that the local Ukranian Greek Catholic priest helped her get an extension on her visa, but Lyuba was less fortunate. The family Lyuba worked for warned her not to take public transit or a police officer could ask her for her documents and put her in prison. They told her there were no Ukrainian Greek Catholic or Ukrainian Orthodox churches in San Francisco. Lyuba said, "I thought I was the only Ukrainian in San Francisco." Dariya nodded, "Lack of information, Cinzia. Write about that. The hardest thing for immigrants is lack of information." Lyuba continued that, here she was, a woman "with a university degree who worked 30 years at school," and she was "cowed and downtrodden." Lyuba nodded to emphasize that it was true. "My husband doesn't believe me. He says why didn't you just pick up the Yellow Pages? Cinzia, who knew about the Yellow Pages?"

One day, Lyuba was home alone with the children, and the TV repairman came into the house. He was a Russian speaker and told Lyuba that there were Ukrainian churches in San Francisco. He returned to the house the next day with an English-language tape so she could learn basic phrases in English. He also encouraged her to walk out the door on her own and go to church. During her free time that following Sunday, Lyuba ventured out by herself for the first time. She stopped someone to ask directions, and it was Dariya. They exchanged phone numbers and have been friends ever since. Lyuba smiled warmly at Dariya, "The next Sunday I got on a bus and went to church. I entered the Ukrainian community and that is how I was extracted from captivity!" Even though the UGCC helped Lyuba find an immigration lawyer, the lawyer warned her that the court could go either way on her case and that getting married was the only sure way to be able to stay. Lyuba had an acquaintance who said she knew a man who was willing to marry, and Lyuba agreed.

They were both whispering now, and Lyuba kept looking over her shoulder to be sure that Myron was not up from his nap. Dariya continued, "Every immigrant has his path. If she had information sooner, maybe it wouldn't have gotten to this." Lyuba said her situation was fine. She worked for the small business that Myron owned, and he paid her. She had been able to go back to Ukraine to visit her children and grandchildren, and she sent them money regularly. They had passed their marriage interview, and Lyuba now had her paperwork. Dariya whispered, "He gets a good pension, but she has signed away her right to it." Lyuba flushed red and explained that she does not want to "steal money from his children and grandchildren." Lyuba felt Myron was good to her and took care of her kids in Ukraine, and this was enough. Dariya looked at me and, with a serious expression, said, "She is too shy and too nice. She thinks everyone is as good as she is!" Lyuba stood up and suggested we move outside. It was getting too warm inside. We moved to the patio and Dariya announced that it was "her turn now."

Dariya explained that in 1996, they would give you a visa if you had an address of a relative in the United States and said you wanted to visit them. You did not need a formal letter of invitation like you do now. Dariya landed in New York City with only an address, but her relatives no longer lived there. She found the same agency that had placed Lyuba, but she walked into their New York office rather than their Kyiv office. They sent her to work with a family in San Francisco and her story is similar to Lyuba's except, whereas Lyuba stayed with the agency for three years, Dariya left after six months. Dariya was able to find work cleaning houses and caring for the elderly on her own. She rented an apartment with another woman who also was "without a social security number" like her.

Dariya had three children and already had two grandchildren when she decided to migrate the first time. Her oldest daughter, Marta, was now 30, her son Nazar was 23, and her youngest daughter, Marianna, was 22. Like Lyuba, they were all, including her oldest daughter's husband and two children, living together in a one-bedroom apartment. Dariya said:

> I came only with the goal of earning some money. But living here for two years, my outlook on life changed. My opinions about life and my relationship to my obligations towards my children, grandchildren, and my family changed. I decided I had to go back and find a way to bring my children here, because I feel that the educational system in Ukraine does not give children a sufficient level of learning, one that is based on current worldwide requirements. … I saw that my children would not be successful in the global marketplace.

If Dariya's first intent was simply to earn money for her children, she came to see that what she wanted to give her children was knowledge about how to navigate the capitalist world. She also saw that in the United States, this was possible.

In fact, Dariya started the process of collecting her family in California right away, telling her son-in-law to apply for the green card lottery. In 1998 Dariya's son-in-law won a green card and came to San Francisco with Dariya's oldest daughter, Marta, and her two grandchildren. Later that year, Dariya returned to Ukraine for her other two children. Dariya says she was tired, bone tired. She had been working night and day in San Francisco, and, once home, she was no longer sure she wanted to return to California. After eight months in Ukraine, Dariya went to church to pray. She told God that she did not know if she was supposed to return to San Francisco, but she would go if it was her destiny. She went back to the consulate and applied for asylum. It was granted. Dariya said she was granted asylum because her family had been partisans in the 1940s and had been, in her words, "suppressed by the Soviet Union." "This means that it was destiny. I was supposed to leave, and so I did." This time she brought Nazar and Marianna with her and Marta was already waiting in San Francisco.

Dariya said she was most concerned about her youngest, Marianna. She was a talented student, had studied well in high school, was already conversant in four languages, and wanted to go to university. Dariya recounted a conversation she had with Marianna:

> [Marianna] said to me, "Mama, I do not see myself in this country. I have to go abroad because in this country I will end up like everyone else. This is what awaits me: get married and this is the end. I don't feel that I want to start a family now; this does not call me. I want to study, Mama. If we wait until Marta becomes an American citizen to get me, then I can wait but my brother cannot because he will be older than 21. When he is grown he will remember that, because of you, he did not have the opportunity to leave." After this conversation, I felt that if I did not go just because it was hard, that I would feel that I did not give my children all the opportunities they wanted. I, their mother, did not want to be the one to stand in their way. I am a mother. If I wanted all my obligations to be easy, then why am I a mother?

Dariya stated that Marianna might never have a family and that was fine with her. I raised my eyebrows, having never heard such a thing from a Ukrainian woman. Dariya's whole family, with the exception of Dariya's mother, was now reunited in San Francisco. Dariya's sister also won a green card in the lottery and was in San Francisco with her husband, children, and grandchildren.

I asked Dariya about her husband. She replied that she had lived with her husband 17 years and then he just "walked away from his family obligations" and had no contact with Dariya or the children. Dariya said, "I understood that I had to take the family role into my hands, become both mother and father for my children, and I divorced him." Dariya had been back to Ukraine recently because her mother passed away. Her ex-husband came to the funeral. He told Dariya that he had changed and wanted her to take him back. I remembered a respondent in Italy who said that she received two to three marriage proposals every time she went back to Ukraine, men hoping that she would support them. Dariya did not mention she suspected a financial motive, but she did say that she told him "No.":

> I think that America has changed me. In America women start to feel that they are women, people, that she is not a thing or object of love of another person or husband. For some reason, in America, women start to believe that their opinions, their feelings are important and should also be taken into account. It is not like this in Ukraine.

Although many women I spoke with, both in Rome and San Francisco, expressed unease with new ethnonationalist ideas that "real Ukrainian women" should marry young and drop out of or not enter the workforce despite their university education, no one else of Dariya's generation spoke about gender relations in this way. The focus was usually on "weak men" who should "protect their families" or women who were "strong," but asked to carry too much on their shoulders without help from husbands or the state. In fact, what these women wanted was for men to want to care for them.[4] But Dariya was talking about something completely different. She was talking about, if not independence, then individuation.

Whereas most participants like Viktoria, who were more "representative" of participants in San Francisco, spoke of localized concerns, Dariya spoke about "world-wide educational requirements," worried about the ability of her children to "compete on the global market," and told me that it was not Russia that was the number one threat to Ukraine but "globalization," which threatened to "eradicate Ukrainian culture" more completely that any Russianization policy through a process of homogenization. Thinking more deeply about Dariya's interview, I realized that what had me most intrigued was how different her presentation of self was from other respondents in San Francisco. It was not just her clothes and hairstyle, although these did set her apart from other participants, but it was the way that she identified with America. She did so not through a "husband," whether it be the U.S. state as pseudo-husband in Viktoria's case, or, much less common, marriage to an American citizen like Lyuba, but rather through an abstract notion of a capitalist Self. Dariya came to understand that what it meant to be capitalist, in large part, was to be a clearly delineated individual. Dariya continued:

> When I arrived the first time and stayed for two years, inside of me I felt I did not know what was happening to me, but it awoke something, something that I never was. I began to look at life differently. I started to analyze what was happening around me differently. And I started to study myself deeply, because I felt my mind and soul were at war with each other. And I started to read a lot of literature. I don't know if this is because … I believe

that all of us who come here as immigrants and arrive in another country, we fall into a vacuum. In the vacuum of the lack of communication, in the vacuum of lack of access to one's own culture, in the full vacuum of isolation from one's family, especially the separation from your children, which for me was very stressful, and when I collected all these factors together, I woke up to my work: I started writing.

Dariya said that, after writing poetry for many months, she realized that her poetry was an important commentary on the "real life circumstances of immigrants." She realized that it was her "destiny" to organize these poems into a book. She had just recently self-published her book of poetry written in Ukrainian. In it, she argued that if the mind and soul are not running in parallel you lose the "meaning of life … If these vectors collide, then we cease to be human." Dariya continued:

> People do not understand that, and I didn't either, until I had to write this book. This book was my destiny and through this destiny I found myself. I hope that every emigrant who has the opportunity to be in the vacuum of extreme situations in life is able to find themselves.

I caught myself thinking, "Whoa, who is this woman?" Some of the women migrants I interviewed in Italy spoke of "reconstructing themselves" (*perestroilis´*) in this post-Soviet era. However, they explained this "reconstruction" by borrowing the language of Mikhail Gorbachev's program of *perestroika*, which was a restructuring or reformation of Soviet policy and economic institutions during the 1980s that some argue led to the dissolution of the Soviet Union. Yet none of the participants in California, had invoked such a deep interior journey of self-discovery. It occurred to me that I had not yet asked Dariya what work she did in Ukraine, perhaps I was speaking with a professor of literature. Dariya had held a high ranking government position as Deputy Director of Economics for her *oblast'* (region). I replied with surprise, "Well that is an entirely different set of questions, isn't it?" Dariya agreed:

> This just awoke in me. This is why I didn't even want to study these questions, because it seemed that I was abandoning my work. But we never know what reserves our organism has. That is why I think that every person, regardless of his professional work, if he finds himself in an extreme situation in life, a second "I" will appear, a second outlook, a second "I" that we did not know before. We appear to ourselves.

Dariya explained that she would not have been able to find her "I" if she had not returned to San Francisco to live, because she would not have had the time and the tranquility needed to think and read if she was either in San Francisco by herself without her family or in Ukraine worrying about her "material conditions." It was through exodus that Dariya was able to find her "I" and cultivate a capitalist subjectivity.

She was quite a contrast to Lyuba whom Dariya had called "Soviet." In Lyuba's narrative there was no "I" only "we" or as Lyuba put it "the collective good." At first I was surprised that Dariya was a former high ranking economist. And yet economics and the construction of selves are deeply connected. Dariya recounted that when she returns to Ukraine to visit, people often tell her, "Come back and show us how to organize ourselves; help improve our country." However, Dariya argued:

> I think if I really was to return, I wouldn't be able to change anything and it would be mentally and physically too difficult for me to explain to these people how to live, understand? There the economic and political environment is different and the worst are the basics of the laws. People are still wasted in the black market. The whole mentality has to change.

Dariya was most critical of Ukraine on questions of "culture," "mentality," and "subject formation." These are inextricably tied to economics, Dariya explained, and this justified her need to bring her children to the United States. Dariya was hyper-aware that Marianna, a bright and talented student, would have little opportunity to find meaningful work in Ukraine, even if she managed to somehow pay for university. The gendered dynamics of Ukraine's economic transformation created conditions that, as Marianna herself noted, encouraged Marianna to abandon ambitions beyond marriage and children. Dariya explained that most of her generation went abroad to Italy, Greece, Poland, wherever they could find work, but most painful was following Marianna's classmates from her high school who specialized in languages. The girls were either "wasted sitting at home" or, those whose parents were not able to go abroad and earn the money to send them to university, went abroad themselves. According to Dariya, one girl was cleaning airplanes in Germany and another was in England working in a bar. "Wasted talent," Dariya said sadly. Dariya continued:

> The second time I came [to San Francisco] I came with the goal of staying and helping my children break away from this information landscape [in Ukraine], this closed circle in which children lose their talent. They cannot reveal themselves because their parents do not have the opportunity to give this to them. We have very intelligent children in Ukraine, but they do not have an educational basis, you understand? They are not given the basis upon which to develop their "I," develop their talent.

Dariya continued that in Ukraine everything is done on bribes. Children enter university and pass exams on bribes. "What kind of specialists can they be?"

Dariya had an intuitive sense that markets are attached to moralities. "What does the market teach kids in Ukraine?" she asked. Although she maintained her poised manner, I could see the force of her conviction: "not religion but corruption" and "not love but pornography" which, she emphasized, "before was forbidden." According to Dariya, Ukrainian children are unable to make it in the "Western market" and this, she explained resolutely, "is the main reason why I left."

Dariya was proud that she was able to pay for Nazar and Marianna to complete university in the United States. She believed that through their American education they now understood and were able to "move in Western markets." Dariya was most interested in speaking about Marianna. Marianna had completed a Masters and would begin a Ph.D. in England where she would study European integration with Ukraine as her case study. Dariya stopped cleaning houses and caring for the elderly in favor of getting her CNA. But she said the work of a nurse's aide was too hard on her and she registered herself as a small business! Although Viktoria was able to pick up part-time government work in the Department of Elections, there were only four people in my sample who were able to move out of performing cleaning and caring labor: Lyuba who worked for her husband; two women who found administrative positions in government agencies delivering social services to Russian speakers; and Dariya.[5] Dariya stood out because she was on the only interviewee to work in the private market rather than the governmental sphere or supplementing clients through IHSS in order to qualify for health care and caring for this income by performing cleaning and caring labor on the black market for cash. Her business still required physically demanding work. At 52, she did not know how much longer she could do it:

> But I have to. My daughter wants to defend her dissertation [in England]. Therefore, I want to continue to support her because I feel my obligation before God and before people to respect my children's talent. Then, when they are able to buy their own bread by their own work, then I will say that my duty is done. Then I will arrange my life as I see fit.

Dariya noted that in Ukraine she would be close to retirement and the life of a full-time *babushka*. "No matter what the country," Dariya exclaimed, "civilization would win if the government gave grandparents the chance to raise their grandchildren." Dariya reasoned that this would be a big help to young women who need to study or are working and studying and it was much better for the children to be with their grandparents after school than with "strangers." After all, "*Babushka* is *babushka*."

Dariya regretted that she had to keep working and had little time to dedicate to the everyday care of her grandchildren. "This is why," Dariya continued, "I do not think it is normal that young people do not marry and have their first child until they are 30–35 years old. In our culture this is not normal." I smiled. First, because I was relieved to finally hear something familiar to my population coming out of Dariya's mouth. Second, because I had suspected that Dariya did hope that Marianna would one day marry and have children. Dariya conceded that she had not yet abandoned her wish for more grandchildren to her understanding of American individualism. And third, because Dariya did not know that I was one of those 30-year-olds who was two months pregnant with my first child.

Dariya continued to speak about how daughters used to defer to their mothers on questions of childrearing. Dariya complained, "Now children say, 'We are smarter than you and will raise our kids alone.'" I could feel the tension that must exist between Dariya and Marta over this question. At the time I did not know how often I would hear my own mother and her Italian immigrant friends make the same complaint about their daughters who "thought they could learn how to raise kids by reading a book" and discounted their advice as "old-fashioned" or "unscientific." The medicalization of infancy where nearly everything – loose bed sheets, crib bars spaced too far apart, and placing a baby to sleep on their stomachs – could lead to the infant's death combined with the American cult of "intensive mothering" (Chapter 1) to which my position as a sociologist did not make me immune, often led my own mother to exclaim in exacerbation, "I raised three children and somehow you three are still alive!"

Although Dariya felt that Marta had become "too American" in her parenting style, Dariya was still committed to her children becoming capitalist subjects. Dariya was also concerned with her own relationship to the United States. For Dariya, her mode of integration was not the state like Viktoria and most other participants, or American culture like her children, but a capitalist Self. Yet, even for Dariya, the internal journey to a capitalist, individuated "I" did not preclude a Soviet understanding of grandmotherly responsibilities. Dariya may have found her "I" in exodus, but that "I" still hoped to be a *babushka*, with all of the Soviet values attached to the term, no matter where she lived.

Kateryna: Defining Children's Success in the Promised Land

Every year at Golden Gate Park in San Francisco, the Ukrainian community celebrates Ukrainian Day (see Figures III.1 and III.2). This year the stage for the 2006 celebration was set up in the grass and people had brought lawn chairs, blankets, and snacks to enjoy during the show. My husband and I arrived with our own chairs and settled in. Kateryna, a respondent who had helped me recruit participants from her Ukrainian Orthodox church, smiled when she saw me. She came over to say hello and exclaimed, "You really *are* pregnant!" At her dining room table two months earlier her husband, Boris, kept offering me vodka, and she joked that she thought I was just saying I was pregnant to get out of drinking. She explained that Americans were always worried about being polite and came up with the strangest excuses for why they could not drink vodka. I laughed and told her of an American colleague who, during her time as a researcher in Russia, incorrectly told people that she was a recovering alcoholic to stop the flow of vodka. "You see, Cinzia! I was right. I understand something about Americans." I thought to myself that I too understood something about Ukrainians.

At four months pregnant, my belly was now starting to show. I waited the three months that is customary among educated, older pregnant women who are hyper-aware of the increased chance of miscarriages before sharing our happy news with family and friends. But, I wasted no time in letting every migrant from the former Soviet Union in San Francisco know I was pregnant. In Rome, getting that first interview was difficult and time-consuming but once the interviews started, they snowballed quickly even if most people I spoke with were undocumented. Interviews in San Francisco were a different story. Although almost everyone had a green card and many were already U.S. citizens, people were afraid to meet with me. Others were simply too busy with work and family to carve out time to speak with an American researcher. Also, I was more "exotic" and interesting to the participants in Rome. Interviews in San Francisco never quite snowballed, and I found interviews in many haphazard ways. I did have two people who helped me greatly, Svitlana, the Ukrainian organizer for the careworkers union and Mila, a placement counselor in San Francisco's IHSS office. I sat in Svitlana's office as she called members and asked if they would speak with me, "Anya, yes, she is a very nice young woman. I've known her for four years already and Anychka, she is pregnant! We have to help to help her finish the dissertation before the baby comes!" I do not believe I would have gotten 41 interviews in San Francisco if I was not pregnant. I did feel guilty that I was using my pregnancy and the cultural norms of Ukrainians around motherhood to speed up my research, but since I was being truthful – I was pregnant, I did need their help, and I was desperate to finish my interviews before the baby came – it was only a vague pang of guilt.

Standing in the middle of a field in Golden Gate Park, I was struck by how different the talent shows I had attended in Rome were from Ukrainian Day in San Francisco. First, in contrast to the hundreds of migrants packed in the Roman auditoriums, here there were about 40 adults plus a handful of children in attendance. The mistress of ceremonies came out dressed in traditional Ukrainian dress: an embroidered peasant top and brightly colored skirt. She spoke English fluently and only occasionally addressed the crowd in Ukrainian. She explained to the audience that on August 24, 1991, Ukraine became an independent country and we celebrate independence from Soviet rule every August 24 with a showing of Ukrainian culture. She went on to talk about the great contributions of Ukrainian-Americans to the United States, a great country made even greater by the presence of so many talented Ukrainians. She had even convinced me that America was the "Promised Land!" The MC then sang a Ukrainian song in operatic style as Kateryna leaned in to explain that she had been a professional singer in Ukraine. A couple of short acts followed: a bandura player, a poem about the friendship between Ukraine and the United States, and another song from our MC. If the talent shows in exile saw teaching Italians about Ukrainian culture as their goal, talent shows in exodus focused on highlighting Ukrainian contributions to America and sought to instill pride in Ukrainian migrants and Ukrainian-Americans about the role of Ukrainians in U.S. history and culture. The heart of the show was a dance troupe of young men and women in their 20s who performed a series of traditional Ukrainian folk dances. They had elaborate costumes and although I know very little about dance, I could tell that these dancers were good. The crowd clapped and cheered as the men on stage leapt in the air and the women twirled. As I clapped I exclaimed, "They are wonderful! Where do they practice?" Kateryna replied, "Canada."

I was at first surprised that they had invited this troupe from abroad to celebrate Ukrainian contributions to America, but it also made sense to me. I could not imagine any of the children of my interviewees dressing in Ukrainian national costumes and performing traditional Ukrainian dances. In a context where the success of children was defined through market relations and "personal connections" were constructed as "Soviet-era *blat*," disassociation from other migrants was part of the definition of "success." This did not foster dance troupes among Ukrainian immigrant youth. There were no "Ukrainian boy bands" in exodus as there were in exile. Chatting with three of the dancers at the reception hosted by San Francisco's UGCC over a plate of *vareniky*, Ukrainian potato dumplings, I learned that they were mostly third generation Ukrainians whose grandparents left for Canada during WWII. They did not speak Ukrainian or Russian and the dancers I spoke with had never been to Ukraine. I asked, "How did you become interested in Ukrainian folk dance?" One woman answered matter-of-factly, "It's just what you do if you are Ukrainian in Canada."[6] She looked at her friends who nodded in agreement as they chewed.

Two months earlier I had arrived at Kateryna's apartment in a secluded corner of San Francisco at 11 a.m. and did not leave until 4 p.m. Kateryna, 56, was a stout woman with brown, curly hair cut short. She was dressed plainly in slacks and a button down short sleeve shirt and smiled warmly as she hustled me in the door. She sat me down at the living room table and poured tea as we chatted. Kateryna was from Eastern Ukraine but had moved to a large city in Central Ukraine outside Kyiv after completing her law degree. Kateryna's city was the capital of the *oblast'*, an administrative center which kept the law firm Kateryna worked for busy. She had worked for this firm almost 30 years before she left for San Francisco.

For the past five years, Kateryna had worked caring for the elderly through IHSS. She worked more hours in the beginning, but now she felt she was supposed to be retired. She worked five hours a day at the home of an elderly client and three evenings a week she cared for a handicapped boy through IHSS. She explained that, at first, she did not want to care for a handicapped child, because she thought it would be too sad. But Kateryna met the boy's grandmother at the Ukrainian Orthodox Church. The family was also from Ukraine, and they were desperate for help. Now Kateryna was so attached to the boy that she said, "At this point I do not watch him for the money. I see that it is very difficult for this family. She [the boy's mother] does not work. He [the boy's father] alone works and they have a second child to care for as well." Kateryna shared the hours needed to care for this client with Natasha who joined us for lunch later on.

Kateryna came to the United States for the first time in 1995 and worked for two years. She said she ended up in San Francisco "by chance." When a Jewish colleague left for San Francisco as a refugee, he sponsored Kateryna on a visitor's visa, paid for her plane ticket, and found her work as a live-in nanny for an infant. It was a difficult adjustment for Kateryna who said that the work was not hard, it was "just housework," but explained that "women of her generation" did not know what it meant to be a housewife, which Kateryna and others referred to as "sitting at home." Although this family was kind to her, and she still saw the child she cared for, now a teenager, Kateryna said:

> The only thing is when I arrived in America and then decided to stay and work, you have to make a break with yourself. You have to forget who you are. You have to forget who you are in this life, what your title and your name is. Because, understand? Yes at home I did something around the house, but I was used to other responsibilities. And to look after a child, someone else's (*chuzhoi*) child as we say, prepare food, clean, take him for a walk, and you know this is not your child – this is very difficult on the morale. And then of course you must reinterpret this to maintain your honor.

IHSS and being "protected" by the government as a "government worker" helped with Kateryna's reinterpretation of carework. Kateryna said she knows of many cases where people ended up working in "bad families – even our Russian-speaking families" that treated workers terribly, but she felt she was fortunate. She had her own room, her own bathroom, but nevertheless:

> It is difficult to live in someone else's house. I know people who couldn't do it and went home [to Ukraine]. During the day it was normal. They [the parents] went to work and I was with the baby all day, but evenings were horrible. They came home, and they had their private things to talk about, their family. They'd say "go relax" both to be kind and to have their family time, and I would feel alone and think about my family and my children. The only thing that kept me going was that I needed to earn that money for my children so that my oldest son finished institute there in Ukraine and the second studied as well. I helped them.

Kateryna had left two sons, Sasha and Vitalik, then 22 and 16, in Ukraine. She noted, "Of course, I earned more money as a nanny in America than working as a lawyer in Ukraine." Kateryna could not have sent her sons to university without the money earned from working abroad.

The friends that sponsored Kateryna also helped her oldest son Sasha enter the green card lottery, which he won. Of the 41 interviews I conducted with Ukrainian careworkers in San Francisco, six came to the United States or were legalized because either they or a relative won a green card in the lottery. However many others reported siblings, in-laws, or married children who had won green cards. The possibility of winning a green card loomed so large in the community that before I actually counted, I would have guessed incorrectly that close to half my respondents arrived through the lottery. Sasha came to San Francisco a year after Kateryna and enrolled at a local community college. Kateryna completed her second year of work, left Sasha in San Francisco, and returned to Ukraine to wait for Sasha to sponsor her through legal channels. After five years Sasha would be eligible to acquire his U.S. citizenship and apply for a green card for his mother.

Kateryna returned to Ukraine in 1997, just as the mass migration to Europe got under way. Kateryna continued:

> Therefore, this was a difficult period. It seemed to me that little-by-little everyone was leaving. They abandoned family, said goodbye to their relatives, and left for different countries, especially to Italy, but also to Spain. A few even went to Moscow to work or outside Moscow there in the government dachas to care for children as we say, other people's children (*chuzhdy*) – you abandon your own. But, what can you do?

Kateryna went back to her old law firm and worked a full year without pay. She said that Sasha was unable to explain to his friends – all Americans – that his mother worked for a year and was not paid. Kateryna explained:

> Americans ask, "She is a volunteer, a saintly woman?" And he says, "She is not a volunteer. She went to work every day and they simply did not pay her." Americans cannot understand. How is it possible that you work but you do not get paid?

During this time, Sasha finished community college in San Francisco. Even though he was raised in the city, Sasha always preferred spending time in the country where his grandmother lived. He found San Francisco both too expensive and too crowded. He found a job as a truck driver delivering tractors and relocated to the Midwest where there is more nature and the great expanses he preferred. Kateryna kept reminding me that Sasha had completed a degree in computer engineering in Ukraine at the Kyiv Polytechnic Institute, but he could not find work in his field. Kateryna said:

> So he started with this work [truck driving], he said he had to. He said
> "Mama, don't worry about this," he said, "I want to see America like this."
> And he did. He has driven to every state. Now that he is married, of course,
> he quit this job because you cannot have just two free days a month. This is
> very difficult. But while he was young and until this interested him, he
> drove. Of course, he earned good money, not bad. He bought himself a
> house there. He managed to build a good life for himself and he tells me
> (laughing) "Mama, soon I will retire!" I reply, "God willing!"

Although Sasha was not working in his profession, Kateryna believed him to be
successful because he earned well and he spoke "beautiful English." She also
emphasized that "he knows more about America than most Americans" because
of all his traveling. Kateryna placed much emphasis on the fact that Sasha had
moved to a place that had no Russian speakers. This was an important marker of
successful integration among my Ukrainian participants in exodus. In fact, when
Sasha became a U.S. citizen and sponsored Kateryna in 2001, she joined him in
the Midwest with her second husband, Boris. But Kateryna and Boris felt too
isolated in a place with hardly any Russian speakers, and they moved to San
Francisco. Kateryna explained:

> My son learned English quickly. He finished college and was able to go there
> where it is rare to meet a Russian speaker. He was able to be absorbed into
> this American life! Of course when you have a language barrier and you are
> unable to express yourself as you want then you have to "boil in your own"
> as we say and you must converse with Russian-speaking people. ... But
> Sasha, he is happy, thank God.

Sasha now works in a factory that produces farm machinery. For Kateryna, the
most important marker of Sasha's success was that there were no other Russian
speakers who worked at that factory. She also noted with pride that Sasha's
friends were American.

Kateryna was proud that Sasha was able to "move among Americans." However, the one American tendency that Kateryna and most other participants
wished their kids would not adopt was delaying having children. Sasha, now 33,
was married but without children. Kateryna shook her head as she exclaimed,
"He says, 'I am still young!' But I say, 'Come on already! Give me grandchildren while I am still able to watch them!'" Kateryna had recently returned
from a trip to Ukraine to visit her mother who was ill and was being cared
for by Kateryna's sister. She noted that her brother and her son also help
provide care. Kateryna sent $100–200 a month to her mother, brother, and sister.
Kateryna said, "Here the government helps the elderly. If someone needs care,
the government pays me. They help the elderly and they help me. There [in
Ukraine] nobody helps. The government no longer takes care of the people."

Kateryna also had several friends to whom she sent money on their birthdays. Once, she said, the people she was working for gave her a whole box of old toys in good condition, so she mailed them to an orphanage in Ukraine. I was surprised to learn that Kateryna does not send money to her son Vitalik except on his birthday and for New Year's. Kateryna says Vitalik works as a lawyer and earns enough to support himself. Nonetheless, Kateryna was consumed with the process of exodus, of reuniting her family in San Francisco. She exclaimed, sobbing, that "it is easier for those who have their whole family here."

When Kateryna got on the plane for her second trip to the United States, she had a green card in hand and sitting next to her was Boris as well as his daughter and ex-wife. But Vitalik was not permitted to go. Kateryna has tried to have Vitalik come to visit them. She was especially concerned that her sons have not seen each other in the ten years since Sasha left. Sasha has never returned to Ukraine and Kateryna thought it unlikely that he ever would. In fact, Kateryna noted that "my generation may go back [to Ukraine] to visit, they might even go back to live, but the younger generation, they are here to stay. They will not go back, not even to visit." Sasha, who was now an American citizen, formally invited Vitalik and completed the paperwork for the visitor's visa. "But," Kateryna explained, "They did not let him go. The consulate didn't let him, because they believed that since he is young, there is a possibility that he will stay here."

Kateryna worried that Vitalik, now 26, may not even want to come to the United States anymore. Kateryna noted that even Sasha hesitated to apply for U.S. citizenship when he became eligible, because he would have to give up his Ukrainian citizenship. However Sasha soon changed his mind. Kateryna recounted their phone conversation, while Kateryna was still in Ukraine waiting for Sasha to sponsor her:

Sasha said to me, "Mama, I don't want to become a U.S. citizen and lose my connection to my country." I answered, "It is nothing bad! If *you* do not become a citizen that means *I* will not be able to come to you and your brother will *never* be able to come." He listened to me, passed the citizenship exam, and filled out the paperwork. Literally four months later, I received my green card. And as soon as I received my green card, I did the papers for family reunification for my youngest son, but it takes time. A unification from brother to brother, before it was fast, but now, [Sasha] as a U.S. citizen, to request his brother for reunification you have to wait 10–12 years. This is very long, understand. And I feel this is not right, but where and with whom do you argue this? I said, I will sit and write a letter to the president. I always have this thought in my mind. I am a government worker … I will write the president and say that I miss my youngest son, I'd like him to come here. Please permit him to come.

Kateryna explained that Sasha thought she was crazy, but Kateryna felt connected to the U.S. government.[7] Kateryna, like most of the California participants, spoke of the U.S. government as "provider," an entity with which she had a personal relationship. Kateryna did not feel she would ever "become American." However, her position as an IHSS careworker allowed her to claim an identity as a "government worker." Through this government worker identity, Kateryna felt she was able to make personal claims on the U.S. state.

In three years, Kateryna will be eligible to apply for U.S. citizenship. Reunification requests for an unmarried child have higher priority and a shorter wait time (see Table 4.2). However, Kateryna worried that Vitalik may marry, and this would make bringing him to the United States more difficult. Not only would it decrease his priority, making the wait to process his green card even longer, but his future wife would also need to agree to come. Kateryna noted that it would be difficult for Vitalik. He would not be able to practice law here and Kateryna was unsure of what work Vitalik could do. Kateryna looked at her hands as she said:

> America is a beautiful and good country, but living here is also not easy. Even here you have to earn money, you have to work. The only thing is what I have already told you, that here if you work your labor is valued.

Sasha is well settled (*ustroilsia*), and Kateryna hoped that God would provide a way for Vitalik to be settled here as well.

I asked Kateryna what her plans were for the future and whether she planned on staying in the United States herself. Kateryna replied:

> Well, you know, look at this apartment. We have it through Section Eight housing and our rent is low, so this worked out. And we work, well of course I told you that here I live 100 times, maybe even 200 times better than I lived there. Even if there I worked, and as a lawyer no less, it doesn't matter. I now look at my classmates, yes, most still have work, but you have to get in contact with them to understand what kind of work. They may even be part of the criminal world there, understand? None of them are tranquil. To say it briefly, they do not give money away easily there either, but here you work and they give you your money. Here there is tranquility.

Kateryna planned on staying in the United States. She continued to say that all of this was possible because God had given her good health. But she also noted that the U.S. government, through her work, had given her health insurance, so that she was not worried if she does get sick. "So," Kateryna continued, "thank God the U.S. government takes care of us." Health insurance was of utmost concern to Kateryna and other participants. It was often mentioned as something they were grateful to the U.S. government for and cited as evidence that the state cared about them personally.

Boris was 63 and Kateryna said he was unable to work and was on welfare. "There [in Ukraine] he was an electrical engineer. He too has higher education … well this is how life turned out. Here you have to forget who you are." Despite what felt like a painful decline in social status, Kateryna noted that there were benefits to performing carework:

> I tell you, for 30 years I worked with my mind. You, I am sure, know what this means to work with your mind and with people. Now I do physical work. Sometimes my legs feel like they will fall off, but morally and in my head I am free, and I feel satisfied with this. Now I can walk in the park, I can travel somewhere, I can go to the ocean and the like. At home, you understand, I always had work on my mind: tomorrow there will be a trial, tomorrow something else is going on in the prosecutor's office, someone has tried to block our work, there someone did something incorrectly … and when your head is tired, it is much more complicated than this life here. Therefore, we can say that I am satisfied with the destiny that God sent me. We can even say that I came back to life here, we can say that.

The theme of "coming back to life" or being "resurrected" through state-sponsored carework was a common one (see Chapter 5, Viktoria).

The doorbell rang and Natasha, a woman in her early 30s, walked in. She was slender with a mop of curly hair and a "don't mess with me attitude." Kateryna was telling me of a friend who went to Italy and her husband left her for another woman. Natasha, who was from Belarus, jumped into the conversation and exclaimed, "Well that is the woman's fault. You cannot leave a man for more than a month." Kateryna nodded, but explained that her friend and women in Italy were working to earn money for their families. Natasha insisted that they were "bad mothers" for leaving their families, but she did acknowledge that the money was not bad. Kateryna, who followed Ukrainian politics, explained how migrants in Italy are for Yushchenko like her.

Kateryna said that when she gets her U.S. citizenship, she will vote in the United States, but for now she was still a Ukrainian citizen and so voted at the consulate for Ukrainian elections. She said that she votes for democracy in Ukraine, therefore she voted Yushchenko. "I am a lawyer, understand. I know how power works." Living in the United States, she said, made her want democracy for Ukraine even more. Vitalik voted for Tymoshenko. Kateryna said that was fine with her, since she liked Tymoshenko too. Kateryna explained:

> Maybe if I did not live in America, maybe I would think that Ukraine should be only for Ukrainians, with their own language. But now, I believe Ukraine should be part of Europe … but follow an American model. The national language should be Ukrainian and everyone should learn Ukrainian. Then if people want to speak Russian or learn three or four other

languages, that is great. If Russians want to live in Ukraine and speak Russian at home like we do here, fine. But at school, in government offices it should be in Ukrainian.

Kateryna's husband Boris had come home from fishing and was sitting at the table already offering me vodka. Natasha told Kateryna that she was ridiculous. "If someone comes to the hospital and tells me they will only speak Belarusian, I tell them I love Russian and get someone else to help them!" Kateryna replied, "Natasha, I love Russian too. That isn't the point." Boris waved at us as if to say, "Hello, I hear you!" Boris was Russian, but had lived in Ukraine 12 years before coming to San Francisco. Kateryna stood behind Boris seated at the table and put her arms around him and said, "We always joke that Boris wants to annex Crimea!"

Natasha went on about how she hated "nationalists." Kateryna sighed as she told us to begin eating. Kateryna complained that when she arrived in California she suddenly became "Russian." She said, "Natasha, just look here in San Francisco. We have Russian newspapers, Russian TV, Russian stores, but there are very few Russians here. I am Ukrainian and you are Belarusian; we are not Russian!" Boris yelled, "I am Russian, and I want to see Cinzia drink vodka!" Kateryna slapped his wrist. "She says she is pregnant. That means 'No thank you' in American. Leave her alone." Boris changed tactics, "Ok, Cinzia, and then you must eat for two. Eat!"

Zhanna: Reinventing *Babushka* across Migration Waves

I met Zhanna, 60, at her place of employment, a private home in San Francisco. Zhanna was a matronly woman with a mass of black hair piled high on her head. She immediately struck me as a *mother* who knew how to get things done. I found myself standing in the foyer resisting the urge to throw myself into her capable arms and ask her to fix all my troubles. Zhanna was dressed in elegant clothes – black pants with a black lace short sleeve cameo and crocheted vest on top. Her clothes, along with her hairstyle, large glasses, and bright pink lipstick were distinct to Soviet women of her generation. She wore a large gold cross around her neck. I was relieved to learn that she was indeed Ukrainian and I silently thanked Mila, the IHSS counselor who referred Zhanna to me. I had come off of a number of referrals from Svitlana, the Ukrainian union organizer, only to realize the person she referred was not actually Ukrainian but from Estonia or Belarus or Kazakhstan and could not be included in my sample. When I went back to Svitlana and explained how grateful I was for her help, but I could only interview people from Ukraine, her response was, "Oh, we are all the same! Just say they are from Ukraine!" Of course I did not take this advice. The opposite also happened. I would be speaking with someone who told me they were Russian, and it was only after some time that I realized that they were actually Ukrainian but thought that "Russian" would be a more understandable label for me as an American. Mistaking a Ukrainian for a Russian or vice versa would be unthinkable among Ukrainians in Rome where Ukrainian nationalism was a defining discourse of migration.

I found that participants had different levels of sensitivity around nationality and identity in San Francisco and whether one spoke of the "Ukrainian community," "Russian community," or the most popular "Russian-speaking community" revealed their perception of where they fit in San Francisco's multi-national, post-Soviet landscape. Dariya and Lyuba (Chapter 5) spoke of the "Ukrainian community." Viktoria (Chapter 5) felt at ease getting the vote out in the Russian-speaking community while Kateryna (Chapter 5) felt, despite being Ukrainian, she was stuck in the "Russian-speaking community." Zhanna joked that before migrating she thought "maybe I'll become American in San Francisco, but I would not have guessed that I would become Russian instead!" In fact, Zhanna, who was ethnically Ukrainian as was her husband, noted that there were many Russians in her home city, many mixed marriages between Ukrainians and Russians, and at times she used "Ukrainian" and "Russian" interchangeably during our conversation. This slippage is also part of Ukraine's post-colonial legacy.

Zhanna was from Odessa, a resort city in Southern Ukraine on the Black Sea. She was a gregarious and rambunctious person, and she described the beauty of her city and its women with drama and flare. After three years in San Francisco, she went back to Odessa for a visit. Now she visits yearly. She explained that Odessa fared better economically than other parts of Ukraine, mostly due to its working naval port, and experienced less emigration. Zhanna's father was a military man and they traveled a lot. Zhanna lived in Germany for seven years as well as Poland and Czechoslovakia. Since they moved around so much, Zhanna's mother, a doctor by training, was unable to practice medicine. Instead she studied to be a fashion designer, and Zhanna proudly stated that her mother was well-known as a designer and even designed gowns for the Miss Ukraine beauty pageants. Zhanna taught German at university and her husband, Viktor, was a doctor. They have two children. Ruslana, 39, was married and had two daughters 17 and 8. She worked as a psychologist in Ukraine. Zhanna's son, Tolya, was 34, unmarried, and worked in San Francisco's finance industry.

After the collapse of the Soviet Union, Zhanna lost her university job. Therefore, Zhanna and her mother decided to open a "private enterprise." She explained the differing effects of the collapse of the Soviet Union on men and women by telling a joke. It was about a foreigner who visits Ukraine and compliments the host on his wife, so beautiful and articulate. Then the foreigner eats a wonderful meal and he says: You have hired a talented cook. The man says: Yes, my wife. And then the man's three beautiful children come in, one works, one studies, and one is still in school. And the foreigner says: You must have a nanny to raise your children. And the man says: Yes, my wife. Then he invites the foreigner to the *dacha* (a country house) and they drive there in a nice car. The foreigner says: You must have another source of income to be able to afford such a car. The man says: Yes, my wife. She works full time. They get to the dacha and the foreigner says: What beautiful flowers and vegetables. You have a talented gardener. And the man replies: Yes, my wife. The foreigner is beside himself and thinks that it is impossible that his wife can do all this and says: Your wife is beautiful, is a wonderful cook, raises three children, works full-time, and gardens at the *dacha*? I have decided what souvenir I want to bring back to my country, a Ukrainian wife! Zhanna nodded her head laughing. She continued:

> And yet it is true that women are not valued there. I tell you truthfully, look even now with all that has happened in our country. When it was difficult times with work, many, many institutions of higher learning were closed down. Men lost their jobs – women also lost their jobs – but women are more tenacious, more enterprising, understand? Each in her own way does what she is able to do. Women baked cakes to sell, went to the collective farms to buy vegetables and then brought potatoes, tomatoes, cucumbers to the city to sell at the bazaar. This is a tragedy, you understand? Imagine putting an American in a Russian woman's place with a husband who still loves to eat, sit on the couch, and watch TV! And yet, he still commands: "Hurry up! Where is dinner? I don't understand why this isn't done and that isn't done." The men fall into a real depression. But the women of course, because they are mothers, they work their way out of it. They find a way.

Zhanna explained that when men lost their jobs, they drank (see Chapter 1 and Conclusion), but when women lost their jobs, they made up a new job. "While the men drank," Zhanna said, "my mother and I organized other mothers who had to feed their children into a sewing cooperative." The rule was that each woman had to have her own sewing machine. They worked with leather goods and Zhanna traveled to Kyiv and even Russia to buy quality leather. They also sewed clothes, and Zhanna went to Turkey to buy cloth. Zhanna declared, "There is no fashion in the United States, none whatsoever! But in Odessa," Zhanna explained, "women always dressed beautifully. Even if at home there was nothing to eat, your clothes were always beautiful and fashionable: beautiful shoes, beautiful dresses. Our women are like this." Therefore, Zhanna's business was doing well, "enough to live on." But then, Zhanna said, the possibility to leave appeared, and they "did not want to lose this opportunity, this chance."

Zhanna's husband, Viktor, has two sisters, one older and one younger. His younger sister, Ivana, married a Ukrainian Jew who later developed lung cancer. His family was already in San Francisco as Jewish refugees, and they wanted him to come to San Francisco and receive cancer treatment in the United States. So Ivana left for San Francisco with her sick husband and young child. Unfortunately, Ivana's husband died of cancer five months later. Before he died, Ivana did the paperwork that made it possible for the whole family, including her brother Viktor, to leave for California. According to Zhanna, Ivana was a civil engineer with a degree from a prestigious school, however in California she found herself "cleaning toilets" and this was "very hard on her morale." Ivana wanted someone to come and watch her son while she studied English and looked for other work. Therefore, Zhanna's mother-in-law left for San Francisco. Yet, she returned to Ukraine after only a few months because her husband, Zhanna's father-in-law, became ill. Ivana then asked Zhanna and Viktor to come to San Francisco. Zhanna says they were surprised, because they had not seriously thought about going to the United States. They felt they were too old to leave their home and besides, they needed to help care for Viktor's father and their grandchildren. They decided instead that their nephew with his wife and child would go to San Francisco to help Ivana. A year later, Viktor's father died. Viktor and his mother joined Ivana in San Francisco. Zhanna stayed in Ukraine and continued to live in a small apartment with her son, daughter, and granddaughters. In fact, Zhanna said, they did not make use of their documents for five years because they lived "normal" in Ukraine:

> How normal? We all worked. My son, Tolya, studied at university in economics and had a very good department. He finished in banking matters, operation of international currency, and he knew English perfectly. He was the best student in his class at university. He created a plan for himself to live in Ukraine, and we thought he had a good future there.

It was not until I had sat in the kitchen for three and a half hours, tasted the cabbage she was preparing for dinner, and suggested a tad more salt, that I finally got the story about why, after five years, they decided to leave Ukraine in 2000. Zhanna had gone on at great length about how intelligent and talented Tolya was. He completed his university degree in economics at the top of his class and then started graduate school. Zhanna remained in Odessa because it seemed Tolya would have a "bright future" in Ukraine, and she did not want to uproot him. According to Zhanna, when the documents finally arrived for her son to leave, the director of the university said, "What are you doing? You are taking away a future economics minister from Ukraine!" Yet, Zhanna felt she was doing the right thing:

> If you are going to have kids, you have to give them everything. You can deprive yourself of something or even lose yourself but give everything to your child so that then you will not have problems in your old age. You won't have shame in front of your children, isn't it like that? If you are not able to do this, then it's better if you don't have kids and that is what I think. That means in my life I have deprived myself of many things because my salary was not enough to give my kids all that I wanted. I wanted to give them always more, give them better knowledge.

Zhanna felt that now she had to give her son America. Zhanna's priest also told her not to go because her "soul would not find sustenance in America." Yet, Zhanna had reason to believe that Tolya's soul (*dusha*), and his life, were in danger in Ukraine. Zhanna said with great sadness, "Ukraine has become a bandit state."

While Tolya continued his graduate studies, he also became finance director of an important firm. Zhanna recounted that there were multiple firms trying to close a contract with a particular client, but it was Tolya's company that succeeded in signing the deal. Zhanna said that Tolya had just left the house to go to work, and she happened to look out the window. She saw two expensive foreign cars with tinted windows on the street. Two men wearing sunglasses stepped out, and Zhanna watched in horror as the men forced Tolya into one of the cars and sped off. Zhanna was beside herself with terror and called Tolya's boss right away. Tolya's boss said, "Oh God, I know who they are. Don't worry!" and hung up. These men brought Tolya to a remote place and wanted to know the details of how his firm got the contract, how much it was for, and what would it take for them to get the contract themselves. They beat Tolya, but Tolya's boss knew who they were and who to call. They let Tolya go. Zhanna wondered:

> But what if he didn't know who to call? Tolya has never in his life accepted a bribe or done anything illegal but after this – I am speaking to you honestly – I thought it was only a matter of time before someone dragged him off the right path and he would be hurt, not just physically but in his soul. I said, "Tolya, you know what? We are going to leave. We are not going to wait for you to finish graduate school or for someone to hurt you. We have this opportunity for you, and we are going to take it."

Zhanna's daughter, Ruslana, was sad to lose her mother and the help Zhanna provided as a *babushka* to her two daughters. Ruslana, Zhanna assured me, understood why she had to go. Zhanna said matter-of-factly, "Do you think that this wasn't also dangerous for my daughter and for my grandchildren? Who was going to protect them when these bandits are on their way to Tolya?"

Zhanna emphasized that they are not refugees in San Francisco, but came as part of family reunification, joining Viktor and his family. Zhanna wanted her mother to come with them, but she refused. Zhanna concluded that maybe in the end it was for the best. She said, "Now I work with these elderly people and coming here at that age is a psychological tragedy for them." Once in San Francisco, Tolya who already spoke "beautiful, elegant, literary English" before migrating, had few problems completing some college courses and earning a finance industry exam certificate. He now works for an auditing company in San Francisco where "he is the only Russian speaker" and he earns "big money." Zhanna explained that everything worked out for Tolya, except that they ended up with a "divided family." Also, Zhanna said expressively, he is 34 and still single. "When Svitlana told me she was sending a nice Italian girl to talk to me about our Ukraine I asked right away: Is she married? Too bad you are married, because I see we understand each other." She jumped out of her chair, "Oh my cabbage! Taste it now, better?"

Zhanna's mother died three years ago. When she was alive, Zhanna sent money to Ukraine for her care and her operations. Zhanna exclaimed:

> The older generation, they were abandoned by the government to die! This is awful! They don't have money for medicine, and you have to pay bribes to the doctors or they will not look at these sick people! Oh, they are left to die.

Zhanna said she sent $10,000 all together for her mother's care. She has tried incessantly to convince her daughter, Ruslana, to bring her family to San Francisco, but she refused. They had all they needed there. Zhanna said she did not send Ruslana money because her husband works for a foreign company and earned well. Zhanna was now trying to convince her oldest granddaughter, who was just starting university and was studying English, to come to San Francisco to study.

Zhanna understands why her daughter refused to come. Zhanna said, "When I got here, I did not know I could hurt so much." Zhanna exclaimed that even with her out-going personality, when she first arrived she was "in shock." She did not like anything in San Francisco. The houses seemed fake, "like a theater," and the whole city seemed closed. She never saw anyone walking on the street except on Geary Boulevard where "our Russian people walk." Other Russian-speaking migrants told Zhanna she was "depressed" and should go on welfare if she was unable to work. But Zhanna answered that she was not used to that:

> When we lived there [in Ukraine], none of us knew what depression was, you know. There you had to survive. You had to work. You had to think about your family. I never had time there to think about "stress." Every once in a while you took a little valerian, maybe a little something else, and then you worked, and you addressed your problems.

The best cure for depression, according to Zhanna, was to work. By her second week in San Francisco she was in the IHSS office saying: "Give me the most difficult and the sickest people you have." Zhanna said, "I need to work with people. I need to see grateful eyes. I need to do some good for people. This is what I am used to." Zhanna took on four different clients right away and worked every day from 7 a.m. to 9 p.m. Over time, one of these four clients was given more and more hours, so Zhanna eventually left her other three clients and now worked full-time caring for Vera. Zhanna was completely enmeshed with the going-on of Vera's family.

Vera was 45, and the daughter of Russian immigrants. She was no longer able to walk, speak, or feed herself due to the debilitating effects of multiple sclerosis. Vera's husband, unable to deal with the disease, left her with two children. Vera's mother, Nina, worked full-time and did the best she could with two teenage grandchildren. Zhanna had been with this family for seven years. She is there Monday through Friday. She was paid to work 8.5 hours a day, but she stayed for 10 since her husband dropped her off in the morning on his way to work and then picked her up in the evening on his way home. IHSS sent another woman to care for Vera on the weekends. Zhanna went into the details of Vera's children's lives, proudly declaring that the older daughter was in college while the son, who Zhanna worried about terribly because he had "fallen in with the wrong crowd," was now back on track since Zhanna convinced his father to send him to military school. Zhanna said the children spoke almost no Russian when she first started working there, and now they speak well. The kids tell Zhanna that they love her like a second mother or grandmother. Zhanna showed me countless pictures of the children, looking at them lovingly. Zhanna explained that, in Ukraine, she lived with her grandchildren and did absolutely everything for them. When she no longer had her grandchildren, Zhanna felt that she had "all this love to give," so she gave it to Vera's children. Zhanna says she did the right thing and has the "good results" to prove it. She said that some people do this work by "putting in their hours and nothing else interests them." Zhanna said the woman who cares for Vera on the weekend comes, does her work, and leaves as quickly as she can, but she was "one of those who has depression":

And I know so many who have this depression. I think depression is an illness of the lazy to tell you the truth. You just have to be occupied with something, you have to be involved with people and live other people's problems not just your own.

Zhanna said she was not able to do carework "half way." She was not able to "close her heart" and Zhanna noted that the results were not only good for Vera's children, but good for her:

This was also medicine for me, positively! Maybe I too would have had depression, I would have missed my granddaughters too much because the love you have for children, your family, it is so strong. But I am here, and I helped these kids. I gave them all the love I would have given to my granddaughters. And I too have received from them. I have received respect, and love, and affection, and everything. Understand?

Interviews in San Francisco were filled with longings to be a *babushka* and for many this seemed out of reach either because grandchildren were left in Ukraine, they moved to other locations in the United States, or because children in

California adopted the late childbearing norms of educated, middle-class Americans. Respondents often wondered out loud if their children were "waiting to have kids until they would need to put Pampers on me and the baby!" For yet others, their children followed American norms of privacy and childrearing keeping *babushki* and their "old fashioned advice" at arm's length (see Chapter 5, Dariya).

Zhanna says that she sometimes goes to the union meetings that Svitlana organized. There they tell her:

> "Zhanna, you cannot do this. You undermine our credibility. You should only occupy yourself with the woman you are paid to care for. Why are you doing anything with these kids? What for?" I said, "Well they are just children. It is not their fault that they are left, we can say, without a mother considering that she is like a doll and does not remember anything. And here we have to work with a conscience."

Zhanna said, at the union meetings, they thought she was "crazy." Vera had a dog. He was an old dog and the "children love him like crazy" and he needed to eat and go for a walk. Zhanna cared for him, too. And then there was a cat, and the cat too needed to eat. Zhanna explained she loves cats. "What am I supposed to do? Not feed the cat?" Zhanna had found a way to be a *babushka* in San Francisco and this has proven to be of vital importance to her.

Vera's family was Zhanna's anchor in California. But Zhanna said the search for a larger community was also important to her. Zhanna explained that she was from Odessa and "people there have a temperament similar to Italians," something she felt I could relate to. "We are emotional and communicative; we care deeply and we live closely." Zhanna exclaimed, "Half the city was my friend and has been to my house for dinner." But San Francisco was different. Zhanna knew that, at her age, she would never learn English and would not have American friends, but she was unprepared for how tricky it would be to find other Russian-speaking friends. On the one hand, she found that the animosity between Western and Eastern Ukrainians was less prominent in San Francisco than inside Ukraine or what I found to be the case in Italy. Zhanna explained that, in Ukraine, language – whether you speak Ukrainian or Russian in your family – was a big issue. Western Ukrainians she met in Odessa would not even consider her Ukrainian because Zhanna speaks Russian but, "Here that doesn't happen. Oh, you are from Ukraine? *Rodnoi, Rodnoi, Rodnoi* (compatriot)." Zhanna explained that in Kharkiv or Odessa people heard that presidential candidate Yanukovych was for the Russian language and they voted for him right away. In San Francisco, however, "we are mostly all for Yushchenko here. It doesn't matter if you are from Odessa, Kharkiv, or L'viv." According to Zhanna, Ukraine had "big problems" to talk about and she asserted that the "language in which we talk about them" was the least of their troubles.

If the divisions between Western and Eastern Ukrainians were less salient among migrants to San Francisco, divisions between migration waves ran deep between these post-1991 migrants and two other groups: WWII Diaspora Ukranians and their descendents and those who Zhanna and others called the "Old Russians" (*starye rysskie*). This was a common theme among participants in San Francisco. "Old Russians" and their descendants, Zhanna explained, are those who left during the Russian Revolution. Since the "Old Russians" arrived first, most Russian-speaking organizations in San Francisco were founded by this previous migration wave. Zhanna explained that Old Russians "do not look at us with respect." She felt that Old Russians believed they came to the United States for lofty moral reasons, whereas the post-1991 migrants were "economic migrants" and money was a crass reason to leave one's homeland according to Old Russians. Zhanna continued that Old Russians "do not love America." Their children do not assimilate, and they still speak Russian and get married "among themselves" while "our children," those of the new arrivals, "become Americans."

Zhanna and others I spoke with, translated the divisions between migration waves via the religious landscape of San Francisco's churches. Zhanna explained that the UGCC, while appealing to a small set of recent migrants, was generally poorly attended. Like the UGCCs in Rome, it was interested in teaching Ukrainians about being "Ukrainian" and was concerned with Ukraine's nation-state building project. Yet, this found few recruits in San Francisco where Ukrainian migrants tended to see the UGCC as a place for Ukrainian-Americans (Chapter 4). My visits to San Francisco's Ukrainian Orthodox Church revealed a similarly small crowd with an elderly congregation and a handful of second and third generation families. The Church offered a buffet lunch after mass and I asked three people in line as we waited for our meal for the priest's name and no one knew. I later spoke with the priest, a kind, elderly man, who was completely disconnected from any of the concerns of recent migrants. He was much more interested in issues such as getting The Great Famine of 1939 recognized as genocide against ethnic Ukrainians. Zhanna could not fathom why anyone would waste their time arguing about hungry people back then, when there were people in Ukraine who were hungry right now. WWII Diaspora Ukrainians and their children, however, saw this as vital to the creation of a Ukrainian ethnic identity. It allowed them to make claims for international recognition and assert that Ukrainians were indeed a separate ethnic group from Russians. It was also a way to create moral distance from a Soviet past in which Ukraine was a colonized victim rather than an independent actor.

A second generation parishioner at the Ukrainian Orthodox Church, Oleg, explained the divisions to me in this way. He felt that his parents and other Diaspora Ukrainians of the WWII generation had made many sacrifices to preserve the Ukrainian language and culture and fight for Ukraine's freedom. Then, in 1991, when Ukraine became independent, the Ukrainian community eagerly welcomed a new wave of migrants. Yet, Oleg felt the new wave of migrants were "opportunists" that behaved "like the Russians we worked so hard to liberate them from." According to Oleg, "new arrivals are 'Ukrainians' when they want services from our organizations, and are 'Russians' when speaking with others." He continued, "They anger us by speaking Russian at our functions. They come without paying for tickets" which, Oleg contended, "They can afford. Just look at how they are dressed!" At the same time he lamented that "our Ukrainian organizations were dying out and going broke." However, recent migrants like Zhanna felt unwelcome in both Ukrainian Diaspora and Old Russian organizations.

Zhanna explained that Tolya studied Ukrainian and speaks it "beautifully," but she was not conversant in Ukrainian. Given that much of present-day Ukraine prefers the Russian language to Ukrainian, this did not make Zhanna feel any less Ukrainian. Zhanna loved to go to the large Russian Orthodox Church on Geary Boulevard. "This was our Church in [Soviet] exile!" She used to attend one of San Francisco's other Russian Orthodox Churches but stopped going when the priest called her and all the recent migrants "communists." Zhanna could barely control her outrage:

> I said, "Well who are you?" The priest said, "I came from *Russia*, you all are *Soviet* and come from communist countries, and we don't want to speak with you." I said, "If I am a communist, then you are a fascist! How did you come here?" He answered it is none of my business how he arrived. I answered, "And you know nothing about how I arrived or why." And I said, "I don't want to speak with Old Russians because your parents and grandparents abandoned their country when they should have stayed and fought for her. We had to live for 70 years with what you Old Russians left us!" I said, "If you didn't abandon your country and your king and fought against the revolution, then maybe the revolution wouldn't have succeeded and we wouldn't have had to live 75 years under all those regimes: Lenin, Stalin, Khrushchev, Brezhnev, then there was Chermenko, then there was the KGB man, what is his name [Andropov], then Gorbachev, Yeltsin … Every time everything changed! Every time the economy collapsed and there was no money and the people scraped bottom!"

Zhanna banged the table in disbelief at how a priest, of all people, could say such a thing. Other people could be "ignorant" but a priest? She felt that his job was to "create connections" and "foster love" between all people from the region. Zhanna's scowl gave way to her customarily boisterous self. She announced, "That is why I like the church on Geary. They send a new priest every two years so he doesn't have time to learn these things."

Zhanna also went to San Francisco's Russian Center a couple of times. But, she felt "it was really for Old Russians, not for us." Zhanna said, "Old Russians are not interested in us. We are more interested in them. They keep their distance and do not want to converse with us." Zhanna laughed that she thought "assimilation" into American society would be a big problem for her. But "assimilating" in the "Russian-speaking community" was the real issue. But now, Zhanna says, she has a "women's collective" here. Of course it is not the same as the friends "back home." In the Soviet Union, Zhanna explained, she and her friends depended on each other for survival. "Friendship needs to be cultivated during hard times. If you do not help each other through hard times, then friendship remains superficial."

This was why, Zhanna said, her connection to Vera's children was so strong. "How much harder of a time could a *babushka* have than leaving her grand-children? And how much harder of a time could children have than to lose a mother slowly over time [to multiple sclerosis] like this?" Zhanna noted that America had changed her. She became a "homecare worker," a job she never thought she would do. She became an "immigrant," a "Russian," and even a "communist" – "I had to come to America to become a 'communist'!" Vera's family were "Old Russians." Therefore, on an individual level, Zhanna managed to bridge the divide between migration waves in becoming a *babushka* to Vera's children. Of all her new identities, *babushka* was the most important one of all.

Halyna: Undocumented but Playing the Green Card Lottery

I met Halyna through her partner, Mycola. Mycola, 56, was about 5'2" with a buzz cut, moustache, and he dressed in the attire of urban youth. He wore an oversized plaid button down and calf-length jean "rapper" pants with wide pant-legs. A chain secured the wallet in his back pocket to the front belt hook. Mycola was animated, smiled a lot, and struck me as having a sunny disposition as he showed me around his apartment. He was a painter and his apartment walls were covered with his artwork. Some paintings were traditional – Ukrainian churches snuggled in a surrounding wood or flowers in green fields – but others more fantastical, such as a portrait of his daughter in jeans shot through with Cupid's arrows and the wind blowing through her hair.

Mycola had arrived in Chicago 10 years earlier. He explained that he grew up in an orphanage in Kyiv, completed his studies at an art institute, and then joined the army where he was stationed in Germany and traveled to many countries. Mycola found a Ukrainian organization that sponsored Ukrainian artists but, upon arriving in Chicago, he instead found himself working in construction with Polish immigrants. He had never done construction work before, but he learned quickly: electricity, plastering walls, putting down parquets, and more. "Everything Americans do not want to do, I can do," Mycola announced.

Mycola did not like the Ukrainian community in Chicago, which he said had few recent migrants and he found it difficult to connect with those from earlier waves. He had a friend in San Francisco and moved to the city. He worked in construction and also provided care to the elderly, because those hours were "more flexible" and gave him more time for his art. Mycola explained:

> I was earning good money in construction, but what is the point if you do
> not do something for your soul (*dusha*)? In the United States you live well
> economically, but your soul suffers. To be an artist you must be happy and
> have lightness in your soul. This is difficult here. Ukrainians here think only
> about money – work and money. But an artist must live life, not just go to
> work and come home, but live for the soul, be in nature, understand?

I asked about his experiences as a caregiver, but he was only interested in talking
about it in terms of what it allowed him to do, namely paint. He did say that the
work was not difficult for him, because he loved to cook, which was also a
"creative act." I was not expecting a meal, our meeting was at 1 p.m., but
Mycola pointed to the pots on the stove and declared that it was already prepared. We continued our conversation over an amazing lunch. I found myself
looking at artwork, talking about politics, and doing the best I could to get
Mycola to share information about his family life over a delicious vegetable
borshch with sour cream (a rich beet soup) followed by *holubtsi* (rolls of cabbage
stuffed with ground beef and rice) that his girlfriend Halyna had made.

Mycola had two daughters, 23 and 26. He said that when he became a U.S.
citizen, he invited both daughters to join him in the United States, but his oldest
daughter had always been "timid," was married with two children, and did not
want to leave Ukraine. She worked as a graphic designer. Her husband worked
in construction. Mycola said that they do not earn much money, but they were
lucky because, after the Soviet Union collapsed, they were able to hold on to
their apartment. Mycola used to send her money, but he no longer did. In fact,
he did not send money to Ukraine at all, repeating what most respondents noted,
that "they do not give money away here either and it is expensive to live here
too." Mycola's younger daughter came to San Francisco three years ago, met a
Ukrainian man, married, moved to Sacramento, and already had a child. Mycola
was rarely in contact with his daughter in Ukraine and did not see his daughter in
Sacramento much either. He continued on at great length about how terrible it
was that Americans put their elderly in nursing homes or paid other people to
care for them. He insisted that one should be surrounded by family and grandchildren in old age; this was the way it was in Ukrainian culture. I asked if he
thought he would live with his daughter in Sacramento when the time came that
he needed care. He replied that he did not know what would happen to him, but
he was positive he would not live with his daughter. Mycola seemed to have a
fantasy about an active family life that he did not have. Mycola and his wife
divorced when the girls were young and, from what I could understand, he had
had little contact with them growing up.

Mycola rents an art studio space and had been producing work he hoped to
sell in Ukraine. Although he had not been back to Ukraine in the past decade, he
planned on going to Ukraine later this year. He had friends in Kyiv and L'viv,
and Mycola hoped he would be able to find a way to sell his artwork in Ukraine.

Mycola explained, as he served me *bliny*, thin pancakes filled with a fresh blueberry sauce, for dessert, "I think that you work for your family until you're 50, and then it is time that you work for yourself. My art, that is for me." I was simply too full to try the two kinds of beautiful bread he had made, one with poppy seeds and one with apples, and he gave me a slice of each to take home. He also sent me home with an invitation to return the following weekend to meet Halyna.

The following week, with Mycola's wonderful appreciation for cooking in mind, I arrived at his apartment with homemade cookies. Halyna was shocked. She did not think Americans baked or cooked anything at all. "Biscotti!" she exclaimed. Halyna looked a youthful 53 with her straight blond hair pulled back from her face in a low ponytail. She completed L'viv University and worked as a high school science teacher in a medium-sized city outside L'viv where she had taught for 25 years.

Halyna was one of only three people in my sample of 41 who was in California without family. The strong connection she had to her 28-year-old daughter, Anna, and almost eight-year-old granddaughter, Natalka, could not have been more different from Mycola's relationship with his daughters. I thought it ironic that Mycola barely saw the daughter he was able to bring to California while Halyna was in constant contact with a daughter she was desperate to have join her in California with no obvious way to make that happen.

We sat at Mycola's kitchen table with tea and cookies, while Mycola went about his business in other parts of the apartment. Halyna repeatedly said that Anna did not want her to go to California and was waiting for her to return. Halyna's greatest sadness was for her granddaughter with whom she had spoken just the day before. Halyna recounted:

> I speak with [Natalka] on the phone very often, at least once a week if not two. Just yesterday she said, "*Baba* (grandmother), come home. Mama is at work, and I have to stay with other (*chuzhoi*) people. It would be better if you were home. You could pick me up from school and we would be together." Natalka stays with a neighbor now after school.

The pain of not being present as a grandmother for Natalka and a help for Anna was constantly with Halyna. Anna graduated from L'viv University in philology with a focus on English. She works for an important newspaper in the L'viv *oblast'* (region) but, according to Halyna, she "works a lot and is paid little," $50–60 dollars a month. Anna's husband also had a university degree. He worked as a tax inspector, but when Yushchenko came to power – "of course we were all very happy Yushchenko came to power" – he "brought his own people" as is "to be expected," leaving her son-in-law unemployed for the past two years. Halyna continued:

Hopefully he will be able to find another job in his field, I don't know. He has been working, so we are lucky. He has not abandoned his responsibilities. He has a friend who started a business selling cars in Poland. It is very difficult now at the Polish border, but my son-in-law drives a truck and is carrying cars back and forth across the border. This is the way it is, Cinzia. You have to support your family somehow.

I asked Halyna what made her decide to come to California. Halyna explained that her father became ill and they could not afford to pay to have the surgeries he needed done. She also wanted to help her daughter build a home in L'viv's periphery, which she said cost less than buying an apartment in L'viv proper where you still would have to contend with L'viv's water problems. I recalled the interviews I conducted in people's apartments in L'viv where bath tubs and buckets were filled with water to use until the next time the water was turned back on. Halyna thought she would try to go to Italy like most of her friends and acquaintances. However a friend who had recently moved to Sacramento as a Baptist refugee told Halyna that she would sponsor her to come to California on a guest visa and Halyna felt that it was an "opportunity" that she could not refuse. Halyna arrived in San Francisco and decided to overstay her visa. Halyna said:

Everyone went abroad then. From just my school I would say 10 of us teachers went abroad. They abandoned everything and went. But most people went to Italy or Spain. Very few people came here to the United States, because it is very difficult to come here if you are Ukrainian and not Jewish. I only have one friend who ended up in the United States.

Halyna shrugged her shoulders joking that "all of Ukraine went to Italy" and she ended up in "America." "No one is jealous if you go to Italy," Halyna explained, "but if you say you are going to America … hoo, hoo, hoo, hoo!" Halyna's head danced and she whistled to indicate that you were a "hot shot" if you went to "America." Halyna's mouth smiled, but her eyes were sad as she explained that her daughter was not impressed:

Anna did not want me to come here, because she says it is too far. Those who go to Europe, they can sit on a bus and go home. Every day she tells me to come home, but I have hopes that I can get a green card. Many people get it and then she can come here. She studied English philology. My dream is that I can do this for her and Natalka.

I am a patriot. I voted for Yushchenko even from here. But it will be a long time before the government will allow its people to support themselves. I wish it was possible for me to live there. Here material life is better, but for my soul, I wish I could live there. It is bad economic times in Ukraine and everyone has left so they can help their children.

Halyna noted, "The first year here I sent $8,000 home. I would send $300 or $500 at a time. Now already I send less; before I sent more."

Halyna's remittances have decreased because her father passed away last year and she no longer needs to send money for his care. But she also sends fewer remittances because she has more expenses in San Francisco. When Halyna first arrived, she worked as a live-in for "very bad people." She made a friend at church who helped her leave this family after five months and she went to work in another family of Ukrainian Jews with a six-year-old daughter and an elderly mother to care for. Halyna said the relationship in this family was good and she stayed a year and a half. Now, however, she has her own apartment. She was unable to care for clients through IHSS because she was undocumented. She hoped that, once she receives her green card, she will be able to work for IHSS where she felt workers were "more protected," because "you have healthcare, and you work for the U.S. government." Currently, Halyna worked full-time caring for an elderly woman who was from Ukraine but arrived in California in the 1950s. Halyna was studying English and had just started a course for her CNA. "I have finally accepted that I will never be a science teacher here!" she exclaimed laughing.

I did not push Halyna for more information about her documents, since she clearly did not want to discuss it, especially with the recorder on. There was nothing I could see in our conversation, however, that suggested that she would be able to apply for a green card unless she married Mycola. Halyna dodged the question about how likely this might be. Despite being undocumented, Halyna's life did not have the unsettled and often frantic air of those in Italy.

Halyna voted during the Orange Revolution elections for Yushchenko and kept up with news in Ukraine. Halyna was Ukrainophone, but said she understood that if you were Russian (*rossiyanin*) or simply a Russophone you wanted to speak Russian. However, "you must learn Ukrainian if you want to live in Ukraine just as I must learn English if I want to live in the United States." Nonetheless, Halyna did not experience a painful connection to Ukraine's nation-state building project like those in exile. She was most concerned with her local situation: work, English classes, and exploring ways to bring Anna and her family to San Francisco. I asked Halyna how she explained to Anna why she was staying in San Francisco. Halyna sighed heavily with great sadness and replied:

I am single. My husband and I divorced long ago, but my daughter is married. She has her husband. She has her own family. Before I left everything was good. I watched the baby, while Anna worked and Mama [Halyna] cooked for everybody. For three and half years we did this. Of course Anna had fewer obligations when I was home. But now I have been gone almost four years and she has gotten used to running the house without me. Mama [Halyna] sent money so it wasn't so bad! [Laughs] Of course materially life is better for them now. What can you do? For me everything is fine so far, except I miss them so very much. Maybe they will win a green card and come here. [Laughs] I don't know. This is our life, Cinzia.

Halyna had Anna and her son-in-law both apply for the green card lottery. "So many win their green card, why not them?" Halyna asked. The promise of exodus was alluring. While other respondents waited for the chain of family reunification to arrive at the point where they could offer a green card to their loved ones, Halyna struggled with how to become the first link in the chain for her family. In the meantime, she lived a life focused on integrating into her local context on the assumption that she will somehow be able to stay in California.

Social Patterns in Exodus

Whereas migrants in Italy were excluded by the Italian state, even those with papers discovered their legal status was temporary, Ukrainian migrants in the United States largely had green cards and even a path to U.S. citizenship. If Yulia Tymoshenko suggested that Italy was a "stepmother" to its Ukrainian migrants, respondents such as Viktoria and Kateryna suggested the U.S. state was their "husband," a good "provider" that gave them work, health insurance, care to their elderly, and for some even state subsidies. This stands in stark contrast to the experiences of Mexicans and other migrant populations of color in the United States and likely is influenced by both the education level of Ukrainian migrants and their racialization into the dominant group as "white" in the U.S. context.[8] For migrants like Viktoria, Kateryna, and nearly all participants in San Francisco, performing carework as "government employees" facilitated a sense of integration, connection, and even loyalty to the U.S. state. Particularly appealing was that this connection did not require learning a new language or the radical "restructuring" of capitalist subjectivities, which were requirements for those in exile. Instead, many participants felt they were "too old" to learn a "new mentality." Their Soviet upbringing had trained them to view capitalism with suspicion, and they believed that their connection to the U.S. state protected them from market forces.

They judged their children, who arrived from Ukraine with them as young adults, by a different standard. Children were expected to cultivate capitalist subjectivities regarding labor practices, consumption, and risk. They should speak "beautiful" English and attain upward economic mobility through a successful navigation of the market. Viktoria and Zhanna both proudly exclaimed that their sons earned "big money." Even Kateryna, who wished her son was able to work in his field as a computer engineer rather than as a truck driver, noted he was financially independent and lived and worked in a place with no other Russian speakers. In California, integration through the capitalist economy for the adult children of respondents translated into disassociation from other Ukrainians or migrants from the former Soviet Union more broadly. Relying on others from the region, exchanging favors, and doing things through connections (*po blatu*) signaled a Soviet subjectivity that could not succeed in the post-Soviet world.

Structurally, exodus, like exile, was implicated in building the new Ukraine transnationally through changes to work and family structures. Many participants had transnational families and, like Kateryna and Halyna, continued to vote in Ukrainian presidential elections and sent back monetary and social remittances, including ideas about capitalist and democratic social orders. In Rome, reinventing oneself as a capitalist subject able to remit this knowledge to family in Ukraine as well as hope that they themselves would one day return to live in a European Ukraine was pervasive. The transnational social field of exile produced intense transnational practices. In San Francisco, deploying discourses of opportunity and luck, participants strategized how to reunite their families in the United States. Even Halyna, undocumented and with no legal claim to regularization, felt winning the green card lottery was possible, and this shaped her practices in exodus.

It was not only federal immigration law that shifted migrants' orientation from Ukraine to the United States. Zhanna noted that the institutional landscape in San Francisco, which included transnational Ukrainian organizations founded by WWII Diaspora Ukrainians, marginalized recent migrants. Unlike Rome UGCCs, Ukrainian and Russian language newspapers, and cultural organizations fostered deep transnational connections to Ukraine, these similar organizations were unable to transcend divisions between migration waves around questions of language and embodied performances of ethnicity and nationality. Therefore, in San Francisco, migrants' transnational practices were private, individual deeds rather than the basis of both a collective identity and collective action.

Dariya reunited her family by bringing all three of her children to the United States. Whereas Zhanna worried about new masculine constructions of toughness, risk, and even corruption as necessary for conducting business in Ukraine's market economy, Dariya worried that new constructions of femininity would leave her daughter unable to fulfill her potential, excluded from the labor market and "sitting at home" as a wife and mother. Dariya was unique in her ability to articulate her gendered process of subject formation through migration. Although Dariya's daughter had engaged in Ukrainian nation-state building as a researcher at Oxford, even Dariya's discovery of her capitalist "I" was deployed to facilitate her and her children's integration into U.S. life rather than to purposely help build a European or capitalist Ukraine.

Motherhood was a dominant discourse in both exile and exodus, but it took on different dimensions. In exile, middle-aged migrant grandmothers were constructed as "prostitutes" against young non-migrant mothers constructed as *Berehyni*. These dominant discourses then shaped migrant practices in Rome as migrants created distinctions between "good" and "bad" mothers. The Ukrainian state did not similarly stigmatize those who migrated to the United States and migrants did not, therefore, engage in the same practices of distinction. Instead, becoming a *babushka* was a dominant discourse. Migrants in San Francisco imbued this role with the power to give focus and meaning to one's life. It was a comforting line of continuity with their previous Soviet world. Zhanna believed that being a *babushka* to the Russian-American children of her client pulled her out of depression and saved her life. The terrain of gendered struggle in California was between generations within the post-1991 migration wave. Kateryna, Zhanna, and most respondents lamented that their children had become "too" American. Children had decided to delay marriage and childbirth, and thus prevented middle-aged migrants from becoming *babushki*. Even when migrants were grandparents, they often needed to continue working and thus were unable to be primary caregivers to grandchildren. Or, like Dariya, they found that their children did not welcome them as Soviet-style *babushki*. Whereas migrants in Italy lived the painful contradictions of building a new Ukraine that had no place for them as *babushki*, migrants in California also found that they had often unwittingly created lives in the United States in which Soviet *babushki* were obsolete.

CONCLUSION

Berehynia Femininities, Cossack Masculinities, and New Nationalisms

Evgeny Afineevky's Oscar-nominated documentary film *Winter on Fire: Ukraine's Fight for Freedom* followed the revolt known as "Maidan" or "Euromaidan" which occurred November 21, 2013 to February 22, 2014. The protests were sparked by Ukrainian President Viktor Yanukovych's failure to sign an expected economic deal with the European Union. He later accepted economic help from Russia which bought $15 billion of Ukrainian debt and reduced the price of Russian gas supplies. This infuriated many Ukrainian citizens because it both signaled an abandonment of the European idea and a submission to Russian power. An estimated 800,000 protesters, united under the banner "For a European Ukraine" and calling for an end to corruption, came together in Kyiv's *Maidan Nezalezhnosti* or Independence Square.[1] The documentary follows the events on the ground with live footage from the perspective of the protestors as the actions in and around Independence Square turned violent. It also relies on retrospective interviews with protestors. More than 100 protestors died in clashes with Ukrainian special police known as the *Berkut*. The protests ousted President Yanukovych who fled to Russia, and the protesters took over the presidential administration buildings. The Ukrainian parliament voted to remove Yanukovych from power in *absentia*.

The Ukrainian nation is often depicted as a woman, vulnerable to Russia's "male" power.[2] *Winter on Fire's* promotional posters depict the fledgling Ukrainian nation as a girl, about 10 years old. She is dressed in the Ukrainian national costume of peasant garb with bright embroidery, and a wreath of yellow and blue flowers on her head, the colors of the Ukrainian flag. The image is of the young girl's back as she faces alone the *Berkut* dressed in riot gear and standing behind a wall of body-length, metal shields. Despite the prominence of the girl's image on the poster, what was striking to me about the documentary was the disconnect between the footage on the ground where we see the bodies of both men and women, and the retrospective interviews in which protestors and clergy, mostly men, provided narratives that erased the presence of women or relegated them to support roles. Men activists spoke about needing to protect women or being galvanized by injuries committed by the *Berkut* against women, but they presented men and not women as the participants in the direct actions for the purpose of nation-state building.

Researchers Olga Onuch and Tamara Martsenyuk as well as Sarah Phillips[3] discovered through survey, interview, and focus group data that Ukrainian women were key organizers of Maidan, and that the protests began with equal numbers of men and women on the streets. As the protests became more violent, fewer women participated in the direct actions, yet women did not willingly leave. Instead, men protestors used patriarchal discourses of protecting "the beautiful women of Maidan" or the "*Berehyni* of the revolution" to push women off the square and into logistical work behind the scenes where their contributions, though vital, were less recognized. Women resisted exclusion by forming their own "Women's Squads" with limited success. *Winter on Fire* follows, among others, the actions of a 12-year-old boy in the middle of heavy fighting who is depicted as learning how to become a man and a patriot. Yet, adult women were deemed incapable of making their own decisions and were turned away by men who said women should not be on the barricades "for their own protection." Therefore, although the Maidan protests unfolded underneath the statue of *Berehynia*, public discourses aimed at "thanking the heroes of Maidan" all but ignored women's contributions.[4]

If the contributions made by women to nation-state building are obscured even when women's bodies are present on Kyiv's Maidan, then women's contributions to nation-state building are even more invisible when they are migrants located outside Ukraine's borders. Yet, as we have seen, gendered migrant subjectivities in exile to Italy and exodus to California are key sites from which we can scale up our analysis. We can bridge levels of analysis by making connections from the experiences of individuals to Ukraine's reorganization of work and family, to larger processes of migration, to the opening to global capitalism, and to the consequences of neoliberalism in Ukraine.

Scaling Up: From Gendered Migrant Subjectivities to Globalization

Although participants expressed varying levels of nostalgia for the Soviet era, all expressed a realization that the world had irrevocably changed. Therefore, participants noted that they would have to "restructure" themselves as neoliberal subjects capable of producing a capitalist and European Ukraine from the outside in. In order to do so, participants asserted that their children in Ukraine would have to embrace capitalist subjectivities to an even greater extent than they themselves in order to simultaneously build Ukraine from the bottom up.

In order to analytically scale up from the narratives from the "gulag" (see Chapter 3), I posit that in exile to Italy, like in Ukraine, motherhood was the language of nation-state building. Participants in Italy, such as Inna, purposefully engaged in cultivating a "European" subjectivity able to fulfill her responsibilities as a good mother by first learning "the rules" for navigating a neoliberal capitalist society and then transferring this cultural knowledge to her sons in Ukraine as social remittances. Inna and her sons engaged in consumption practices that were imbued with nationalist meanings. Even the house she was building in Ukraine was Inna's "monument" to a Ukraine that was destined to be "Europe" and not "Africa." Although Tatiana did not present herself as building the new Ukraine, she too experienced expulsion when her daughter-in-law unexpectedly had a second child and lost her job. She realized that her son did not need her to care for the grandchildren; he needed money. As Tatiana navigated the laws governing carework, strategized how to earn the most money she could while in Italy, and maximized her monetary remittances, she too was an agent in transnational nation-state building. Tatiana's migration and labor helped make possible the new "Ukrainian" family form by subsidizing her son's attainment of the breadwinner ideal and her daughter-in-law's status as a *Berehynia of the Ukrainian people.*" Inna, Tatiana, and their children in Ukraine participated in the transnational social field of exile. In this social field, knowledge about capitalist institutions, the kind of individual subject needed to navigate them, and how to make capitalist sub-jectivities *Ukrainian* traveled between Italy and Ukraine and back again. Inna and Tatiana did not want their children to immigrate to Italy where they would likely be unable to pursue their professional careers. Instead, they asked their children to help make their sacrifices as mothers and grandmothers worthwhile by helping to build the new Ukraine. Inna and Tatiana's children participated in the protests for a European Ukraine with a clearer understanding of what the political, social, and economic institutions of a European Ukraine might look like due to their mothers' migration. When these actions take place collectively and by large groups of people to produce social patterns, we can scale up our analysis moving from gendered migrant subjectivities to national level gendered discourses of ethnonational identity. We can then scale up again to transnational nation-state building and finally to the gendered restructuring of work and family as well as state institutions that produce neoliberal globalization from the bottom up.

Oksana, although not a mother herself, embraced women's "special position" as mothers and symbols of the Ukrainian nation. Indeed the poignant contra-dictions between the nuclear family on stage at the talent show in Rome that Oksana declared "*is* Ukraine" and the transnational families of the migrants in the audience was a powerful reminder of how many of us live in the painful gap between gendered expectations and aspirations and the limitations of our material conditions. Nevertheless, dominant discourses still powerfully shape our ideas and practices. Even Lydmyla, who managed to bring her whole family to Italy, saw herself as engaged in transnational nation-state building. She realized her children would have to be socialized differently than she was under the Soviet regime, and learn the capitalist values of "risk" and "consumption." Lydmyla also felt enmeshed in transnational nation-state building and was invested in Ukraine's Europeanization project, in part because the exclusionary policies of the Italian state might mean her family will one day have to return to Ukraine. These narratives from exile, with a focus on gendered migrant subjectivities, give us a window into the ground-level workings of global capitalism and the production of capitalist subjects through participation in the transnational field of exile.

Similarly, starting with the narratives from the "Promised Land" (see Chapter 5), we can scale up our analysis to national discourses of nationhood. This scaling up from gendered migrant subjectivities in exodus to California reveals not only Ukrainian discourses of nationhood, but also highlights U.S. national ideals and how U.S. discourses of nationhood are shaped by neoliberal capitalist moralities. Migrants in exodus to California were implicated in Ukrainian nation-state building and contributed to the structural changes in Ukraine through migration. Although migrants in California worked to bring their family to the United States, many, such as Lyuba, Dariya, Kateryna, and Zhanna, lived in transnational families either permanently or temporarily for decades as they waited for the bureaucratic process of family reunification to be completed. In the meantime, much like migrants to Italy, these migrants helped produce housewife–breadwinner nuclear families in Ukraine both by removing themselves from households in Ukraine and through participating in the transnational social field of exodus by sending monetary and social remittances to those still in Ukraine. Respondents in California sent social remittances about capitalist subjectivities and institutions that aided in nation-state building from the bottom up and the outside in. However, California respondents also had a contradictory aspiration. Shaped by dominant discourses in exodus that asserted mothers migrated in order to give their children a better life in the United States, middle-aged migrant women asked their children to help them bolster their honor as mothers by finding a way to immigrate to California.

Despite the influential role of WWII Diaspora Ukrainians in Ukrainian nation-state building, post-1991 migrants in this study were often excluded from these organizations in San Francisco. This exclusion increased the importance participants attached to the U.S. state's policies of inclusion toward this migrant population through both legal status and paid work with healthcare benefits as homecare workers. This combination of exclusion and inclusion made the daily transnational practices that were obligatory in exile optional in exodus. Viktoria was a homecare worker and, like most participants in exodus to California, understood her relationship with the U.S. state in gendered terms. The U.S. state took care of Viktoria "like a husband," protecting her from the uncertainty of the capitalist market. By comparison, the Ukrainian state was a "failed provider." Although Viktoria did not have to engage in the deep introspection of capitalist subject formation that accompanied those in exile to Italy, she did not expect her children to follow the same state-based integration strategy of those in her generation. Instead, she expected her children and other young adult Ukrainian migrants to engage in market-based integration strategies where speaking "beautiful" English and cultivating capitalist subjectivities as well as their racialization as "white," gave them access to earning "big money" through market mobility. Having more than one's neighbor was frowned upon in the Soviet moral order. But Viktoria and the other participants realized that, in neoliberal capitalist America, a large salary was not just about having the funds to engage in American consumer culture, but it gave their children high social status, honor, and defined them as "successful." Although Viktoria and her generation in exodus were dependent on the U.S. state and "connections" with other migrants from the region, Viktoria's children and the younger generation adopted American ideologies of individualism that suggested they had to achieve success on their own. After all, Viktoria noted that in a socialist economy where consumer goods were scarce, one needed friends and "connections" to acquire both basic needs and small luxuries. In the United States, however, people do not need friends or family for survival. An individual who earns a wage can simply buy what is needed or desired.

In contrast to Viktoria, Dariya presented the process of subject formation she experienced through migration as discovering her capitalist "I." She transferred this knowledge to her three children in Ukraine, also part of the transnational social field of exodus, before finding piecemeal ways to bring her children to the United States. One daughter was relaunched in what Dariya called the "global market," writing her Ph.D. dissertation in England on Ukraine–EU relations. The other daughter, Dariya lamented, learned capitalist subjectivities *too* well, rejecting Dariya's attempts to enact the role of Soviet *babushka*. Kateryna was also caught in the contradictions of wanting her son to become American by experiencing market mobility, which in the U.S. often requires postponing marriage and first births, without infringing on her ability to be a young *babushka* able to care for her grandchildren. Her second son, who had been waiting in Ukraine over a decade for papers, still had long to wait. Kateryna chose to act transnationally, voting in Ukrainian elections through the consulate and sending back to Ukraine ideas about an "American" model of ethnic and linguistic social organization as a possibility for the new Ukraine her son must continue to live in. Even Halyna, alone and undocumented in the United States, found the discourse of "luck" seductive in exodus and maintained one foot in Ukraine, voting to make Ukraine better for her daughter and granddaughter, while playing the green card lottery in the hopes her family could be reunited in the "Promised Land." For Dariya and Zhanna, bringing a daughter who aspired to a career beyond motherhood and a son who might lose his soul or his life in Ukraine's masculinized economic context of "bandits" and "bribes" was both a reaction to and perpetuation of transnational practices that contributed to the gendered reorganization of work and family structures that continue to build the new Ukraine from the outside in. Therefore, scaling up analytically from migrant gendered subjectivities in exodus allows us to see the transnational and global processes of both Ukrainian nation-state building and neoliberal capitalism in action.

Limitations of the Metaphors of Destination

Participants framed their migrations as "forced" exile to the Italian "gulag" and "voluntary" exodus to California, the "Promised Land" (see Table 0.1, Introduction). Although these framings give the impression that California is a "better" destination than Italy, the ethnographic and interview data may suggest a surprising inversion.

Italy or California: Which is Better?

I am often asked, where is life better for migrants: Italy or California? This question makes me uncomfortable for two reasons. First, it is hard to know what the questioner means by "better" (Earn more money? Have more labor protections? Experience less discrimination? Spend more time with family? Are able to go home to Ukraine more frequently?). Second, I could not possibly know which location is better for each individual migrant who, assuming they had deep knowledge of post-1991 migrant life in each destination, might give weight to different factors than I would. And yet, I find I cannot avoid the question entirely. I can say that if I were in the difficult position of having to walk in the shoes of my participants as a migrant domestic worker, I would prefer to walk the streets of Rome. My interlocutors are often surprised that I would choose the "gulag" over the "Promised Land." It is true that migrants in Italy felt expelled from Ukraine, and the feeling that they were kicked out of their own country was heart-wrenching. Because they all started out without documents, migrants felt trapped in Italy as if it were a prison. This feeling was compounded by doing live-in caring labor where migrants were only allowed free time on Thursday afternoons and Sundays, so that many felt their confinement in their elderly ward's home was a 24/7 forced labor system. Migrants in exile were vulnerable to the vices of individual employers and dependent on their kindness. Even for those migrants who acquired documents, they could only stay in Italy if they continued working, because they needed proof they were still employed in order to renew their documents every one or two years. Migrants in exile lived ascetic lives and sent economic and social remittances back home, and thus bolstered not only their families but a Ukraine to which they longed to return. However, Ukraine's structural and discursive changes, which they themselves as migrants helped produce, left no social space for them in Ukraine as Soviet people. Respondents cried for hours into my recorder while they reported missing family back home and the everyday indignities of working as live-in caregivers with no private space to call their own. This certainly is a coercive labor system. The

Italian state was doing gendered work through quota systems that created domestic workers as a preferred category but also confined migrant women to this work if they had any hopes of acquiring documents that allowed them to return to Ukraine.[5] And yet there are limitations to "gulag" as a metaphor of destination.

Migrant domestic workers in Italy had a national contract with impressive labor protections when compared to migrants in California. They had rights to a month of paid vacation each year, a yearly holiday bonus equal to one month's pay, and a severance payment when they were let go adjusted for the length of time of employment. Although they experienced racialization in Italy as a "Slavic race" and therefore could never "become Italian" (migrants in California identified as "white" and therefore with the dominant racial group), participants often said they felt "like a person" in Italy. They did a job and had wages to show for it. Several adult children I interviewed in Ukraine reported that their mother "looked 10 years younger" since migrating to Italy. Participants also had access to Italy's universal healthcare system, whereas access to healthcare was a constant worry that weighed heavily on the minds of participants in California.

In exile to Italy, participants watched family members age via photographs, which was heartbreaking, and the loneliness for their families was always palpable despite visits home for those with documents. Although one interviewee, with her family in Italy, complained that she had to spend her time off from work cooking and cleaning for her family and wished she was "free" like those in Italy without their family to visit museums and congregate in piazzas. Even with just Thursday afternoons and Sundays off, migrants in Rome created a vibrant and dense community united by a common nationalist goal. As a sociologist, I am a sucker for a collective project that gives meaning to actions and relationships. I do not romanticize this community of dense networks nor the nationalist project itself. It was the kind of camaraderie I have heard men who have been to war talk about, a camaraderie forged in times of adversity, deprivation, and fear. After this field experience in Rome, I better understand how a U.S. veteran when asked, "Why would you want to go back to Afghanistan?" could offer an answer that often included "because my buddies, my brothers are there." (The experiences of women veterans have been less reported.) Elements of the "gulag" were present in Rome, and yet with the heartache there was also joy in providing for one's family, coming together for community events, and struggling together to create a better Ukraine.

The "Promised Land" also has limitations as a metaphor of destination. Although migrants in both places earned comparable amounts of money, the SEIU in San Francisco, at the time I was in the field, was just beginning to suggest a fight for one week of paid vacation for homecare workers. Holiday bonuses or severance pay were not even imaginable. Without a universal healthcare system in the United States, access to healthcare was a constant worry for migrants in California, which encouraged them to work long after their health suggested they should retire. Unlike migrants in Italy, those in California were able to go home to their own apartment at the end of the work day and be with some if not all of their family. They did not cry for hours into my recorder, yet many more California participants than participants in Italy expressed feeling depressed and lonely. Not only did migrants in California have loose networks, they often felt disconnected from their own children, the object of their migration sacrifice, because their children became *too* American. On the one hand, participants were proud of their children's success, and their children *were* successful by U.S. standards with good jobs and growing families. And yet, this also meant these children moved away when better job prospects came up elsewhere. They bought homes in the suburbs or moved to other cities and other states, taking grandchildren with them. Even if children remained nearby, respondents complained that their children's "American" ways denied them the ability to be a *babushka*. One California respondent told me, "My daughter is waiting for me to be in diapers before she makes a baby! I'll be too old to change either of our diapers!" If respondents did have grandchildren, then they often spoke sorrowfully of quarreling with their children because living in the United States had turned their already significant generation gap into a chasm. Respondents lamented that their parenting advice was ignored because "that's not how they do it in America" and reported language barriers that sometimes made deep connections to grandchildren challenging. I cannot decide for others which location is "better," but what *is* clear is that not everything was terrible in the "gulag" and much was far from rosy in the "Promised Land." Nevertheless, respondents in both destinations were part of a transnational social field that meaningfully contributed to Ukrainian nation-state building. These grandmothers carried Ukraine on their shoulders.

The Paradoxical Soviet Gender Legacy

The rise and fall of communism was one of the defining events of the twentieth century. Of equal magnitude and significance for the twenty-first century is the transformation of those post-socialist countries, many engaged in the process of building democratic societies and capitalist economies. The advent of neoliberal capitalism has produced a drastic transformation of gender discourses as well as gender relations not only between men and women, but also between citizens and states and states and the global community of nations. Contemporary nation-state building in Ukraine must deal with a paradoxical Soviet legacy in which "strong" women are linked to "weak men," producing what both scholars and lay people in the region call a "crisis of masculinity."

Soviet authorities devoted more attention to the social position of women than of men, heightening the visibility of gender as a system of social organization and control.[6] The Soviet "emancipation" of women, while by many measures illusive, did produce high levels of education for women, full-time workforce participation, and decreased if not eliminated women's economic dependence on men. Thus, the labor collective was the primary site of integration into Soviet society for both men and women.[7] Soviet gender identities for women as "mother-workers" were coupled with Soviet gender identities for men founded on public work for the Soviet State rather than private patriarchal power.[8] Soviet motherhood was grounded in a biological view of "natural" sex differences. However, the role accorded to women as transmitters of the new ideology and culture combined with the Soviet state's hostility toward the private family as a threat to state power did enhance the private position of Soviet women. The Soviet State made an alliance with women. Sociologist Sarah Ashwin notes that:

> This contrasts with the practice of many conservative regimes, in particular theocracies, where men's private control over women is seen as a crucial buttress of the existing order: gender is likewise used as an organizing principle of state power, but the state's alliance is with men rather than with women.[9]

This produced a paradoxical Soviet gender legacy in which women were perceived as strong and independent, but who nevertheless ended up doing all the cleaning and caring labor and men were perceived as weak and feminine, but who had the autonomy to relax, drink, and exist on the margins of domestic life. This notion of "weak" men created a "crisis of masculinity" that underlies the current belief that men must reclaim their position as heads of the family as a restoration of pre-Soviet, ethnic Ukrainian culture.[10]

A neofamilial discourse that suggests a gendered division of labor in which women are relegated to the private sphere as caregivers and men to the public sphere as breadwinners has been adopted across the post-Soviet region even if the economic realities prevent the widespread adoption of this familial arrangement.[11] Nevertheless, these discourses are rooted in the structural material reality of neoliberalism in which a retreat of the state and the elimination of state services (including free, state-subsidized education, medical care, childcare, and housing) have disproportionately increased the burdens of reproductive labor for women in the region. This has created structural barriers for women's entrance into the formal labor market. In Ukraine, like in many post-colonial contexts, neofamilialism has also been interwoven with the strengthening of national and ethnic identities. The fate of the emerging nation is currently inextricably intertwined with the fate of its women and is embodied in the national symbol of *Berehynia*.

The rise of *Berehynia* and the accompanying fetishization of motherhood, although presented by Ukrainian policymakers and elites as defining Ukrainianess "since the beginning of time," only began in the 1980s and 1990s and is used to mark the European and modern character of Ukraine.[12] Although contradictory at first glance, in the ethnographic and folkloristic work of Ukrainian scholars, women in Ukraine have always had a privileged position in Ukraine's "domestic matriarchy" where they enjoyed "equality in difference."[13] Therefore, even many in Ukraine's contemporary women's movement embrace *Berehynia*. In Western feminism, paid work for women has been equated with emancipation and indeed communism did claim that it would liberate women through work. However, near full employment rates for women in the Soviet Union did not leave Soviet women feeling "liberated." Instead, the post-Soviet shift to Ukrainian "matriarchs," represented by the *Berehynia* discourse, is seen by many as "women's empowerment."[14] Indeed, Sociologist Tatiana Zhurzhenko finds that young women with little or no work experience accepted the new role of housewife without many "inner conflicts."[15]

The post-Soviet social construction of young women as housewives did, however, produce extreme inner conflicts for the middle-aged migrant women in this study as well as tensions for many of the young women I met in Ukraine. The intersection of gendered nationalism and neoliberal capitalism has *doubly marginalized* grandmothers in particular from both the labor market and the home. Post-Soviet and national discourses now suggest children should be cared for by young mothers charged with conveying the values and culture of the new Ukraine to the next generation, something a Soviet *babushka* can not do. The confluence of these national, transnational, and global level processes produced the expulsion of many grandmothers from Ukraine and created painful contradictions for this older generation of women (see Chapter 1).

Migrants I met in both Italy and California were extremely ambivalent about the rise of the housewife–breadwinner family model in Ukraine. Migrants did not want remittances from their paid domestic labor abroad facilitating their daughters performing unpaid domestic labor in Ukraine and "sitting at home." In fact, earning money to pay for the university education of sons and daughters with an eye to fulfilling professional careers was a key motivating factor in individual decisions to migrate. The return of men as heads of family, however, was less contested by respondents than the notion of daughters as housewives. The majority of participants believed from their observations in Rome and San Francisco that both the involved parenting practices of middle-class European and American men and these men's integration into families as partners with their wives was preferable to the Soviet legacy of "weak" men unwilling or unable to provide and care for their families.

Where are the Grandfathers?

A gendered global perspective helps us see what the adoption of neoliberal economic principles look like on the ground in Ukraine. At its most stark, it means grandmothers migrate to Europe and the United States. But what about grandfathers? Some middle-aged men are migrating, most often east toward Russia, but also to Portugal and Spain to work in construction.[16] Others stay in Ukraine like Inna's husband Dmytro (Chapter 3), who oversaw the building of their new house, "the monument," bought a car to start an informal taxi service with Inna's remittances, and watched over their two young adult sons. However, men in Ukraine have not fared well by health indicators after the Soviet collapse.[17] Neoliberal reforms of the socialist welfare state caused economic insecurity and mass impoverishment as well as contributed to Ukraine's "demographic crisis" of depopulation.[18]

Ukrainian nationalists see depopulation as a result of the abandonment of traditional family values by ethnic Ukrainians and, as in other post-Soviet countries, demography is at the core of reconstructing the nation.[19] The demographic crisis has three key manifestations. The first is emigration, and the emigration of mothers and grandmothers without their families is particularly stigmatized. The second is low fertility and, in Ukrainian nationalist discourse, women are made responsible for low fertility because they selfishly prefer a professional career to their familial responsibilities.[20] As we have seen, this is addressed by the Ukrainian state with pro-natalist policies and the glorification of motherhood. The third is high mortality rates, which is considered a men's issue. In 1994, men's life expectancy fell to 57.7 years and, after briefly rallying to 61.3 years in 1998, was 58.8 years in 2003.[21] In Ukraine as of 2007, men's life expectancy was only 62.3 years compared to 73.6 for women, the largest gender gap in Europe after Russia, and the death rate for working-age men 20–45 years old is three times higher than for women.[22] Men's deaths exceed women's deaths by six to one and scholars attribute this to a post-Soviet rise in violent death, alcoholism, and stress-related disease such as heart attack, stroke, and high blood pressure; furthermore, men's suicides outnumber women's by five to one.[23] Although many factors, including a collapsing healthcare system, increased psychological stress, and the collapse of institutions following the dissolution of the Soviet Union all contribute to declining health in post-Soviet countries, men may have been harder hit than women because men's Soviet identity was solely tied to state-based work that linked men's status in relation to the Soviet state.[24] Therefore, when men lost jobs, they lost everything: their social position, status, and their livelihood. As a result, many men simply could not accept performing a lower status job. In contrast, when women lost jobs, respondents like Zhanna (see Chapter 5) noted that women still had to wake up every morning to make breakfast for children and grandchildren. Even if women could no longer find work in their field of expertise, they accepted lower status work to support their family. They did not, according to Zhanna, give up and drink vodka like the men did. As a result, many of the migrant women in my sample reported that husbands or ex-husbands were dead or incapable of working due to alcoholism or other illness. In post-Soviet discourse, Ukrainian men are an "endangered species."[25]

Cossack Masculinities in the New Ukraine

In addition to men's health, the gendered intersection of neoliberal capitalism and nation-state building has also affected the social identities of Ukrainian men. In

Western ideology, the spread of global capitalism was supposed to liberate women everywhere by granting them economic independence, but in the former Soviet Union where women were already considered "too empowered" by the Soviet state, the coming of capitalism was supposed to liberate men. Instead, neoliberal capitalism has further aggravated the problems associated with the "crisis in masculinity" where Ukrainian men, almost exclusively defined by earning a wage, are largely unable to provide economically for their families.

If the ideal Ukrainian woman should be *Berehynia*, then the ideal Ukrainian man should be a *Cossack*. Cossacks constituted a male-dominated, democratic military community that formed a Ukrainian-Cossack state in the mid-seventeenth century. In contemporary discourse, Cossacks are credited with founding Ukraine's democratic traditions and, like *Berehynia*, are a pre-Soviet symbol of Ukrainian identity.[26] The Cossack ideal stands in sharp contrast to the post-colonial Soviet legacy of "weak," "feminized" men. The new post-Soviet Ukrainian man should accept the responsibility of being the family's breadwinner and patriarch by engaging in market capitalism, which requires the "masculine" traits of risk-taking, competition, and toughness.[27] Young men in present-day Ukraine, pushed into unstable capitalist markets, do perceive a link between their ability to earn wages and their status at home.[28] However, men often find they have limited economic opportunities to fulfill this breadwinner ideal, causing a painful dissonance and intensifying the "crisis of masculinity."[29] For men like Yuriy (Chapter 3) working in Rome and unable to send back remittances, gendered shame further distanced him from his son and daughter in Ukraine. Yuriy could not face his son Kostya's question: Why are you far from us if you do not provide financially for us? For others like Kolya (Introduction), who supplemented his low earning potential as a doctor in L'viv by engaging in various "business" deals, the stress of navigating corruption in this period of "Wild West capitalism" was inscribed on his face; the nerves had collapsed on one side of it. Understanding men's gendered subjectivities helps us see how the new gendered economic landscape can translate into poor health outcomes, high mortality rates, and new social expectations for men that are often agonizingly unattainable.

Women also navigated corruption. Many women migrants informed me that when university professors or doctors learned their student or patient had a family member abroad, they expected bribes in order for children to pass exams and for elderly parents to receive medical care. However, men were expected to be breadwinners by engaging in "business," and therefore often had qualitatively different and more constant interactions with corruption. This narrative was most prominent in the interviews with young men in Ukraine and the migration stories of mothers like Zhanna (Chapter 5) concerned for their sons. Zhanna thought of Ukraine as a "bandit state;" scholars use the term "predatory" state, to describe the landscape of daily corruption that occurs when the state is unable to fairly enforce contract law and public officials such as police officers, doctors, and teachers are paid so little that bribes become part of their salary. Zhanna feared her son was in a lose–lose situation. Should he not attain the Cossack ideal, his perceived lack of toughness could result in his murder by business associates. Yet succeeding in becoming a "Cossack" required that he engage in corrupt practices that Zhanna worried would lead to moral bankruptcy and damage his soul. This "crisis of masculinity" and widespread corruption has fueled nationalist projects such as Euromaidan.

A Resurgence of Nationalism in Ukraine, Europe, and the United States

Some argue we are post-nation-states or even post-nationalism and suggest that nationalism is an anachronism best suited to a previous historical era.[30] But for the newly independent former Soviet countries as well as many newly independent countries in Africa, creating national identities linked to nation-states is of utmost importance and even a matter of survival as Russia's recent incursion into Ukraine suggests.[31] These new states struggle to constitute themselves in a current context of globalization and mass migration rooted in the global political system of modern nation-states.

Recent scholarship on a resurgence of nationalism focuses on nationalism as more than a political ideology but as a cognitive, affective, and discursive category and draws our attention to the United States and the established democracies of Europe as right-wing movements in particular seek to strengthen borders against migrants and refugee populations in the name of protecting the nation.[32] In the United States, Donald Trump, in his successful campaign for president, used a nationalist vision of the nation that emphasized the superiority of the American people (understood as white), the threat posed by immigrants and ethnic, racial, and religious minorities,[33] and a misogynist vision of gender relations. This form of nationalism, including Britain's 2016 decision to exit the European Union, is often framed as a backlash against globalization.[34] Now more than ever we must understand the transnational dynamics of nation-state building and the new nationalisms of recently independent countries in the former Soviet Union and other regions because they give us insight into these global processes of nationalism from which the established countries of the United States and Europe are not exempt.

Wealthy and poor countries are inextricably linked through global processes of economic restructuring and migration, and international migrants are increasingly women. Between 1960 and 2000, the number of women migrants worldwide more than doubled from 35 million to 85 million and in 2013 the number of women migrants increased further to 111.32 million.[35] According to the World Bank, women comprise half of the world's migrants with expectations that both the number and the percentage of women migrants will continue to increase.[36] Both Italy and the United States have experienced an increased demand for migrants to provide cleaning and caring labor due to trends associated with global economic restructuring such as raising wage inequality,[37] a decline in manufacturing,[38] increasing numbers of middle- and upper-class women in the paid labor force,[39] and neoliberal polices that have led to the reduction of the welfare state.[40] However, rather than recognize these gendered global economic forces, many citizens in the United States and Europe continue to love capitalism but hate those, such as migrants, that capitalism has displaced.[41]

Reorienting Migration Studies

Just as focusing on nationalist, anti-immigrant sentiments without looking at the workings of global capitalism can lead to poor social policy, so too does attempting to understand migrant subjectivities and practices solely from the perspective of the receiving site provide a limited and at times distorted perspective. Feminist ethnographers have called for multi-sited ethnographies that take the transnational lens seriously despite the cost, time, and language skills involved in conducting such projects.[42] However, I further argue that simply comparing receiving sites could be misleading, because more than the contexts of reception affect migrant outcomes. Exile and exodus are concepts that can be applied to other cases besides Ukraine and their application changes how we study migration by highlighting migrant subjectivities and practices, the effects of migration in both sending and receiving countries, and its links to global and transnational processes.

Rhacel Parreñas's book *Servants of Globalization: Women, Migration and Domestic Work* makes an important contribution by comparing migrant Filipina domestic workers in two destinations, Italy and California.[43] She discovered that, despite migration scholars' predictions that different contexts of reception lead to different migrant experiences, Filipina migrant domestic workers in Italy and California lived "parallel lives" with similar migrant subjectivities. According to Parreñas, this sameness is due to migrant women's similar structural position in globalization.[44] I build on this finding by adding depth to the structural explanation of why we might find in some cases that migrants from the same sending country in two different receiving countries have radically different subjectivities and outcomes as in the case of Ukrainian migrants in Italy and California, and in other cases find they have similar migrant subjectivities as in the case of Filipinas to these same receiving countries.

First, I suggest that the intersection of sending and receiving countries does not mean that each country has equal weight in shaping the transnational field. In the case of Filipina migration, sociologist Robyn Rodriguez found that the Philippine state closely manages its migrations through a bureaucratic system that produces migrants for export.[45] Therefore, we can infer that the Philippine state strongly influences both the structural and discursive dimensions of the transnational social fields produced through Filipina migration to Italy and California. As a result, I suggest that a comparison of the transnational social fields of the two Filipina migrations in which the Philippines is analytically connected to both Italy and California as part of the research design would likely allow us to see that the two migrations are a comparison of exile to exile. As a result, the production of similar migrant subjects is expected rather than surprising in this approach to migration studies.

In *On the Shoulders of Grandmothers*, I uncovered two divergent transnational social fields, exile and exodus, which produced different gendered migrant subjectivities. The experience of migration, including the type and intensity of transnational ties to Ukraine, the construction of national and civic identities, and relationships to the receiving countries all differed between Ukrainian migrants in Italy and those in California. Once again the sending and receiving countries, although both essential for explaining migrant subjectivities and practices, did not equally shape the transnational social fields produced. In the migration from Ukraine to Italy, the social conditions and context inside Ukraine likely exerted greater weight in shaping the transnational field of exile, while in shaping the transnational social field of exodus the opposite was likely true with California exerting greater influence. Therefore, this study of transnational nation-state building in Ukraine suggests that a gendered global and transnational approach, and the concepts of exile and exodus in particular, can be useful for explaining differences and similarities in migrant subjectivities and practices in other cases where a country sends migrants to multiple destinations.

A New Map of Europe: Deploying a Gendered Global and Transnational Perspective

The September/October 2014 issue of *Foreign Affairs Magazine* included an essay by political scientist John J. Mearsheimer titled, "Why the Ukraine Crisis is the West's Fault: The Liberal Delusions That Provoked Putin."[46] In it, Mearsheimer argues that prevailing wisdom in the West blames the ongoing Ukrainian–Russian War following the protests of Euromaidan on Russian President Vladimir Putin. The story in the West is that Putin used the protests as an excuse to annex Crimea, a region of the sovereign Ukrainian state and the first annexation of a European country's territory since WWII, in an attempt to fulfill his long-standing desire of reviving the Russian empire. Mearsheimer asserts that this interpretation is incorrect. Instead, he argues that the United States and Europe provoked Russia by pushing NATO and EU expansion as well as democratization projects in the region. He writes that the West has a flawed view of international politics. The West believes that realpolitik, a system of politics or principles based on practical rather than moral or ideological considerations, has given way to governance based on liberal principles such as rule of law and economic interdependence. However, Russia has shown that realpolitik is alive and well. Therefore, Mearsheimer concludes that Ukraine should not be incorporated into either the West or Russia, but instead act as a neutral buffer between the two. Appeals to Ukraine's right to self-determination, he concludes, ignore the "real" in realpolitik.

This launched a heated debate that led the *Foreign Affairs* Staff to conduct a poll of their pool of experts. In the piece, "Who is at Fault in Ukraine: *Foreign Affairs'* Brain Trust Weighs In," *Foreign Affairs* published 29 responses in which experts agreed or disagreed with the statement: "*The West provoked Russian President Vladimir Putin's aggression in Russia's near abroad by expanding NATO and the EU after the Cold War.*"[47] The responses assessed whether Russia or the West was to blame. Notably, only one expert even mentioned Ukraine as an actor in the context of meetings with the EU and the United States that may have caused Russia concern. Only two experts objected to the use of the Soviet-era term "near abroad" used to denote Republics distinct from Russia but still part of the Soviet Union and one of these two experts reminded the *Foreign Affairs'* Staff that, as of yet, Ukraine is a sovereign country.

If we are interested in Ukrainian nation-state building, the above international relations approach seems to miss the mark. As we have seen, Ukraine's transnational nation-state building process, uncovered by gendered global ethnography, is both structurally and discursively creating a new Ukraine whose institutions, including family structure, labor market, and economy, increasingly look more like Europe than Russia; and Russia has noticed.

Russia has taken the transformative potential of migration seriously. For years Russia has been issuing passports to Ukrainian citizens in Eastern and Southern Ukraine.[48] Migrants traveling to Russia to work from Ukraine often find themselves with two passports, yet Moscow views a Russian citizen as anyone with a Russian passport and refuses to recognize an individual with the passport of another country as having dual citizenship. Russia's aims were to bolster economic and social ties of control with Ukraine through migration. Later, this situation was used by Russia to frame the current war as Russia's obligation to protect Russians in Ukraine, where "Russian" was expansively defined. I am not suggesting the international relations account of interactions between the West and Russia is unimportant, but rather that it tells a limited narrative of Ukrainian nation-state building and tells us nothing of what these processes mean for individuals on the ground.

The intersectional analysis of the transnational social fields of exile and exodus help us see what Putin intuits: Ukraine is being reinvented transnationally and this places Ukraine on a trajectory toward Europe. Gendered global ethnography allows us to grasp, through the lives of increasing numbers of women and men in exile and exodus, the dynamics of a neoliberal imposition of a global economic system based on a nuclear family with an unequal gendered division of labor. With the redrawing of the contemporary map of Europe in the balance, the stakes for accurately understanding these global politics from the bottom up and the outside in could not be higher.

APPENDIX

At the outset of this project, I believed I would be interviewing migrants from multiple sending countries in the former Soviet Union. While there is a growing recognition that post-Soviet countries have taken different trajectories since the collapse of the Soviet Union, many Western scholars still tend to think of peoples and countries from the region as more or less the same and perceive distinctions between nationalities as relatively insignificant given the processes of homogenization in their Soviet past. Western scholars also tend to study Russia and then generalize to the region. I too ascribed to this view at the start of this project and assumed distinctions between migrant domestic workers from the region would be slight. It did not take much time in the field to disabuse me of this assumption. Furthermore, it became painfully obvious that post-Soviet countries with a colonial legacy such as Ukraine have different sets of struggles especially around nation-state building than post-Soviet Russia.

Gaining Access

Gaining access to participants was different in each of my three sites. In Italy it took almost two months of laying the groundwork before I had my first recorded interview with a migrant. I attended church services, spent time at the Garbatella, conducted interviews with priests, and spent countless hours in ACLI offices observing as domestic workers and employers came in for assistance. I met with the leaders of the Italo-Ukrainian Christian Cultural Association who are in charge of organizing the Garbatella on Sundays. I volunteered at *Forum*, a Ukrainian and Russian language newspaper and with the Association of Ukrainian Woman Workers that was run out of the same office. I even worked in a Caritas soup kitchen, hoping to meet Ukrainian migrants with little luck.

Then several things came together. First I met Inna at the Community of Sant'Egidio (Chapter 3) and then Oksana at the Ukrainian Festival. Both women helped recruit interviewees. Also the Ukranian Greek Catholic priests, interested in studies of Ukrainians in Italy, agreed to introduce me to parishioners, many of whom had already seen me at church services on a weekly basis for months. After months of attending the Russian Orthodox Church (ROC) and having Sunday lunch with the same migrant women week after week, many now felt comfortable speaking into a recorder. *Forum* published my picture and a piece about my research in their newspaper, which also helped legitimize my presence in this community. For a population that was both largely undocumented and had familial experiences with the Soviet gulags for discussing some of the very issues I was asking them to discuss with a recorder present, I was amazed at how quickly referrals came once they started. Formal interviews lasted anywhere from two hours to all day and often led to repeated meetings at the Garbatella, community events, or church basements. I was invited to birthday parties, political demonstrations, poetry readings, and cultural shows. I was deeply embedded in this community and found that the hours of tears and the painful contradictions with which individuals struggled affected me physically in chronic stomach pain that finally dissipated with my first pregnancy. I was warned by a kind Ukranian Greek Catholic priest that I might find that I would come to carry the collective pain of those I came to care for "in my gut." This was an embodied cost of ethnographic work.

In contrast, interviews in San Francisco never truly snowballed. I attended Svitlana's SEIU union meetings for Russian-speaking careworkers, church services, enlisted the help of priests, and attended cultural events. I even spent a day lobbying in Sacramento on behalf of the homecare workers' union. While in Italy interviewees were happy to recommend friends for an interview, this rarely happened in San Francisco. Interviewees, often willing to set me up on dates with their sons or the sons of friends or relatives while I reiterated that I really was married, said they did not know anyone else doing homecare work or did not have friends that were close enough that they could bother with such a request. As a result, many interviews came through my contact at In-home Supportive Services (IHSS) and the homecare workers' union. I also conducted interviews through people I met at the various local churches I attended. These formal, recorded interviews occurred after several months of informal interactions through attending services and lunches on a weekly basis as well as cultural events. Men are under-represented in this sample with respect to the overall pool of Ukrainian migrants in California where the population was roughly half women and half men. However, men were a minority of domestic workers in California and therefore were a justifiably small part of this sample as well.

Perhaps the easiest site in terms of participant recruitment was L'viv. I con-ducted a total of 39 interviews with the adult children of migrants and other family members. Ten of these interviews were with the children of migrants I had interviewed in Rome. These interviews were some of the most informative about the ways migration was experienced both by migrants and those left behind. I also spent extensive time with the families of six migrant women who I had met in Rome. This allowed me to learn about daily life, remittances, and negotiations with migration from the point of view of non-migrants in Ukraine. Some interviewees came from referrals by participants from Rome visiting L'viv at the time I was in the field. They helped to recruit the children of their friends who worked abroad in either Italy or the United States to speak with me. I also found interviewees through the Italian Center at L'viv University. Since I also wanted to interview people who had a parent or parents in the United States, I also visited English-language classes at the university and was permitted to recruit interviewees in classes. I found that Italian and English classes had many students with parents abroad. The snowball method worked well especially among students. My identity as a dual citizen of Italy and the United States who grew up in "America" made me a person of interest. Young Ukrainians were full of questions about life in Italy and the United States, some were curious to know how typical their family experiences were, and still others were happy to have a native speaker with whom to practice English or Italian.

As a result, my sample in L'viv was skewed toward young students with parents abroad. Some did not yet have children of their own or nieces or nephews by older siblings, but many did. I do not recall ever seeing a pregnant undergraduate student during my time at Berkeley or during my own time as an undergraduate. Therefore, walking into L'viv University and seeing young pregnant women sitting in classes and walking through the halls was striking to me but of course ordinary for the Ukrainians around me. I also conducted a handful of interviews with grandmothers who were caring for grandchildren in L'viv while their daughters worked in Italy or the United States.

Becoming *Nasha*

I am not Ukrainian or of Ukrainian descent. However, all ethnographers seek to forge connections of trust with their participants. There were many ways participants signaled that I had gained their trust and the most obvious was when I was referred to or introduced as *nasha* or "one of ours." There are many paths to becoming *nasha*. Sometimes becoming *nasha* was an event. For example, at San Francisco's UGCC, I found that the women in the parish quickly became comfortable having me around, while I felt the men still checked their political discussions when I was at the table. When discussions switched from politics to soccer with the 2006 World Cup, I suddenly became a person of great interest to the men as Italy continued to advance in the competition. As an Italian, I was the recipient of many handshakes and congratulations at church on the Sunday after Italy became World Cup Champions. I was standing with a group of Ukrainian men in the church basement when one participant looked at me and said in Russian, "Do you know who Shevchenko is?" I replied, "The soccer player or the poet?" The men burst into laughter, exclaiming to each other, "She's *nasha*! She's *nasha*!" The following week I began interviewing men who had, until then, deflected my requests. Of course becoming *nasha* did not make me Ukrainian. I likely missed some cultural references, but I also benefited from my outsider status. I was able to ask questions about cultural meanings and their understandings of national identity that would seem strange coming from someone who was from the region themselves. Participants also assumed that I would not understand many cultural references and provided cultural translations of events that enriched my data.

More typically in my research, becoming *nasha* was a process and not an event. In Rome, for example, I came to belong at the Sunday lunch at the ROC because I went every Sunday over a period of six months; in San Francisco, I came to belong at union meetings because I attended them over an extended period of time. Participants learned my personal story, because I shared it with them, and they became invested in my life events as I became invested in theirs. I was also a young researcher, the same age as many of the respondents' children, and I framed the interviews as help for a student conducting a university-based project. For women of this age and generation, many of them school teachers, a plea from a student for help was a request they could not refuse once they knew me.

Not only was I negotiating my position as "insider" and "outsider" as all ethnographers must, but I found myself actively highlighting either my Italian or U.S. identity depending on the situation. I also found that participants assigned me an Italian or U.S. identity at different times. In Rome, emphasizing my Italian heritage and citizenship was advantageous in the many Italian bureaucratic and social services agencies to which I would not have had access without fluent Italian and some insider currency. However, among Ukrainian participants in Rome, I tended to downplay my Italian identity. Participants often exclaimed, "You are not an Italian presence" or "You do not *feel* Italian." This was frequently a relief to participants. Those who began interviews saying that Italy was a wonderful place and treated them well, felt they could be more honest in their assessment as they came to feel I was not *really* Italian.[1] In a profound cultural sense, this was a correct observation. I did not grow up or receive my schooling in Italy and my dress and body language were different from women raised in Rome. Participants in the United States also varyingly perceived me as Italian and/or American. It was less likely that I was considered "not American" in California, however I was often introduced as a "nice Italian girl" and informants often perceived me as "American" like their children who came to the United States as teenagers or young adults were "American" despite the fact that I was born and raised in the United States.

Choosing the Research Sites

Although I do not compare Italy and California as receiving sites, but rather the transnational social fields of exile and exodus, in the Introduction I explain why

Italy and California are valuable research sites for the study of post-1991 Ukrainians migration. In this section, I offer the demographic data that supports this decision. At the time I was in the field, 2004–2006, and as of 2011, Italy was the largest receiving country of post-1991 Ukrainians in the European Union.[2] In 2005, there were 93,441 foreign-born Ukrainians in Italy.[3] However, researchers note, including the undocumented population likely doubles the documented population, placing the number of Ukrainian migrants in Italy closer to 197,000.[4] In that same year, only looking at migrants who arrived from 1991–2005, there were 237,483 foreign-born from Ukraine in the United States and 42,037 lived in California.[5] Within the United States, California is second only to New York as a receiving state for Ukrainian migrants.[6] New York is the established center of Jewish refugee services for Soviet Jews. California's attraction for migrants, however, resulted from global economic restructuring beginning in the mid-1970s and 1980s. The privatization of public goods, explosive growth in service-sector jobs, increased workforce casualization, and declines in unionization are changes that came sooner and were more extreme in California than elsewhere in the United States and created a greater demand for cheap, migrant labor; as a result, in the decades following Ukrainian independence, there was a large increase in immigration to California more broadly.[7]

As an ethnographer, I had to choose a city in each geographical location as my research site. Rome not only had a large concentration of Ukrainian migrants, but was also the organizational center of the Ukrainian community in Italy. In 2004, Rome had 2,968 registered Ukrainian migrants, along with a significant undocumented population that likely brought the number closer to 6,000.[8] The social world of Ukrainian migrants was often organized through religious institutions and the seats of both the UGCC and ROC were located in Rome. Rome was also the hub of domestic worker organizations and unions. Similarly, San Francisco had a significant concentration of post-1991 Ukrainian migrants. In 2005, 5,718 foreign-born Ukrainians, who migrated between 1991 and 2004, lived in the San Francisco metro area.[9] Therefore, there were close to an equal number of post-1991 migrants in both Rome and San Francisco. However, post-1991 Ukrainian migrants in San Francisco were part of a much larger community. Excluding Ukrainians, there were 11,317 people from other former Soviet countries who immigrated between 1991 and 2004 and were living in the San Francisco metro area in 2005.[10] As we learned in Chapters 4 and 5, recent migrants from other post-Soviet countries or what participants called the Russian-speaking community were integrated into the lives of recent Ukrainian migrants and likely damped the nationalist emphasis on Ukrainian language and religion that were the hallmarks of Rome's Ukrainian community. A refusal to speak Russian meant severing ties with other recent migrants from the region. Additionally, the children and other descendants of WWII Diaspora Ukrainians were also part of the lives of post-1991 Ukrainian migrants. In 2005, 14,038 people in the San Francisco metro area claimed Ukrainian as their first ancestry on the census.[11]

Like Rome, San Francisco also had a developed organizational infrastructure. This included the headquarters of the ROC in America and other community and union groups. Although the Ukrainian community in San Francisco was the same size and part of a much larger Russian-speaking community than in Rome, it was nevertheless less densely organized (for explanations why, see Chapters 1, 4, and 5). However, the constellation of organizations in San Francisco facilitated my ability to access this difficult to reach population.[12]

The Data Sets

The extensive participant observation I conducted is detailed in the Introduction. In what follows are tables of the formal interviews I conducted.

Exile to Italy

Table A.1 is a list of 61 interviewees, all domestic workers in Italy with the exception of Yuriy (Chapter 3) who attempted to acquire work as a domestic but never performed this work. Not included in the list below are a total of 16 interviews: six formal interviews with Ukranian Greek Catholic priests and one active church volunteer; two religious leaders from the ROC; three interviews with representatives from different unions; the representative of migrants to Rome's local government, who was herself a Russian-speaking migrant; the director of the Italo-Ukrainian Christian Cultural Association; a regional director of ACLI; and the director of the Association of Ukrainian Women workers.

TABLE A.1 Migrant interviewees in Rome, Italy

Name	Age	# of yrs. in Italy	Occupation in Ukraine	Documents (Permesso di soggiorno) Y/N
Anastasiya	42	4	Manager in factory	N
Inna	50	4	High school teacher (Languages)	Y
Larisa	53	3	Head accountant	Y
Bohdanna	62	2	Supermarket cashier	N
Rita	29	3.5	Nurse	N
Bianca	42	5	Electrical engineer	N
Rosaline	40	4	Housewife	N
Alexandra	54	3	Librarian	N
Lydmyla	42	8	Accountant	Y
Kalyna	53	7	Nurse	Y
Lidiya	47	7	Factory worker	Y
Oksana	51	4	University teacher; Editor; Journalist	Y
Diana	57	7	Factory worker	N
Margarita	52	6	Electrical engineer	Y
Yalena	45	8	Accountant	Y
Tatiana	54	4	Factory worker	Y
Valentina	34	4	Cashier	N
Yana	53	3	High school teacher (Russian language and literature)	N
Klara	52	4.5	Music teacher; Professional musician	N
Evgenia	54	4	Accountant	Y

Name	Age	# of yrs. in Italy	Occupation in Ukraine	Documents (Permesso di soggiorno) Y/N
Sonya	50	5	Head accountant	Y
Marika	50	4	Therapist (Disabled children)	N
Veronika	50	4	High school teacher (Ukrainian language and literature)	N
Dina	58	5	High school teacher (Ukrainian language and literature)	N
Valeriya	52	3	Publishing house editor	N
Hanna	24	2	Nurse	N
Zina	48	4	Customer service (Airline industry)	N
Valya	52	3	Accountant	N
Hennady	48	2	Chemical engineer	N
Marusya	46	3	University teacher (Fashion design)	N
Daniela	55	3	High school teacher (Geography)	N
Yulia	35	5	Housewife (University degree in information sciences)	Y
Vasylyna	54	3	Chemist	Y
Natasha	36	1	Music teacher (Conservatory); Professional choir director	N
Khrystyna	27	3	Accountant	N
Svetlana	52	4	High school teacher (History)	N
Katya	54	4	Librarian; Newspaper editor	N
Margarita	53	4	Electrical engineer	Y
Alyona	45	4	Grocery store clerk; Factory worker	Y
Rada	48	4.5	High school teacher (Ukrainian language and literature)	Y
Miloslava	55	5	High school teacher (Science)	N
Lesia	40	5	High school teacher (Math)	Y
Maks	28	6	Archeologist	Y
Valentin	48	3.5	Locomotive mechanic	N
Oleksiy	51	3	Military	N
Ostap	21	1	University student (Computer programmer)	N
Volodymyr	34	4	Military	Y

Name	Age	# of yrs. in Italy	Occupation in Ukraine	Documents (Permesso di soggiorno) Y/N
Inna	50	6	High school teacher (Music)	Y
Slavo	54	3	University professor (Poetry)	N
Milyena	35	7	High school teacher (Russian language and literature)	Y
Andriy	58	4	Supplier (Electronics factory)	N
Valery	29	3	Sailor (Cook)	N
Evgenii	23	1	University student	N
Pavla	40	2	Tourist agent	N
Yuriy	43	3	Factory worker (TV and radio)	N
Galya	53	3	University instructor; Journalist	N
Roksana	54	3	High school teacher (Russian language and literature)	N
Tetyana	50	5	High school teacher (History and music)	Y
Arina	48	4	High school teacher (Language)	N
Manya	58	6	High school teacher (Science)	Y

Exodus to California

Table A.2 is a list of the 41 recorded interviewees, all domestic workers, I conducted in San Francisco. The list does not include two interviews: one with a Ukranian Greek Catholic priest and one with a lay person associated with the ROC and on the board of many of the social service outreach programs to migrants from the former Soviet Union in San Francisco.

TABLE A.2 Migrant interviewees in San Francisco, California

Name	Age	# of yrs in U.S.	Occupation in Ukraine	Stage of Family Migration*	Documents (Green card or U.S. citizen)
Kateryna	56	7	Lawyer	Transnational family	N then Y
Zhanna	60	7	University instructor (Languages)	Transnational family	Y
Mycola	56	10	Military	Transnational family	Y
Oleksandra	55	11	Pediatrician	Family unit in U.S.	Y
Ganna	56	2	High school teacher (Russian language and literature)	Family unit in U.S.	Y

Name	Age	# of yrs in U.S.	Occupation in Ukraine	Stage of Family Migration*	Documents (Green card or U.S. citizen)
Elyzaveta	46	12	Factory worker	Family unit in U.S.	Y
Lada	62	12	Hairstylist	Transnational family (husband)	Y
Halyna	53	4	High school teacher (Chemistry)	Individual migrant	N
Olena	56	11	Manager (Grocery store)	Individual migrant	N
Yadviga	62	11	Nurse	Transnational family U.S./Canada	Y
Raina	59	6	High school teacher (Physics)	Transnational family	Y
Agata	66	26	Nurse	Family unit in U.S.	Y
Agnessa	48	10	High school teacher (History)	Transnational family	Y
Maks	60	2	Engineer (Quality assurance for consortium of 5 factories)	Transnational family	N
Dariya	52	10	Deputy Director of Economics (Regional Office)	Family unit in U.S.	Y
Lyuba	63	9	High school teacher (Ukrainian and Russian language and literature)	Transnational family	Y
Emiliya	59	8	High school teacher (History)	Family unit in U.S	Y
Tereza	28	3	Accountant	Family unit in U.S.	Y
Kyrylo	70	8	Engineer	Individual migrant	N
Tanya	59	5	Hydroelectric engineer; Instructor at Technical Institute	Family unit in U.S.	Y
Susanna	53	6	Chef	Transnational family	N then Y
Nadezhda	68	7	Factory worker	Transnational family	Y
Ida	63	7	Civil engineer	Family unit in U.S.	Y
Eleonora	70	5	Orchestra conductor; music librarian	Transnational family	Legal status in flux
Arkady	60	8	Physicist	Family unit in U.S.	Y
Nastya	51	6	Seamstress	Family unit in U.S.	Y

Name	Age	# of yrs in U.S.	Occupation in Ukraine	Stage of Family Migration*	Documents (Green card or U.S. citizen)
Vladimir	60	6	Factory worker	Family unit in U.S.	Y
Anita	55	9	Engineer	Family unit in U.S.	Y
Klarysa	50	17	Housewife	Family unit in U.S.	Y
Lavra	48	8	Grocery store clerk	Family unit in U.S.	Y
Karyna	54	10	Photographer	Family unit in U.S.	Y
Alisa	54	8	Scientist (Electrical research)	Family unit in U.S.	Y
Marina	45	>1	Music critic	Family unit in U.S.	Y
Oliya	51	4	Civil engineer	Transnational family	Y
Tosha	42	18	Nurse	Transnational family (husband)	Y
Vladislava	62	8	English teacher; Technical editor	Family unit in U.S.	Y
Anzhela	68	11	Photographer	Family unit in U.S.	Y
Mychailo	63	6	Engineer	Family unit in U.S.	Y
Bohuslava	53	6	Chemical engineer	Transnational family	Legal status in flux
Marko	55	6	Pediatrician (Sports medicine)	Transnational family	Legal status in flux
Viktoria	58	10	High school teacher (Russian language and literature); Hotel management	Family unit in U.S.	Y

Total Interviewees: 41

*Transnational family means interviewee has one child in U.S. and one or more children and likely grandchildren in Ukraine unless specified that it is the husband who is in Ukraine.

L'viv: The Children and Families of Exile and Exodus

Table A.3 is a list of the 39 interviews I conducted with the children of exile and exodus and other family members left behind (30 women and nine men). Thirty were teenage and adult children with parent(s) abroad; four were *babushki* with adult children abroad; three had a spouse abroad; one was supported by an aunt abroad; and one had a sister abroad. Not included is an interview with a return migrant.

TABLE A.3 Respondents who had family member(s) abroad

Name	Age	Occupation in Ukraine	Family Member(s) abroad
Sviatoslav	38	Factory worker	Wife and mother in Italy/Aunt in California
Olena	70	Retired/ cared for teen-age and young adult grandchildren	Daughter (47) in Italy
Oleksandr	23	Medical student	Mother in Italy
Roman	27	Sales	Mother in Italy
Tetyana	70	Retired/cared for teen-age and young adult grandchildren	Daughter (48) in Italy; Son (43) plans to go to U.S.
Kostya	19	University student	Father in Portugal then Italy
Ivan	28	Military	Mother in Italy
Nadya	23	Translator for Italian clothing company	Mother and older sister in Italy
Valentina	33	University instructor	Older sister in U.S.
Dana	19	University student	Mother and aunt in Italy
Bohdan	22	University student	Mother in Italy
Olga	51	Unemployed, trying to get visa for Italy	Husband in U.S. and son's mother-in-law in Italy
Sofiya	23	Housewife	Mother in Italy
Iryna	19	University student	Mother and grandmother in Italy
Ela	19	University student	Grandmother in Israel, Mother hopes to migrate when grandmother returns
Justyn	18	University student	Mother in Italy
Tonya	17	University student	Mother in Italy
Lena	18	University student	Aunt in U.S.
Gala	19	University student	Mother, father, aunt in Italy
Vadym	28	Medical doctor	Mother in Italy, uncle in U.S.
Ionna	18	University student	Mother in Italy
Ihor	24	Computer programmer/ university student	Mother in Italy
Cristina	26	Housewife/consultant	Mother in Italy
Sergei	27	Furniture maker	Mother in Italy
Elisabetta	23	Completed university/ unemployed	In Italy and brother in Portugal
Oles	23	University student	Mother in Italy

Name	Age	Occupation in Ukraine	Family Member(s) abroad
Olessia	16	University student	Mother and father were in U.S.; now mother in U.S. and father in Spain
Igor	19	University student	Mother in Italy
Nina	69	Retired/cared for teenage and young adult grandchildren	Son (50) was in U.S. and now in L'viv; daughter (45) in Italy
Alessia	32	Housewife/part-time museum worker	Mother, father, and brother and sister-in-law in Italy
Kiril	48	Unemployed/cared for teenage children	Wife in Italy
Jaroslav	23	Medical student	Mother went to Greece then Italy
Masha	21	University student	Mother in Italy
Olha	16	University student	Mother in Italy
Mariya	65	Retired/cared for teenage grandchildren	Daughter (43) in Italy with son-in-law
Lina	18	University student	Mother and father in Italy
Ira	16	University student	Mother in Italy
Nataliya	17	University student	Mother in Italy and Father in Portugal
Kolya	24	Medical student/ businessman	Mother, father, and sister in U.S.

Total Interviewees: 39

NOTES

Introduction

1 For a specific look at Ukrainian women in the Gulag system, see Kis (2015).
2 In the U.S. context, scholars most often use the terms "immigrant" and "immigration," because U.S.-centric social science research is usually produced from the point of view of the United States as a receiving country. The framing of this book is "migration." I examine both sending and receiving countries. Therefore, I will refer to Ukrainians in both Italy and the United States as "migrants."
3 I use the term "domestic work" or "domestic labor" to indicate both cleaning and caring labor and sometimes use the term "careworker" to emphasize the priority given to providing personal bodily and emotional care to elderly clients. In San Francisco, the most popular term was "homecare worker."
4 The diminutive of Viktoria.
5 See Horn and Schweppe (2016) for studies on aging transnationally.
6 Migrants to the United States experienced the same structural forces that doubly marginalized older women from work and family structures. Therefore, I put the word "voluntary" in quotation marks to remind the reader that in the U.S. context, we tend to over-emphasize individual "choice" and under-emphasize the structural constraint that limits the choices available to individuals (see Bellah et al. [1991]). "Forced" is also in quotation marks, because these migrants might have stayed in Ukraine even if they understood their choices as so constrained that they reported they were "forced" to migrate.
7 Kukhterin (2000).
8 Reproductive labor refers to the unpaid labor women are expected to perform such as caring for and educating children, cleaning, cooking, and other domestic tasks. Although Karl Marx had little to say about gender as a relation of power, women's work in Marxist analyses was rendered invisible, because it was not considered "productive labor" such as labor in a factory that produced an object. Marxist feminists rejected the categorization of the work women performed as "unproductive labor" and instead called it "reproductive labor" because this labor produces the working class. The expectation that women will perform reproductive labor for free places women in a subordinate position to men.
9 Ashwin (2000a), Kis (2005).

10 Hrycak (2011a), Kindler (2011).
11 Kis (2005), Volodko (2015).
12 Zhurzhenko (2004b).
13 Parsons and Bales (1955).
14 This is similar to what Stone and Lovejoy (2004) found in a study of professional women in the United States who "opt out" of the labor market once they have a child. They discovered that these women encountered so many structural obstacles at work and at home that, although women reported "choosing" to be stay-at-home mothers, they first struggled to keep their jobs and be mothers. Only after realizing how structurally limited their "choices" were, did women find opting-out a desirable "choice."
15 Glick Schiller (2009, 20).
16 Ashwin (2000a), Kuehnast and Nechemias (2004b), Rubchak (2015).
17 Kupets et al. (2013, 36, 39).
18 Bureychak (2013).
19 Hrycak (2011a).
20 For a look at grandmothers who stay behind, see Lutz and Palenga-Mollenbeck (2012).
21 Levitt and Glick Schiller (2004, 1009).
22 Levitt (1998, 927).
23 In European scholarship, the Ukrainian migration is considered unique and "transnational" because of the constant movement of bodies between Ukraine and other European countries, which European scholars refer to as "circulation" as opposed to "permanent" migration; see Fedyuk and Kindler (2016). Although useful, this is a different approach than the one I take here.
24 Ambrosetti et al. (2014, 178, 205, 49), Ratha et al. (2011).
25 Ratha et al. (2011).
26 McClintock et al. (1997), Yuval-Davis (1997).
27 Mahler and Pessar (2006), Schmitter Heisler (2008).
28 See Fitzgerald (2009), Massey et al. (1998), Rodriguez (2010), Vollmer (2015).
29 Portes and Rumbaut (2014).
30 Oishi (2005, 141).
31 Some scholars argue for two different definitions of transnational and global (see Mahler and Pessar [2001]). However, in this study where global processes such as neoliberal capitalism and transnational processes such as migration were so intertwined, I found disentangling them a purely academic exercise that in this instance did not help illuminate the study's findings.
32 Glick Schiller (2009, 17).
33 Wimmer and Glick Schiller (2002).
34 Ibid.
35 Levitt and Jaworsky (2007), Solari (2014).
36 Basch et al. (1994), Levitt (2001).
37 Blair (2010), Hoang (2015).
38 For notable exceptions see Burawoy and Verdery (1999), Mandel and Humphrey (2002).
39 Foucault (1983).
40 Foucault (1972).
41 Parreñas (2001, 31).
42 Enloe (1989), Radhakrishnan and Solari (2015).
43 Vollmer (2015), Wanner (2005).
44 Transnationalism is still a contested concept. Some scholars wonder if the phenomenon of transnationalism meaningfully exists (see Waldinger and Fitzgerald [2004]). Instead, Hondagneu-Sotelo and Avila (1997) argue that transnationalism has been understood too narrowly. They critique this literature for focusing too much on the physical flow of people without paying enough attention to the transnational practices of settled

migrants who, for example, may be in the United States permanently but continue to mother transnationally.

45 Solzhenitsyn (1973).
46 Kas'ianov (2011), Satzewich (2002).
47 See Gold (1995), Slezkine (2004).
48 See Mukhina (2009).
49 Burawoy (2000b), (2001).
50 Marchetti and Venturini (2014, 4–6); The authors contrast this finding with migrants from Moldova, also mostly women doing caring labor in Italy, whose largest age bracket is 30–34.
51 Solari (2006a).
52 Burawoy (1998), Reinhartz and Davidman (1992), Naples (2003).
53 Kulyk (2011).
54 This is in line with studies that show cultural production decreased in Ukraine post-1991, while the flow of cultural imports from the West and Russia in English and Russian languages dramatically increased (Holmes [2007]). Interestingly, women, considered the cultural carriers of the Ukrainian language, were more critical of Ukrainian language than men and preferred Russian. Historically, Ukrainian was considered a "backward," "peasant" language and even today in the context of increased gender discrimination, greater prestige is given to women on the labor market who speak Russian, see Bilaniuk (2003). Nevertheless, Ukrainian language was important to many of my participants as a marker of ethnicity and an indicator of political positions in the contests spectrum of new nationalisms. Also see Arel (2002).
55 Migration Policy Centre (2013a). The top receiving countries are the United States, Israel, and Italy in that order. Because of Soviet-era persecution of Jews and complicated regional nationality politics in which many, including some Jews, may not consider Jews "Ukrainian" even if they were born in Ukraine, Ukrainian Jews are beyond the purview of this study on Ukrainian nation-state building.
56 Camarota (2011), Milkman (2006).
57 Delp and Quan (2002).
58 See Solari (2014).
59 Sassen (1988).

Chapter 1

1 This is an overestimation. See the Appendix for documented numbers of Ukrainians in Italy and Rome. These statistics are often inflated or minimized for political reasons (Vollmer [2011]).
2 Andall (2000b), Anderson (2000), Chang (2000), Hochschild (2000), Tolstokorova (2010), Dreby (2010), Vianello (2009).
3 Enloe (1989), Kimmel (2003).
4 Mandel and Humphrey (2002).
5 Wanner (2005).
6 There is debate about how "capitalist" Ukraine is and many scholars challenge the notion that there are no other alternatives to capitalism in the post-Soviet region. Nevertheless, it is clear that although there are both market and non-market-based economic practices in Ukraine, the meta-narrative of market capitalism produces tangible effects inside Ukraine. See Burawoy (2000b), Williams and Round (2008), and Zhurzhenko (2001).
7 Fitzgerald (2009).
8 Kubicek (2008), Ambrosetti et al. (2014).
9 Korek (2007a), Riabchuk (2012b).
10 White and McAllister (2008).

11 Velychenko (2007), Riabchuk (2015). There is a rich literature on Ukrainian ethnic and linguistic relations and its implications for Ukrainian nation-state building. Zhurzhenko (2002) notes that while the "two Ukraines" do vote differently, have different histories, and therefore different relationships to the national idea; she seeks to deconstruct what she believes is a false dichotomy between Europe and Russia in order to forge new paths forward. For more on this debate see Kuzio (2015). Furthermore, language is a deeply contested marker of nationality, ethnicity, and culture in Ukraine, as in many post-Soviet countries. The terms Ukrainophile and Russophile are at times used interchangeably with Ukrainophone (Ukrainian-speaking) and Russophone (Russian-speaking), while at other times they refer solely to one's political stance about, for example, whether Ukraine should be politically tied to Russia or to Europe. In my fieldwork I met many Russophones who were also Ukrainophiles.

12 There is some debate about who should be considered "Ukrainian." This is a complex identity and there is variation between how scholars label different groups in Ukraine and how people from this region self-identify. Although not all people born and raised in Ukraine consider themselves Ukrainian, all participants in this study, even the Russian speakers, did consider themselves Ukrainian.

13 Oksana Kis (2011), in her study of women's political attitudes, uncovered differences by region that echo the findings presented here. Kis found that Western Ukrainian women in her study were critical of the former Soviet Union, which they cited as limiting freedom. They cited ethnic discrimination that included forced Russianization and disdain of Ukrainians. Instead, they saw the independent Ukrainian state as liberating them so that they could speak Ukrainian and reclaim Ukrainian culture. However, women interviewed in Eastern and Southern Ukraine did not talk about the former Soviet Union as limiting freedom and civil rights. Instead, as Russians or Ukrainian Russophones, they presented themselves as culturally superior to the "backward peoples" residing on the peripheries of the Russian empire. They exhibited anxiety over the loss of their once-favored status as Russians or Russian speakers. They supported Russian as the region's universal language and resisted speaking Ukrainian. Consequently, they were more critical of both the Ukrainian state and Ukrainian independence.

14 Magocsi (2002), Wolczuk (2000, 672).

15 The UGCC was established in 1596 as the Uniate Church at a time when Western and Central Ukraine was part of the Polish-Lithuanian Commonwealth. In an attempt to move closer to their Roman Catholic rulers, Metropolitan Mikhail Rohoza of Kyiv and other Orthodox bishops signed the Union of Brest, pledging allegiance to the Vatican but retained Eastern rites and practices.

16 Plokhy and Sysyn (2003).

17 Solari (2006b), Solari (2006a).

18 Gromadzki et al. (2010), Kubicek (2008).

19 For more on the contested region of Galicia and Ukrainian nationalism see Magocsi (2002).

20 Motyl (2015), Wolczuk (2000).

21 Riabchuk (2015); Leonid Kuchma, the second president of an independent Ukraine (1995–2005), was elected by Russophone regions of Ukraine. He originally rejected Galician nationalism arguing instead that Ukraine's place was in Eurasia. Yet, he too softened his position over time and ultimately proclaimed Ukraine's place in Europe.

22 Riabchuk (2007), Wanner (1998).

23 Gromadzki et al. (2010).

24 Torbakov (2014).

25 Kubicek (2008).

26 Wapiński (2014).

27 Medish (2009).

28 For more on Euromaidan, see Bachmann and Lyubashenko (2014), Stepanenko and Pylynskyi (2015).

29 Taras et al. (2004).
30 Arel (2008).
31 Kuzio (2009).
32 Ibid.
33 Ashwin (2002).
34 Gerasymenko (2006).
35 Kukhterin (2000).
36 Riabchuk (2012a).
37 Kiblitskaya (2000b).
38 Einhorn (1993), Hankivsky and Salnykova (2012).
39 Lissyutkina (1999).
40 Utrata (2011).
41 Kuehnast and Nechemias (2004a), Zdravomyslova (2010).
42 World Bank (2014).
43 Comparable poverty rates for the Philippines were 30 percent and Mexico 40 percent (CIA World Factbook 2011).
44 Kupets et al. (2013), United Nations Development Programme (2008).
45 Kis and Bureychak (2015), United Nations Development Programme (2003).
46 Kupets et al. (2013, 36).
47 Ibid.
48 Ibid., 20–21, 36.
49 LaFont (2001).
50 Perelli-Harris (2008).
51 Ibid., Zdravomyslova (2010).
52 Attwood (1996).
53 Verdery (1994, 254) writes, "The chief alternative Eastern Europe's women might anticipate is what has happened in more-advanced economies: the commodification of household tasks into services (day care, cleaning, meal provision, and so forth) for which a working couple pays something closer to their real cost than is paid when these are housework. Until the commodity economy becomes as pervasive in Eastern Europe as it is in the developed world, however, post-socialist Eastern-Europe will be returning to the housewife-based domestic economy superseded at least in part by both socialism and advanced capitalism."
54 Ashwin and Lytkina (2004); Einhorn (1993).
55 Gorbachev (1988, 102).
56 Marsh (1996).
57 Attwood (1996), Kuehnast and Nechemias (2004a).
58 Zhurzhenko (2004a); Gal and Kligman (2000) and Verdery (1996) further argue that nationalist policies of driving women back to their "proper" nurturant role as well as an increasingly visible ethnonationalism coupled with an anti-feminist and pro-natalist politicking are features common to post-Soviet Eastern European countries and tied to the post-Soviet experience.
59 Zhurzhenko (2004b).
60 Predborska (2005, 356–357).
61 Perelli-Harris (2008).
62 Zhurzhenko (2004b).
63 Hrycak (2002), Kukhterin (2000).
64 Issoupova (2000), Riabchuk (2012a), Zhurzhenko (2004b).
65 LaFont (2001).
66 Predborska (2005), Zherebkin (2006).
67 Chari and Verdery (2009), Korek (2007b), Riabchuk (2012b), Smolyar (2006).
68 Gromadzki et al. (2010), Solari (2015).
69 Funk (2004), Hrycak (2011b).

70 Hrycak (2002), Phillips (2008).
71 Rubchak (1996), Zhurzhenko (2001).
72 Pavlychko (1996).
73 Hrycak (2005), Kis (2005).
74 Hrycak (2006), Kis (2012), Phillips (2008).
75 Kiblitskaya (2000a).
76 Ibid., 102.
77 Rubchak (2005).
78 Bureychak (2013).
79 Hrycak (2011a), United Nations Development Programme (2003).
80 Ashwin (2000b), Rotkirch (2000), Utrata (2015).
81 Solari (2011).
81 Zdravomyslova (1996).
83 Bezrukov and Foight (2004).
84 Portes and Rumbaut (2014).
85 McClintock (1995).
86 Abu-Lughod (1998), Einhorn (1993), Radhakrishnan (2011).
87 Oishi (2005, 100).
88 Nixon (1997), Pateman (1988).
89 I use the terms "First World" and "Third World" both because my participants used these terms and because they are the terms used in the sociology of migration literature. The former Soviet Union is "Second World" in this framework because it produced modern subjects who might not have access to basic economic comforts such as running water. As such it is an implicit critique of the First/Third World dichotomy used to frame migration flows.
90 Zhurzhenko (2012), Hays (1996).
91 Correll et al. (2007).
92 This number includes mothers in the United States who reported being disabled or in school and therefore is an overestimation of mothers who stay home to care for children full-time, see Cohn et al. (2014) and Collins (1997).
93 Correll et al. (2007), Stone and Lovejoy (2004).
94 Chesley (2011).
95 Kotusenko (2007), Lutz (2010), Tolstokorova (2009).
96 Solari (2010).
97 Kuchma's comments reinforce a meta-narrative in the public media that young women are emigrating from Ukraine as sex workers in large numbers. Hrycak (2011a) argues that although evidence suggests that sex workers constitute a small percentage of the labor migration from Ukraine to Europe, the vast majority are middle-aged women doing cleaning and caring labor. She argues that both Western policies and NGOs address the needs of migrant women mainly by funding anti-trafficking initiatives. In order to gain access to these funds, Ukrainian women's organizations produce trafficked women.
98 Ambrosetti et al. (2014, 147), Gropas et al. (2015, 36).
99 Parreñas (2005).
100 Feminism is considered a "dirty word" in the post-Soviet contexts, see Funk (2004), Radhakrishnan and Solari (2015), and Zhurzhenko (2011).

Chapter 2

1 Zontini (2008).
2 Kofman et al. (2000).
3 Ibid., King (2000).
4 Pastore (2004).

5 King (2000).
6 Capone (2004), Kofman et al. (2000), Markov (2008).
7 Sarti (2004).
8 Andall (2000b).
9 Andall (1998).
10 Andall (2000a).
11 Eurostat (2015), Sciortino (2004).
12 Alemani (2004), Scrinzi (2004).
13 Andall (2000a).
14 Chell (2000, 109), CIA World Factbook (2014).
15 Ambrosini (2014a), Da Roit et al. (2013), Scrinzi (2004).
16 Ribas-Mateos (2004).
17 Sciortino (2004, 178).
18 Gagliardi et al. (2012, 96).
19 Ibid.
20 Gropas et al. (2015); Although *badanti* is the term used in the media and on the street, among Italian academics there is some debate about this word. The verb *badare* is usually used in reference to children. Therefore, the noun *badante* may be offensive, not to the worker, but to the elderly Italian receiving care.
21 See Gagliardi et al. (2012).
22 Ibid., 97.
23 In 2004, the average exchange rate for Euros to U.S. dollars was 1.244143. In conversations and interviews, participants switched between currencies, especially Euros and U.S. dollars, and therefore I report costs and wages in the currency that the participant(s) provided.
24 Contratto Nazionale (2001–2005).
25 Personal communication of the author.
26 Gropas et al. (2015), ISTAT (2004), Marchetti and Venturini (2014); Furthermore, in a survey study based in Rome, the largest age bracket of Ukrainian women migrants was found to be 40–55; see Shehda and Horodetskyy (2004). Another study concluded that the mean age of Ukrainian women migrants in Italy was 43.5 years-old, see Ambrosetti et al. (2014). This placed most Ukrainian women at the point in their life-course when they were or were poised to become grandmothers.
27 Fonseca (2008), Marques and Gois (2007).
28 Lissyutkina (1999), Utrata (2008).
29 Most Ukrainian women I met in Rome could not drive. Attending driving school and applying for a driver's license was an important activity for a subset of participants.
30 Colombo and Sciortino (2003).
31 Ambrosini (2014b).
32 Capone (2004).
33 Ibid., ISTAT (2004).
34 Montefusco (2008).
35 Marchetti and Venturini (2014).
36 Colombo and Sciortino (2003, 66).
37 King (2000, 14).
38 Solari (2006a).
39 The UGCC is part of the Universal Catholic Church and is in full communion with Rome. There are 22 Catholic churches that make up the universal Catholic Church. One of these is the Roman Catholic Church, which follows the Latin rite and has about 800 million followers worldwide. The remaining 21 Catholic churches, including the UGCC, follow the Byzantine rite and have a combined total of about 15 million followers. In fact, the late Pope John Paul II, himself from post-communist Poland, possessed a keen awareness of the problems facing post-Soviet republics. The

UGCC received special attention from the Vatican under John Paul. This institutional support from the Roman Catholic Church helped the UGCC provide services to Ukrainian migrants in Italy.

40 The role of Catholics in the Orange Revolution was acknowledged at a press conference in Poland on April 4, 2005, following Pope John Paul II's death. Newly elected Ukrainian President Viktor Yushchenko said, "I know that millions of people and Pope John Paul II personally prayed for the Orange Revolution. Without his prayers, the revolution would undoubtedly not have had such success," see Religious Information Service of Ukraine (2005).

Chapter 3

1 About half of the sample embraced global poverty discourses as honor shields like Tatiana, and half rejected poverty discourses as incompatible with notions of Ukraine as a European country like Inna. It is possible that the latter group was overrepresented in my sample, because I recruited participants through organizations such as churches and Ukrainian migrant organizations where people committed to the cultural work of nation-state building tended to congregate. It is also possible that a portion of migrants, who at the time of my interviews and participant observations embraced global poverty discourses, could come to reject them at some later date as they become more involved with the UGCC and other Ukrainian migrant organizations that emphasized nation-state building.
2 Ehrenreich and Hochschild (2002).
3 Hochschild (1983).
4 Colombo and Sciortino (2003).
5 Ibid.

Chapter 4

1 Portes and Rumbaut (2014).
2 Auclair and Batalova (2013).
3 Ibid., McKay (2003).
4 McKay (2003).
5 Gold (1995), Lewin-Epstein et al. (2013), Markowitz (1993), Orleck (1999).
6 See Gitelman (2012).
7 See Solari (2006b).
8 I actively tried to screen out Ukrainian Jews from my sample. In the Soviet Union "Jew" was treated as a nationality like "Ukrainian" or "Russian," therefore they are often treated as a separate group in the area studies literature. I also felt the complexity of post-Soviet Jewish identity was beyond the scope of this study on transnational Ukrainian nation-state building. Nevertheless, I found that Ukrainian Jews were often referred to me as Ukrainians and eight found their way into my sample. Three of the eight I interviewed reported experiencing discrimination in Ukraine because they were Jews as well as economic hardships. These three cut ties with Ukraine and highlighted their relationship with the U.S. state. The remaining five reported the same economic pressures to leave as the non-Jewish respondents and noted family reunification and access to refugee status as facilitating their decision. They felt they has just as much right as Christians or non-believers to claim a Ukrainian identity. Although their narratives, with the exception of access to Jewish resettlement services, fit within the range of responses from the ethnic Ukrainian respondents, here I highlight the experiences of non-Jewish Ukrainians.
9 U.S. Department of State (2015); I chose to compare Ukraine's wait-times to Mexico and the Philippines because they are quintessential examples of family-based and female-led migrations respectively. See the Conclusion for a discussion of Philippines

migration as "exile." For more on the comparison between these three sending countries, see Solari (2014).
10 Bureau of Labor Statistics (2017).
11 Reddy (2005).
12 Wheeler (2015).
13 Delp and Quan (2002).
14 Solari (2006b).
15 Satzewich (2002).
16 Ibid.
17 Holmes (2007).
18 Gold (1992), Orleck (1999).
19 Wanner (2007).
20 Markowitz (1993).
21 Kasinitz (2008).
22 In the literature, those that left the region as political refugees before Soviet power solidified are given the more prestigious title of "émigrés" rather than "(im)migrants."
23 One participant put it this way: "Why is it that when a Russian says, 'I love my country' he is a patriot, but if a Ukrainian says 'I love my country' he is a nationalist?" The difference in connotation in the Soviet context is a fundamental one. A soldier fighting for Mother Russia during World War II was a *patriot* and might have been rewarded with a medal. A *nationalist*, on the other hand, was considered a threat to the very existence of the Soviet Union, which was an entity composed of many nationalities and therefore maintained "internationalism" as an official policy. Being labeled a *nationalist* was the state's reason for sending thousands to the gulags.

Chapter 5

1 Glenn (1986), Hondagneu-Sotelo (2001), Romero (1992).
2 See Fedyuk (2012).
3 In Russian it is: *Myshka za koshku, koshka za Zhuchku, Zhuchka za vnuchku, vnuchka za babku, babka za dedku, dedka za repku, tianut-potianut – vytianuli repku!*
4 Kiblitskaya (2000b).
5 This should be understood in the context of my sample where I was specifically looking for careworkers to the elderly.
6 For a comparative discussion of immigration, ethnicity, and multiculturalism in the United States and Canada, see Bloemraad (2006).
7 This is reminiscent of women in the gulags writing letters to Stalin. They assumed Stalin did not know about the gulags and would rescue them once informed, see Ginzburg (1964).
8 De Genova (2004), Kasinitz (2008), Marrow (2011), Ong (2003).

Conclusion

1 Vollmer (2015, 152).
2 Van Meter (April 20, 2015).
3 Onuch and Martsenyuk (2014), Phillips (2014).
4 Phillips (2014, 415).
5 Calavita (2006).
6 Gender is more visible to us when we think about women because the dominant group, men, is often unmarked and therefore invisible. This is the same reason why when we think of race, we think of brown and black people and when we think of sexual orientation we think of LGBTQ people. It makes it seem that men do not have a

gender, white people do not have a race, and straight people do not have a sexual orientation since they are the standard category against which everyone else is measured.
 7 Ashwin (2000b).
 8 Kukhterin (2000).
 9 Ashwin (2000b, 13).
10 Zdravomyslova and Temkina (2013).
11 Gal and Kligman (2000), Kuehnast and Nechemias (2004b).
12 Kis (2005).
13 Ibid., Zhurzhenko (2001).
14 Rubchak (2001).
15 Zhurzhenko (2001, 41).
16 Fedyuk and Kindler (2016), Hormel and Southworth (2006).
17 Abbott et al. (2006).
18 Becker and Bloom (1998), Romaniuk and Gladun (2015).
19 Zhurzhenko (2012).
20 Janey et al. (2009).
21 Cockerham et al. (2006).
22 Riabchuk (2012a, 207).
23 Hinote and Webber (2012), Janey et al. (2009).
24 Meshcherkina (2000).
25 Zhurzhenko (2012).
26 For more on how the Cossack image is used by state actors, see Yushchenko (2008).
27 Janey et al. (2009).
28 Ibid.
29 Ashwin and Lytkina (2004), Kukhterin (2000).
30 Hobsbawm (1990), Soysal (1994).
31 Brubaker (2011), Leenco (2004).
32 Bonikowski (2016).
33 Bonikowski and DiMaggio (2016).
34 Sassen (1998).
35 Oishi (2005), United Nations (2013).
36 Morrison et al. (2008).
37 Milkman et al. (1998), Osterman (1999).
38 Ambrosini (2014a), Freeman (1994).
39 Campani (2000), Hochschild (2000), Lutz (2011).
40 Kofman et al. (2000), Radhakrishnan and Solari (2015).
41 Kimmel (2003).
42 Mahler and Pessar (2006).
43 Parreñas (2001).
44 Ibid., 3–4.
45 Rodriguez (2010).
46 Mearsheimer (2014).
47 *Foreign Affairs* Staff (2014).
48 *The New York Times* Staff (2008), Arel (2008).

Appendix

 1 This was also true among Italians. In Chapter 2 I discussed delivering a paper in Trento about my research. I was introduced as a colleague from the United States, but my family was from Italy "so we can call her one of our own." As the conference continued and I was perceived, I believe incorrectly, as taking sides with foreign migrants against Italians, panelists no longer even used my name but rather called me "*la Americana*," the American.

2 Migration Policy Centre (2013a), OECD (2001); The most recent data suggests that in 2012, Italy was second to Poland by a small margin Migration Policy Centre (2013b).
3 ISTAT (2005a).
4 Montefusco (2008), Vollmer (2011).
5 Ruggles et al. (2015).
6 Ibid.
7 Milkman (2006), Camarota (2011).
8 ISTAT (2005b).
9 Ruggles et al. (2015).
10 Ibid.
11 Ibid.
12 More recent data show that in 2015, 230,728 Ukrainians were officially registered in Italy, see ISTAT (2016), and 341,837 foreign-born Ukrainians were legally in the United States, see U.S. Census Bureau (2015).

BIBLIOGRAPHY

Abbott, Pamela A., Sergei Turmov and Claire Wallace. 2006. "Health World Views of Post-Soviet Citizens." *Social Science & Medicine* 62: 228–238.

Abu-Lughod, Lila. 1998. "The Marriage of Feminism and Islamism in Egypt: Selective Repudiation as a Dynamic of Postcolonial Cultural Politics." Pp. 243–269 in *Remaking Women: Feminism and Modernity in the Middle East*, edited by L. Abu-Lughod. Princeton, NJ: Princeton University Press.

Alemani, Claudia. 2004. "Le Colf: Ansie e Desideri delle Datatrici di Lavoro." *Polis: Ricerche e Studi Su Società e Politica in Italia* 18: 107–136.

Ambrosetti, Elena, Eralba Cela, Wadim Strielkowski and Josef Abrhám. 2014. "Ukrainian Migrants in the European Union: A Comparative Study of the Czech Republic and Italy." *Sociology & Space* 53(2): 141–166.

Ambrosini, Maurizio. 2014a. "Migration and Transnational Commitment: Some Evidence from the Italian Case." *Journal of Ethnic and Migration Studies* 40(4): 619–637.

Ambrosini, Maurizio. 2014b. "Non tutti gli Insuccessi Regolativi Vengono per Nuocere: La Costruzione di un Welfare Parallelo e l'Immigrazione Irregolare." *Sociologia del Lavoro* 135: 109–125.

Andall, Jacqueline. 1998. "Catholic and State Constructions of Domestic Workers: The Case of Cape Verdean Women in Rome in the 1970s." Pp. 124–142 in *The New Migration in Europe: Social Constructions and Social Realities*, edited by K. Koser and H. Lutz. New York: Macmillan Press.

Andall, Jacqueline. 2000a. "Organizing Domestic Workers in Italy: National Trends and Local Perspectives." Pp. 145–171 in *Gender and Migration in Southern Europe: Women on the Move, Mediterranea series*, edited by F. Anthias and G. Lazaridis. New York: Berg.

Andall, Jacqueline. 2000b. *Gender, Migration and Domestic Service: The Politics of Black Women in Italy*. Aldershot, England: Ashgate.

Anderson, Bridget. 2000. *Doing the Dirty Work?: The Global Politics of Domestic Labour*. New York: Zed Books.

Arel, Dominique. 2002. "Interpreting 'Nationality' and 'Language' in the 2001 Ukrainian Census." *Post-Soviet Affairs* 18(3): 213–249.

Arel, Dominique. 2008. "Ukraine Since the War in Georgia." *Survival* 50(6): 15–25.

Ashwin, Sarah, ed. 2000a. *Gender, State, and Society in Soviet and Post-Soviet Russia*. New York: Routledge.

Ashwin, Sarah. 2000b. "Introduction: Gender, State and Society in Soviet and Post-Soviet Russia." Pp. 1–29 in *Gender, State, and Society in Soviet and Post-Soviet Russia*, edited by S. Ashwin. New York: Routledge.

Ashwin, Sarah. 2002. "'A Woman is Everything': The Reproduction of Soviet Ideals of Womanhood in Post-communist Russia." Pp. 117–133 in *Work, Employment and Transition: Restructuring Livelihoods in Post-communist Eastern Europe*, edited by A. Rainnie, A. Smith and A. Swain. London: Routledge.

Ashwin, Sarah and Tatyana Lytkina. 2004. "Men in Crisis in Russia: The Role of Domestic Marginalization." *Gender & Society* 18(2): 189–206.

Attwood, Lynne. 1996. "The Post-Soviet Woman in the Move to the Market: A Return to Domesticity and Dependence?" Pp. 255–266 in *Women in Russia and Ukraine*, edited by R. Marsh. Cambridge: Cambridge University Press.

Auclair, Gregory and Jeanne Batalova. 2013. "Green-Card Holders and Legal Immigration to the United States." Retrieved: June 12, 2015 (http://www.migrationpolicy.org/article/green-card-holders-and-legal-immigration-united-states).

Bachmann, Klaus and Igor Lyubashenko, eds. 2014. *Maidan Uprising, Separatism and Foreign Intervention: Ukraine's Complex Transition*. Frankfurt: Peter Lang AG.

Basch, Linda, Nina Glick Schiller and Cristina Szanton Blanc. 1994. *Nations Unbound: Transnational Projects, Postcolonial Predicaments, and Deterritorialized Nation-states*. Langhorne, PA: Gordon and Breach.

Becker, Charles and David Bloom. 1998. "The Demographic Crisis in the Former Soviet Union: Introduction." *World Development* 26(11): 1913–1919.

Bellah, Robert N., Richard Madsen, Steven M. Tipton, William M. Sullivan and Ann Swidler. 1991. *The Good Society*. New York: Knopf.

Bezrukov, Vladislav V. and Natalia A. Foight. 2004. "The Impact of Transition on Older People in Ukraine: Looking to the Future with Hope." Pp. 71–96 in *Living Longer: Ageing, Development and Social Protection*, edited by P. Lloyd-Sherlock. New York: Zed Books.

Bilaniuk, Laada. 2003. "Gender, Language Attitudes, and Langauge Status in Ukraine." *Language in Society* 32(1): 47–78.

Blair, Jennifer. 2010. "On Difference and Capital: Gender and the Globalization of Production." *Signs: Journal of Women in Culture & Society* 36(1): 203–226.

Bloemraad, Irene. 2006. *Becoming a Citizen: Incorporating Immigrants and Refugees in the United States and Canada*. Berkeley: University of California Press.

Bonikowski, Bart. 2016. "Nationalism in Settled Times." *Annual Review of Sociology* 42: 427–449.

Bonikowski, Bart and Paul DiMaggio. 2016. "Varieties of American Popular Nationalism." *American Sociological* 81(5): 949–980.

Brubaker, Rogers. 2011. "Nationalizing States Revisted: Projects and Processes of Nationalization in Post-Soviet States." *Ethnic and Racial Studies* 34(11): 1785–1814.

Burawoy, Michael. 1998. "The Extended Case Method." *Sociological Theory* 16(1): 4–33.

Burawoy, Michael and Katherine Verdery. 1999. "Introduction." Pp. 1–17 in *Uncertain Transition: Ethnographies of Change in the Postsocialist World*, edited by M. Burawoy and K. Verdery. New York: Rowman & Littlefield Publishers, Inc.

Burawoy, Michael. 2000a. "A Sociology for the Second Great Transformation?" *Annual Review of Sociology* 26: 693–695.

Burawoy, Michael. 2000b. "Introduction: Reaching for the Global." Pp. 1–40 in *Global Ethnography: Forces, Connections, and Imaginations in a Postmodern World*, edited by M. Burawoy, J. A. Blum, S. George, Z. Gille and M. Thayer. Berkeley: University of California Press.

Burawoy, Michael. 2001. "Manufacturing the Global." *Ethnography* 2(2): 147–159.

Bureau of Labor Statistics, U.S. Department of Labor. 2017. "Occupational Outlook Handbook, 2016–2017 Edition, Personal Care Aides." Retrieved: December 8, 2016 (http://www.bls.gov/ooh/personal-care-and-service/personal-care-aides.htm#tab-6).

Bureychak, Tetyana. 2013. "Zooming In and Out: Historical Icons of Masculinity Within and Across Nations." Pp. 219–238 in *Rethinking Transnational Men: Beyond, Between and Within Nations*, edited by J. Hearn, M. Blagojevi and K. Harrison. New York: Routledge.

Calavita, Kitty. 2006. "Gender, Migration, and Law: Crossing Borders and Bridging Disciplines." *International Migration Review* 40(1): 104–132.

Camarota, Steven A. 2011. "A Record Setting Decade of Immigration: 2000 to 2010.". Retrieved: October 19, 2016 (http://cis.org/2000-2010-record-setting-decade-of-immigration).

Campani, Giovanna. 2000. "Immigrant Women in Southern Europe: Social Exclusion. Domestic Work and Prostitution in Italy." Pp. 147–169 in *Eldorado or Fortress?: Migration in Southern Europe*, edited by R. King, G. Lazaridis and C. G. Tsardanides. New York: St. Martin's Press.

Capone, Francesca Romana. 2004. "Immigrati: Oltre 2,5 Milani gli Extracomunitari in Italia." Retrieved: October 16, 2011 (www.labitalia.com).

Chang, Grace. 2000. *Disposable Domestics: Immigrant Women Workers in the Global Economy*. Cambridge, MA: South End Press.

Chari, Sharad and Katherine Verdery. 2009. "Thinking between the Posts: Postcolonialism, Postsocialism, and Ethnography after the Cold War." *Comparative Studies in Society and History* 51(1): 6–34.

Chell, Victoria. 2000. "Female Migrants in Italy: Coping in a Country of New Migration." Pp. 103–123 in *Gender and Migration in Southern Europe: Women on the Move*, edited by F. Anthias and G. Lazaridis. New York: Berg.

Chesley, Noelle. 2011. "Stay-at-Home Fathers and Breadwinning Mothers: Gender, Couple Dynamics, and Social Change." *Gender & Society* 5: 642–664.

CIA World Factbook. 2011. "Population Below Poverty Line (2003) by Country." Retrieved October 10, 2013 (http://www.NationMaster.com/graph/eco_pop_bel_pov_lin-economy-population-below-poverty-line&date=2003).

CIA World Factbook. 2014. "Total Fertility Rate by Country." Retrieved November 3, 2016 (http://www.indexmundi.com/g/r.aspx?c=it&v=31).

Cockerham, William C., Brian P. Hinote, Geoffrey B. Cockerham and Pamela Abbott. 2006. "Health Lifestyles and Political Ideology in Belarus, Russia, and Ukraine." *Social Science & Medicine* 62: 1799–1809.

Cohn, D'Vera, Gretchen Livingston and Wendy Wang. 2014. "After Decades of Decline, a Rising Share of Stay-at-Home Mothers." Pew Research Center. Retrieved November 8, 2016 (http://www.pewsocialtrends.org/2014/04/08/after-decades-of-decline-a-rise-in-stay-at-home-mothers).

Collins, Patricia Hill. 1997. "The Meaning of Motherhood in Black Culture and Black Mother–Daughter Relationships." Pp. 264–275 in *Through the Prism of Difference:*

Readings on Sex and Gender, edited by M. B. Zinn, P. Hondagneu-Sotelo and M. Messner. Boston: Allyn and Bacon.

Colombo, Asher and Giuseppe Sciortino. 2003. "Italian Immigration: The Origins, Nature, and Evolution of Italy's Migratory Systems." *Journal of Modern Italian Studies* 9(1): 49–70.

Contratto Nazionale. 2001–2005. "Contratto Collettivo Nazionale del Lavoro Sulla Disciplina del Rapporto di Lavoro Domestico." Retrieved: November 24, 2009 (http://www. filcams.cgil.it/lavoro-domestico-ccnl-8-03-2001-7-03-2005-testo-ufficiale).

Correll, Shelley J., Stephen Benard and In Paik. 2007. "Getting a Job: Is There a Motherhood Penalty?" *American Journal of Sociology* 112(5): 1297–1338.

Da Roit, Barbara, Amparo González Ferrer and Francisco Javie Moreno-Fuentes. 2013. "The Southern European Migrant-based Care Model." *European Societies* 15(4): 577–596.

De Genova, Nicholas. 2004. "The Legal Production of Mexican/Migrant 'Illegality'." *Latino Studies* 2(2): 160–185.

Delp, Linda and Katie Quan. 2002. "Homecare Worker Organizing in California: An Analysis of a Successful Strategy." *Labor Studies Journal* 27(1): 1–23.

Dreby, Joanna. 2010. *Divided by Borders: Mexican Migrants and Their Children*. Berkeley, CA: University of California Press.

Ehrenreich, Barbara and Arlie Russell Hochschild, eds. 2002. *Global Woman: Nannies, Maids, and Sex Workers in the New Economy*. New York: Metropolitan Books.

Einhorn, Barbara. 1993. *Cinderella Goes to Market: Citizenship, Gender and Women's Movemenets in East Central Europe*. New York: Verso.

Enloe, Cynthia. 1989. *Bananas, Beaches, and Bases: Making Feminist Sense of International Politics*. Berkeley: University of California Press.

Eurostat. 2015. "Employment and Activity by Sex and Age – Annual Data for 2015, Table lfsi_emp_a." (http://appsso.eurostat.ec.europa.eu/nui/show.do?query=BOOKMARK_ DS-053312_QID_13369B2A_UID_-3F171EB0&layout=SEX,L,X,0;GEO,L,Y,0;AGE, L,Z,0;UNIT,L,Z,1;TIME,C,Z,2;INDIC_EM,L,Z,3;INDICATORS,C,Z,4;&zSelection =DS-053312INDIC_EM,EMP_LFS;DS-053312TIME,2015;DS-053312UNIT,PC_P OP;DS-053312INDICATORS,OBS_FLAG;DS-053312AGE,Y15-64;&rankName1=T IME_1_0_-1_2&rankName2=UNIT_1_2_-1_2&rankName3=GEO_1_2_0_1&rankN ame4=AGE_1_2_-1_2&rankName5=INDICATORS_1_2_-1_2&rankName6=SEX_1 _2_0_0&rankName7=INDIC-EM_1_2_-1_2&rStp=&cStp=&rDCh=&cDCh=&rDM =true&cDM=true&footnes=false&empty=false&wai=false&time_mode=FIXED&time _most_recent=true&lang=EN&cfo=%23%23%23%2C%23%23%23.%23%23%23).

Fedyuk, Olena. 2012. "Images of Transnational Motherhood: The Role of Photographs in Measuring Time and Maintaining Connections between Ukraine and Italy." *Journal of Ethnic and Migration Studies* 38(2): 279–300.

Fedyuk, Olena and Marta Kindler, eds. 2016. *Ukrainian Migration to the European Union: Lessons from Migration Studies*. Switzerland: Springer International Publishing.

Fitzgerald, David. 2009. *A Nation of Emigrants: How Mexico Manages its Migration*. Berkeley: University of California Press.

Fonseca, Maria Lucinda. 2008. "New Waves of Immigration to Small Towns and Rural Areas in Portugal." *Population, Space and Place* 14(6): 525–535.

Foreign Affairs Staff. 2014. "Who Is at Fault in Ukraine?: *Foreign Affairs'* Brain Trust Weighs In." *Foreign Affairs Magazine*. Retrieved: March 28, 2015 (http://www.foreignaffairs. com/articles/142345/who-is-at-fault-in-ukraine).

Foucault, Michel. 1972. *The Archeology of Knowledge*. New York: Tavistock.

Foucault, Michel. 1983. "Afterward: The Subject and Power." Pp. 208–228 in *Michel Foucault: Beyond Structuralism and Hermeneutics*, edited by H. L. Dreyfus and P. Rabinow. Chicago, IL: University of Chicago Press.

Freeman, Richard. 1994. "How Labor Fares in Advanced Economies." Pp. 1–28 in *Working Under Different Rules*, edited by R. Freeman. New York: Russell Sage Foundation.

Funk, Nanette. 2004. "Feminist Critiques of Liberalism: Can They Travel East? Their Relevance in Eastern and Central Europe and the Former Soviet Union." *Signs: Journal of Women in Culture & Society* 29(3): 695–726.

Gagliardi, Cristina, Mirko Di Rosa, Maria Gabriella Melchiorre, Liana Spazzafumo and Fiorella Marcellini. 2012. "Italy and the Aging Society: Overview of Demographic Trends and Formal/Informal Resources for the Care of Older People." Pp. 85–104 in *Advances in Sociology Research. Volume 13*, edited by J. A. Jaworski. New York: Nova Science Publishers, Inc.

Gal, Susan and Gail Kligman, eds. 2000. *Reproducing Gender: Politics, Publics and Everyday Life after Socialism*. Princeton, NJ: Princeton University Press.

Gerasymenko, Ganna. 2006. "The Development of Feminist Traditions in Ukraine." Pp. 383–395 in *Women's Movements: Networks and Debates in Post-communist Countries in the 19th and 20th Centuries*, edited by E. Saurer, M. Lanzinger and E. Frysak. Vienna: Böhlau Verlag Köln Weimar.

Ginzburg, Eugenia. 1964. *Journey into the Whirlwind*. Orlando, FL: Harcourt, Inc.

Gitelman, Zvi. 2012. *Jewish Identities in Postcommunist Russia and Ukraine: An Uncertain Ethnicity*. New York: Cambridge University Press.

Glenn, Evelyn Nakano. 1986. *Issei, Nisei, War Bride: Three Generations of Japanese American Women in Domestic Service*. Philadelphia: Temple University Press.

Glick Schiller, Nina. 2009. "A Global Perspective on Migration and Development." *Social Analysis* 53(3): 14–37.

Gold, Steven J. 1992. *Refugee Communities: A Comparative Field Study*. Newbury Park, CA: Sage Publications.

Gold, Steven J. 1995. *From the Workers' State to the Golden State: Jews from the Former Soviet Union in California*. Boston, MA: Allyn and Bacon.

Gorbachev, Mikhail. 1988. *Perestroika: New Thinking for our Country and the World*. New York: Harper & Row.

Gromadzki, Grezegorz, Veronika Movchan, Mykola Riabchuk, Iryna Solenenko, Susan Stewart, Oleksandr Sushko and Kataryna Wolczuk. 2010. *Beyond Colours: Assets and Liabilities of "Post-Orange" Ukraine*. Kyiv: International Renaissance Foundation.

Gropas, Ruby, Laura Bartolini and Anna Triandafyllidou. 2015. "Country Report Italy: ITHACA Research Report N. 2/2015." 1–72. Retrieved: April 7, 2016 (http://cadmus.eui.eu//handle/1814/37865).

Hankivsky, Olena and Anastasiya Salnykova, eds. 2012. *Gender, Politics, and Society in Ukraine*. Toronto: University of Toronto Press.

Hays, Sharon. 1996. *The Cultural Contradictions of Motherhood*. New Haven, CT: Yale University Press.

Hinote, Brian P. and Gretchen R. Webber. 2012. "Drinking toward Manhood: Masculinity and Alcohol in the Former USSR." *Men and Masculinities* 15(3): 292–310.

Hoang, Kimberly Kay. 2015. *Dealing in Desire: Asian Ascendancy, Western Decline, and the Hidden Currencies of Global Sex Work*. Berkeley: University of California Press.

Hobsbawm, Eric J. 1990. *Nations and Nationalism since 1870: Programme, Myth, Reality*. New York: Cambridge University Press.

Hochschild, Arlie Russell. 1983. *The Managed Heart: Commercialization of Human Feeling.* Berkeley: University of California Press.

Hochschild, Arlie Russell. 2000. "Global Care Chains and Emotional Surplus Value." Pp. 130–146 in *On the Edge: Living with Global Capitalism*, edited by W. Hutton and A. Giddens. London: Jonathan Cape.

Holmes, Marcus. 2007. "Culture without the State? Reinvigorating Ukrainian Culture with Diasporic Efforts." *Review of Policy Research* 24(2): 133–154.

Hondagneu-Sotelo, Pierrette and Ernestine Avila. 1997. "'I'm here, but I'm there': The Meanings of Latina Transnational Motherhood." *Gender & Society* 11(5): 548–568.

Hondagneu-Sotelo, Pierrette. 2001. *Domestica: Immigrant Workers Cleaning and Caring in the Shadows of Affluence.* Berkeley: University of California Press.

Hormel, Leontina and Caleb Southworth. 2006. "Eastward Bound: A Case Study of Post-Soviet Labour Migration from a Rural Ukrainian Town." *Europe-Asia Studies* 58(4): 603–623.

Horn, Vincent and Cornelia Schweppe, eds. 2016. *Transnational Aging: Current Insights and Future Challenges.* New York: Routledge.

Hrycak, Alexandra. 2002. "From Mothers' Rights to Equal Rights Post-Soviet Grassroots Women's Associations." Pp. 62–79 in *Women's Activism and Globalization: Linking Local Struggles and Global Politics*, edited by N. Naples and M. Desai. New York: Routledge.

Hrycak, Alexandra. 2005. "Coping with Chaos: Gender and Politics in a Fragmented State." *Problems of Post Communism* 52(5): 69–81.

Hrycak, Alexandra. 2006. "Foundation Feminism and the Articulation of Hybrid Feminisms in Post-Socialist Ukraine." *East European Politics and Societies* 20(1): 69–100.

Hrycak, Alexandra. 2011a. "Women as Migrants on the Margins of the European Union." Pp. 47–64 in *Mapping Difference: The Many Faces of Women in Contemporary Ukraine*, edited by M. Rubchak. New York: Berghahn Books.

Hrycak, Alexandra. 2011b. "The 'Orange Princess' Runs for President: Gender and the Outcomes of the 2010 Presidential Election." *East European Politics and Societies* 25(1): 68–87.

Issoupova, Olga. 2000. "From Duty to Pleasure? Motherhood in Soviet and Post-Soviet Russia." Pp. 30–54 in *Gender, State and Society in Soviet and Post-Soviet Russia*, edited by S. Ashwin. New York: Routledge.

ISTAT. 2004. "I Permessi di Soggiornio, 2001, 2002." Retrieved: February 22, 2012 (http://demo.istat.it).

ISTAT. 2005a. "Cittadini Stranieri. Bilancio Demografico Anno 2004 e Popolazione Residente al 31 Dicembre – Tutti i Paesi di Cittadinanza." Retrieved: January 5, 2017 (http://www.demo.istat.it/str2004/index.html).

ISTAT. 2005b. "Stranieri Residenti al 1° Gennaio – Cittadinanza per Regioni e Comuni." Retrieved: June 21, 2016 (http://dati.istat.it).

ISTAT. 2016. "Stranieri Residenti al 1° Gennaio – Cittadinanza." Retrieved: December 26, 2016 (http://dati.istat.it).

Janey, Bradley A., Sergei Plitin, Janet L. Muse-Burke and Valintine M. Vovk. 2009. "Masculinity in Post-Soviet Ukraine: An Exploratory Factor Analysis." *Culture, Society and Masculinities* 1(2): 137–154.

Kas'ianov, Georgii. 2011. "The Holodomor and the Building of a Nation." *Russian Social Science Review* 52(3): 71–93.

Kasinitz, Philip. 2008. "Becoming American, Becoming Minority, Getting Ahead: The Role of Racial and Ethnic Status in the Upward Mobility of the Children of Immigrants." *The Annals of the American Academy of Political and Social Science* 620: 253–269.

Kiblitskaya, Marina. 2000a. "'Once we were kings': Male Experiences of Loss of Status at Work in Post-Communist Russia." Pp. 90–104 in *Gender, State, and Society in Soviet and Post-Soviet Russia*, edited by S. Ashwin. New York: Routledge.

Kiblitskaya, Marina. 2000b. "Russia's Female Breadwinners: The Changing Subjective Experience." Pp. 55–70 in *Gender, State, and Society in Soviet and Post-Soviet Russia*, edited by S. Ashwin. New York: Routledge.

Kimmel, Michael S. 2003. "Globalization and its Mal(e)contents: The Gendered Moral and Political Economy of Terrorism." *International Sociology* 18(3): 603–620.

Kindler, Marta. 2011. *A Risky Business? Ukrainian Migrant Women in Warsaw's Domestic Work Sector.* Amsterdam: Amsterdam University Press.

King, Russell. 2000. "Southern Europe in the Changing Global Map of Migration." Pp. 3–26 in *Eldorado or Fortress?: Migration in Southern Europe*, edited by R. King, G. Lazaridis and C. G. Tsardanides. New York: St. Martin's Press.

Kis, Oksana. 2005. "Choosing without Choice: Dominant Models of Femininity in Contemporary Ukraine." Pp. 105–136 in *Gender Transitions in Russia and Eastern Europe*, edited by M. Hurd, H. Carlback and S. Rastback. Stockholm: Gondolin Publishers.

Kis, Oksana. 2011. "Biography as Political Geography: Patriotism in Ukrainian Women's Life Stories." Pp. 89–108 in *Mapping Difference: The Many Faces of Women in Ukraine*, edited by M. J. Rubchak. New York: Berghahn Books.

Kis, Oksana. 2012. "(Re)Constructing Ukrainian Women's History: Actors, Agents, and Narratives." Pp. 152–179 in *Gender, Politics, and Society in Ukraine*, edited by O. Hankivsky and A. Salnykova. Toronto: University of Toronto Press.

Kis, Oksana. 2015. "Remaining Human: Ukrainian Women's Experiences of Constructing 'Normal Life' in the Gulags." Pp. 121–137 in *Gender and Peacebuilding: All Hands Required*, edited by M. P. Flaherty, T. Matyok, S. Byrne and H. Tuso. New York: Lexington Books.

Kis, Oksana and Tetyana Bureychak. 2015. "Gender Dreams or Sexism? Advertising in Post-Soviet Ukraine." Pp. 110–140 in *New Imaginaries: Youthful Reconstruction of Ukraine's Cultural Paradigm*, edited by R. Marian. New York: Berghahn Press.

Kofman, Eleonore, Annie Phizacklea, Parvati Raghuram and Rosemary Sales. 2000. *Gender and International Migration in Europe: Employment, Welfare and Politics.* New York: Routledge.

Korek, Janusz, ed. 2007a. *From Sovietology to Postcoloniality: Poland and Ukraine from a Postcolonial Perspective.* Stockholm: Södertörns Högskola.

Korek, Janusz. 2007b. "Central and Eastern Europe from a Postcolonial Perspective." Pp. 5–22 in *From Sovietology to Postcoloniality: Poland and Ukraine from a Postcolonial Perspective*, edited by J. Korek. Stockholm: Södertörns Högskola.

Kotusenko, Victor. 2007. "Labour Migration from Ukraine and its Ethical Implications." *Oikonomia* 3: 9–13. Retrieved: November 24, 2009 (http://oikonomia.it/old/pages/2007/2007_Ottobre/studi_1.htm).

Kubicek, Paul. 2008. *The History of Ukraine.* Westport, CT: Greenwood Press.

Kuehnast, Kathleen and Carol Nechemias, eds. 2004a. *Post-Soviet Women Encountering Transition: Nation Building, Economic Eurvival, and Civic Activism.* Baltimore, MD: Johns Hopkins University Press.

Kuehnast, Kathleen and Carol Nechemias. 2004b. "Introduction: Women Navigating Change in Post-Soviet Currents." Pp. 1–20 in *Post-Soviet Women Encountering Transition: Nation Building, Economic Survival, and Civic Activism*, edited by K. Kuehnast and C. Nechemias. Baltimore, MD: Johns Hopkins University Press.

Kukhterin, Sergei. 2000. "Fathers and Patriarchs in Communist and Post-Communist Russia." Pp. 71–89 in *Gender, State, and Society in Soviet and Post-Soviet Russia*, edited by S. Ashwin. New York: Routledge.

Kulyk, Volodymyr. 2011. "Language Identity, Linguistic Diversity and Political Cleavages: Evidence from Ukraine." *Nations & Nationalism* 17(3): 627–648.

Kupets, Olga, Volodymyr Vakhitov and Svitlana Babenko. 2013. *Ukraine Case Study: Jobs and Demographic Change*. World Development Report.

Kuzio, Taras. 2009. "Russia's Ideological Crusade Against Ukraine." *Eurasia Daily Monitor*. Retrieved: September 1, 2012 (http://www.jamestown.org/single/?no_cache=1&tx_ttnews[swords]=8fd5893941d69d0be3f378576261ae3e&tx_ttnews[any_of_the_words]=kuzio&tx_ttnews[pointer]=1&tx_ttnews[tt_news]=35123&tx_ttnews[backPid]=7&cHash=d8d06d1b2b).

Kuzio, Taras, ed. 2015. *Independent Ukraine: Nation-state Building and Post-communist Transition*. New York: Routledge.

LaFont, Suzanne. 2001. "One Step Forward, Two Steps Back: Women in Post-Communist Societies." *Communist and Post-Communist Studies* 34: 203–220.

Leenco, Lata. 2004. *The Horn of Africa as Common Homeland: The State and Self-determination in the Era of Heightened Globalization*. Waterloo, Ont.: Wilfrid Laurier University.

Levitt, Peggy. 1998. "Social Remittances: Migration Driven Local-Level Forms of Cultural Diffusion." *International Migration Review* 32(4): 926–948.

Levitt, Peggy. 2001. *The Transnational Villagers*. Berkeley: University of California Press.

Levitt, Peggy and Nina Glick Schiller. 2004. "Conceptualizing Simultaneity: A Transnational Social Field Perspective on Society." *International Migration Review* 38(3): 1002–1039.

Levitt, Peggy and B. Nadya Jaworsky. 2007. "Transnational Migration Studies: Past Developments and Future Trends." *Annual Review of Sociology* 33(1): 129–156.

Lewin-Epstein, Noah, Paul Ritterband and Yaacov Ro'i, eds. 2013. *Russian Jews on Three Continents: Migration and Resettlement*. New York: Routledge.

Lissyutkina, Larissa. 1999. "Empancipation without Feminism: The Historical and Socio-cultural Context of the Women's Movement in Russia." Pp. 168–187 in *Women and Political Change: Persepctives from East-Central Europe*, edited by S. Bridger. New York: St. Martin's Press, Inc.

Lutz, Helma. 2010. "Gender in the Migratory Process." *Journal of Ethnic and Migration Studies* 36(10): 1647–1663.

Lutz, Helma. 2011. *New Maids: Transnational Women and the Care Economy*. New York: Zed Books.

Lutz, Helma and Ewa Palenga-Mollenbeck. 2012. "Care Workers, Care Drain, and Care Chains: Reflections on Care, Migration, and Citizenship." *Social Politics: International Studies in Gender, State & Society* 19(1): 15–37.

Magocsi, Paul Robert. 2002. *The Roots of Ukrainian Nationalism: Galicia as Ukraine's Piedmont*. Toronto: University of Toronto Press.

Mahler, Sarah J. and Patricia R. Pessar. 2001. "Gendered Geographies of Power: Analyzing Gender Across Transnational Spaces." *Identities* 7(4): 441–459.

Mahler, Sarah J. and Patricia R. Pessar. 2006. "Gender Matters: Ethnographers Bring Gender from the Periphery toward the Core of Migration Studies." *International Migration Review* 40(1): 27–63.

Mandel, Ruth and Caroline Humphrey. 2002. "The Market in Everyday Life: Ethnographies of Postsocialism." Pp. 1–16 in *Markets & Moralities: Ethnographies of Postsocialism*, edited by R. Mandel and C. Humphrey. New York: Berg.

Marchetti, Sabrina and Alessandra Venturini. 2014. "Mothers and Grandmothers on the Move: Labour Mobility and the Household Strategies of Moldovan and Ukrainian Migrant Women in Italy." *International Migration* 52(5): 111–126.

Markov, Ihor, ed. 2008. *Ukrainian Labour Migration in Europe: Findings of the Complex Research of Ukrainian Labour Immigration Processes.* L'viv: Caritas Ukraine.

Markowitz, Fran. 1993. *A Community in Spite of itself: Soviet Jewish Émigrés in New York.* Washington: Smithsonian Institution Press.

Marques, Jose Carlos and Pedro Gois. 2007. "Ukrainian Migration to Portugal. From Non-existence to the Top Three Immigrant Groups." *Migrationonline.cz*. Retrieved: June 21, 2016 (http://www.migrationonline.cz/e-library/?x=1963795).

Marrow, Helen B. 2011. *New Destination Dreaming: Immigration, Race, and Legal Status in the Rural American South.* Stanford, CA: Stanford University Press.

Marsh, Rosalind, ed. 1996. *Women in Russia and Ukraine.* New York: Cambridge University Press.

Massey, Douglas S., Joaquin Arango, Graeme Hugo, Ali Kouaouci, Adela Pellegrino and J. Edward Taylor. 1998. *Worlds in Motion: Understanding International Migration at the End of the Millenium.* Oxford: Clarendon Press.

McClintock, Anne. 1995. *Imperial Leather: Race, Gender and Sexuality in the Colonial Contest.* New York: Routledge.

McClintock, Anne, Aamir Mufti and Ella Shoha, eds. 1997. *Dangerous Liaisons: Gender, Nation, and Postcolonial Perspectives.* Minneapolis: University of Minnesota Press.

McKay, Ramah. 2003. "Family Reunification." Migration Information Source. Retrieved: December 22, 2016 (http://www.migrationinformation.org/article/family-reunification).

Mearsheimer, John J. 2014. "Why the Ukraine Crisis is the West's Fault: The Liberal Delusions That Provoked Putin." *Foreign Affairs Magazine* 93(5). Retrieved: March 28, 2015 (www.foreignaffairs.com/articles/141769/john-j-mearsheimer/why-the-ukraine-crisis-is-the-wests-fault).

Medish, Mark. 2009. "The Difficulty of Being Ukraine." In *The New York Times,* December 22.

Meshcherkina, Elena. 2000. "New Russian Men: Masculinity Regained?" Pp. 105–117 in *Gender, State, and Society in Soviet and Post-Soviet Russia,* edited by S. Ashwin. New York: Routledge.

Migration Policy Centre. 2013a. "Migration Facts: Ukraine." Retrieved: June 23, 2016 (http://www.migrationpolicycentre.eu/publications/migration-profiles-fact-sheets/).

Migration Policy Centre. 2013b. "Migration Profile: Ukraine." Retrieved November 29, 2016 (http://www.migrationpolicycentre.eu/docs/migration_profiles/Ukraine.pdf).

Milkman, Ruth, Ellen Reese and Benita Roth. 1998. "The Macrosociology of Paid Domestic Labor." *Work and Occupations* 25(4): 483–510.

Milkman, Ruth. 2006. *L.A. Story: Immigrant Workers and the Future of the U.S. Labor Movement.* New York: Russell Sage Foundation.

Montefusco, Cristina. 2008. "Ukrainian Migration to Italy." *Journal of Immigrant & Refugee Studies* 6(3): 344–355.

Morrison, Andrew R., Maurice Schiff and Mirja Sjöblom, eds. 2008. *The International Migration of Women.* New York: The World Bank and Palgrave Macmillan.

Motyl, Alexander. 2015. "State, Nation, and Elites in Independent Ukraine." Pp. 3–16 in *Independent Ukraine: Nation-state Building and Post-communist Transition,* edited by T. Kuzio. New York: Routledge.

Mukhina, Irina. 2009. "New Losses, New Opportunities: (Soviet) Women In The Shuttle Trade." *Journal Of Social History* 43(2): 341–359.

Naples, Nancy A. 2003. *Feminism and Method: Ethnography, Discourse Analysis, and Activist Research*. New York: Routledge.

Nixon, Rob. 1997. "Of Balkan and Bantustans: Ethnic Cleansing and the Crisis in National Legitimation." Pp. 69–88 in *Dangerous Liaisons: Gender, Nation, and Postcolonial Perspectives*, edited by A. McClintock, A. Mufti and E. Shohat. Minneapolis: University of Minnesota Press.

OECD. 2001. "Trends in International Migration: Continuous Reporting System on Migration." Retrieved: March 11, 2003 (https://www.oecd.org/migration/mig/2507635.pdf).

Oishi, Nana. 2005. *Women in Motion: Globalization, State Policies, and Labor Migration in Asia*. Stanford, CA: Stanford University Press.

Ong, Aihwa. 2003. *Buddha is Hiding: Refugees, Citizenship, the New America*. Berkeley: University of California Press.

Onuch, Olga and Tamara Martsenyuk. 2014. "Mothers and Daughters of the Maidan: Gender, Repertoires of Violence, and the Division of Labour in Ukrainian Protests." *Social, Health, and Communication Studies Journal* 1(1): 80–101.

Orleck, Annelise. 1999. *The Soviet Jewish Americans*. Westport, CT: Greenwood Press.

Osterman, Paul. 1999. *Securing Prosperity: The American Labor Market, How It Has Changed and What We Can Do About It*. Princeton, NJ: Princeton University Press.

Parreñas, Rhacel. 2001. *Servants of Globalization: Women, Migration and Domestic Work*. Stanford, CA: Stanford University Press.

Parreñas, Rhacel. 2005. *Children of Global Migration: Transnational Families and Gendered Woes*. Stanford, CA: Stanford University Press.

Parsons, Talcott and Robert F. Bales. 1955. *Family Socialization and Interaction Process*. Glencoe, IL: The Free Press.

Pastore, Ferruccio. 2004. "Italy's Migration Contradiction." Retrieved: July 7, 2005 (http://www.opendemocracy.net/people-migrationeurope/article_1744.jsp).

Pateman, Carole. 1988. *The Sexual Contract*. Stanford, CA: Stanford University Press.

Pavlychko, Solomea. 1996. "Feminism in Post-Communist Ukrainian Society." Pp. 305–314 in *Women in Russia and Ukraine*, edited by R. Marsh. New York: Cambridge University Press.

Perelli-Harris, Brienna. 2008. "Family Formation in Post-Soviet Ukraine: Changing Effects of Education in a Period of Rapid Social Change." *Social Forces* 87(2): 767–794.

Phillips, Sarah. 2014. "The Women's Squad in Ukraine's Protests: Feminism, Nationalism, and Militarism on the Maidan." *American Ethnologist* 41(3): 414–426.

Phillips, Sarah D. 2008. *Women's Social Activism in the New Ukraine: Development and the Politics of Differentiation*. Bloomington: Indiana University Press.

Plokhy, Serhii and Frank E. Sysyn. 2003. *Religion and Nation in Modern Ukraine*. Toronto: Canadian Institute of Ukrainian Studies Press.

Portes, Alejandro and Rubén Rumbaut. 2014. *Immigrant America: A Portrait, Updated and Expanded*. Berkeley: University of California Press.

Predborska, Irina. 2005. "The Social Position of Young Women in Present-day Ukraine." *Journal of Youth Studies* 8(3): 349–365.

Radhakrishnan, Smitha. 2011. *Appropriately Indian: Gender and Culture in a New Transnational Class*. Durham, NC: Duke University Press.

Radhakrishnan, Smitha and Cinzia Solari. 2015. "Empowered Women, Failed Patriarchs: Neoliberalism and Global Gender Anxieties." *Sociology Compass* 9(9): 784–802.

Ratha, Dilip, Sanket Mohapatra and Ani Silwa. 2011. "Migration and Remittances Factbook 2011." Washington, DC: The International Bank for Reconstuction and Development/The World Bank. Retrieved June 23, 2011 (http://go.worldbank.org/U1S23A9QR0).

Reddy, Raahi. 2005. "The Value of Care: Homecare Workers went from being an Invisible Workforce to one of the most Vibrant Sectors in the Labor Movement." *Color Lines Magazine*. Retrieved: October 16, 2011 (www.thefreelibrary.com/The+value+of+care%3a+homecare+workers+went+from+being+an+invisible ... -a0136254609).

Reinhartz, Shulamit and Lynn Davidman. 1992. *Feminist Methods in Social Research*. New York: Oxford University Press.

Religious Information Service of Ukraine. 2005. "Yushchenko Notes Pope's Role in 'Orange Revolution'." Retrieved: January 15, 2006 (http://www.risu.org.ua/eng/news/article;5150/).

Riabchuk, Anastasia. 2012a. "Homeless Men and the Crisis of Masculinity in Contemporary Ukraine." Pp. 204–221 in *Gender, Politics and Society in Ukraine*, edited by O. Hankivsky and A. Salnykova. Toronto: Toronto Press.

Riabchuk, Mykola. 2007. "In Bed with an Elephant: Cultural Wars and Rival Identities in Contemporary Ukraine." Pp. 155–176 in *From Sovietology to Postcoloniality: Poland and Ukraine from a Postcolonial Perspective*, edited by J. Korek. Stockholm: Södertörns Högskola.

Riabchuk, Mykola. 2012b. "Ukraine's 'Muddling Through': National Identity and Postcommunist Transition." *Communist and Post-Communist Studies* 45(3–4): 439–446.

Riabchuk, Mykola. 2015. "Civil Society and Nation Building in Ukraine." Pp. 81–98 in *Independent Ukraine: Nation-state Building and Post-communist Transition*, edited by T. Kuzio. New York: Routledge.

Ribas-Mateos, Natalia. 2004. "How Can We Understand Immigration in Southern Europe?" *Journal of Ethnic and Migration Studies* 30(6): 1045–1063.

Rodriguez, Robyn M. 2010. *Migrants for Export: How the Philippine State Brokers Labor to the World*. Minneapolis: University of Minnesota Press.

Romaniuk, Anatole and Oleksandr Gladun. 2015. "Demographic Trends in Ukraine: Past, Present, and Future." *Population and Development Review* 41(2): 315–337.

Romero, Mary. 1992. *Maid in the U.S.A.* New York: Routledge.

Rotkirch, Anna. 2000. *The Man Question: Loves and Lives in Late 20th Century Russia*. Helsinki: University of Helsinki.

Rubchak, Marian, ed. 2015. *New Imaginaries: Youthful Reconstruction of Ukraine's Cultural Paradigm*. New York: Berghahn Press.

Rubchak, Marian J. 1996. "Christian Virgin or Pagan Goddess: Feminism versus the Eternally Feminine in Ukraine." Pp. 315–330 in *Women in Russia and Ukraine*, edited by R. Marsh. New York: Cambridge University Press.

Rubchak, Marian J. 2001. "In Search of a Model: Evolution of a Feminist Consciousness in Ukraine and Russia." *The European Journal of Women's Studies* 8(2): 149–160.

Rubchak, Marian J. 2005. "Yulia Tymoshenko: Goddess of the Revolution." Retrieved: March 1, 2007 (http://eng.maidanua.org/node/111).

Ruggles, Steven, Katie Genadek, Ronald Goeken, Josiah Grover and Matthew Sobek. 2015. "Integrated Public Use Microdata Series: Version 6.0 [American Community Survey (ACS) 2005]." Retrieved: January 6, 2017 (http://usa.ipums.org/usa).

Sarti, Raffaella. 2004. "'Noi Abbiamo Visto Tante Città, Abbiamo un'Altra Cultura.' Servizio Domestico, Migrazione e Identità di Genere in Italia: Uno Squardo di Lungo Periodo." *Polis* 18: 107–136.

Sassen, Saskia. 1988. *The Mobility of Labor and Capital: A Study in International Investment and Labor Flow.* New York: Cambridge University Press.

Sassen, Saskia. 1998. *Globalization and its Discontents.* New York: New Press.

Satzewich, Vic. 2002. *The Ukrainian Diaspora.* New York: Routledge.

Schmitter Heisler, Barbara. 2008. "The Sociology of Immigration: From Assimilation to Segmented Assimilation, from the American Experience to the Global Arena." Pp. 83–111 in *Migration Theory: Talking Across Disciplines,* edited by C. Brettell and J. F. Hollifield. New York: Routledge.

Sciortino, Giuseppe. 2004. "Immigration in a Mediterranean Welfare State: The Italian Experience in Comparative Perspective." *Journal of Comparative Policy Analysis* 6(2): 111–128.

Scrinzi, Francesca. 2004. "Professioniste Della Tradizione. Le Donne Migranti nel Mercato del Lavoro Domestico." *Polis* 18(1): 107–136.

Shehda, Natalia and Oleksandr Horodetskyy. 2004. "Ucraini in Italia: Una Realtà Sempre Più Presente." Pp. 299–307 in *Europa Allargamento a Est e Immigrazione,* edited by O. Forti, F. Pittau and A. Ricci. Rome: Caritas Italiana.

Slezkine, Yuri. 2004. *The Jewish Century.* Princeton, NJ: Princeton University Press.

Smolyar, Lyudmyla. 2006. "The Ukrainian Experiment: Between Feminism and Nationalism or the Main Features of Pragmatic Feminism." Pp. 397–411 in *Women's Movements: Networks and Debates in Post-communist Countries in the 19th and 20th Centuries,* edited by E. Saurer, M. Lanzinger and E. Frysak. Vienna: Böhlau Verlag Köln Weimar.

Solari, Cinzia D. 2006a. "Professionals and Saints: How Immigrant Careworkers Negotiate Gendered Identities at Work." *Gender & Society* 20(3): 301–331.

Solari, Cinzia D. 2006b. "Transnational Politics and Settlement Practices: Post-Soviet Immigrant Churches in Rome." *American Behavioral Scientist* 49(11): 1528–1553.

Solari, Cinzia D. 2010. "Resource Drain vs. Constitutive Circularity: Comparing the Gendered Effects of Post-Soviet Migration Patterns in Ukraine." *Anthropology of East Europe Review* 28(1): 215–238.

Solari, Cinzia D. 2011. "Between 'Europe' and 'Africa': Building the New Ukraine on the Shoulders of Migrant Women." Pp. 23–46 in *Mapping Difference: The Many Faces of Women in Ukraine,* edited by M. J. Rubchak. New York: Berghahn Books.

Solari, Cinzia D. 2014. "'Prostitutes' and 'Defectors': How the Ukrainian State Constructs Women Emigrants to Italy and the USA." *The Journal of Ethnic and Migration Studies* 40(11): 1817–1835.

Solari, Cinzia D. 2015. "Disarticulated Nation-state Building: Theorizing Postcolonial Ukrainian Nationalisms from the Perspective of Global Ethnography." Paper presented at the American Sociological Association, Chicago.

Solzhenitsyn, Aleksandr. 1973. *The Gulag Archipelago.* London: Fontana.

Soysal, Yasemin Nuhoglu. 1994. *Limits of Citizenship: Migrants and Postnational Membership in Europe.* Chicago, IL: University of Chicago Press.

Stepanenko, Viktor and Yaroslav Pylynskyi, eds. 2015. *Ukraine After the Euromaidan: Challenges and Hopes.* Switzerland: Peter Lang.

Stone, Pamela and Meg Lovejoy. 2004. "Fast-Track Women and the 'Choice' to Stay Home." *The Annals of the American Academy of Political and Social Science* 596: 62–83.

Taras, Ray, Olga Filippova and Nelly Pobeda. 2004. "Ukraine's Transnationals, Far-away Locals and Xenophobes: The Prospects for Europeanness." *Europe-Asia Studies* 56(6): 835–856.

The New York Times Staff. 2008. "More Russian Passports in Ukraine?" In *The New York Times*, August 18.

Tolstokorova, Alissa. 2009. "Who Cares for Carers?: Feminization of Labor Migration from Ukraine and its Impact on Social Welfare." *International Issues & Slovak Foreign Policy Affairs* 17(1): 62–84.

Tolstokorova, Alissa. 2010. "Where have all the Mothers Gone? The Gendered Effect of Labour Migration and Transnationalism on the Institution of Parenthood in Ukraine." *Anthropology of East Europe Review* 28(1): 184–214.

Torbakov, Igor. 2014. "'This is a Strife of Slavs among Themselves': Understanding Russian-Ukrainian Relations as the Conflict of Contested Identities." Pp. 183–205 in *Maidan Uprising, Separatism and Foreign Intervention: Ukraine's Complex Transition*, edited by K. Bachmann and I. Lyubashenko. Frankfurt: Peter Lang AG.

U.S. Census Bureau. 2015. "Place of Birth for the Foreign-Born Population in the United States, B05006."

U.S. Department of State. 2015. "Visa Bulletin for May 2015." 11(10). Retrieved: May 5, 2015 (http://travel.state.gov/content/visas/english/law-and-policy/bulletin/2015/visa-bulletin-for-may-2015.html).

United Nations. 2013. "International Migration Report 2013." Department of Economic and Social Affairs, Population Division.

United Nations Development Programme. 2003. "Gender Issues in Ukraine: Challenges and Opportunities." Kyiv: United Nations Development Programme, UN in Ukraine.

United Nations Development Programme. 2008. "Human Development and Ukraine's European Choice." Kyiv: United Nation Development Programme in Ukraine.

Utrata, Jennifer. 2008. "Keeping the Bar Low: Why Russia's Nonresident Fathers Accept Narrow Fatherhood Ideals." *Journal of Marriage and Family* 70(5): 1297–1310.

Utrata, Jennifer. 2011. "Youth Privilege: Doing Age and Gender in Russia's Single-Mother Families." *Gender & Society* 25(5): 616–641.

Utrata, Jennifer. 2015. *Women without Men: Single Mothers and Family Change in the New Russia*. Ithaca, NY: Cornell University Press.

Van Meter, Matthew. April 20, 2015. "Gender, Nation, and Revolution: The Rise of Women in the Euromaidan Protests." in *Harriman Institute Russian, Eurasian, and East Europen Studies*. New York: Columbia University.

Velychenko, Stephen, ed. 2007. *Ukraine, the EU and Russia: History, Culture and International Relations*. New York: Palgrave Macmillan.

Verdery, Katherine. 1994. "From Parent-State to Family Patriarchs: Gender and Nation in Contemporary Eastern Europe." *East European Politics and Societies* 8(2): 225–255.

Verdery, Katherine. 1996. "Nationalism, Postsocialism, and Space in Eastern Europe." *Social Research* 63(1): 77–95.

Vianello, Francesca A. 2009. *Migrando Sole: Legami Transnazionali tra Ucraina e Italia*. Milan: FrancoAngeli.

Vollmer, Bastian A. 2011. "Policy Discourses on Irregular Migration in the EU-'Number Games' and 'Political Games'." *European Journal of Migration and Law* 13(3): 317–339.

Vollmer, Bastian A. 2015. *Ukrainian Migration and the European Union: Dynamics, Subjectivity, and Politics*. New York: Palgrave Macmillan.

Volodko, Viktoriya V. 2015. "Homemaker and Breadwinner Roles in the Eyes of Female Labor Migrants." Pp. 191–210 in *New Imaginaries: Youthful Reinvention of Ukraine's Cultural Paradigm*, edited by M. Rubchak. New York: Berghahn Press.

Waldinger, Roger and David Fitzgerald. 2004. "Transnationalism in Question." *American Journal of Sociology* 109(5): 1177–1195.

Wanner, Catherine. 1998. *Burden of Dreams: History and Identity in Post-Soviet Ukraine.* University Park: Pennsylvania State University Press.

Wanner, Catherine. 2005. "Money, Morality and New Forms of Exchange in Postsocialist Ukraine." *Ethnos* 70(4): 515–537.

Wanner, Catherine. 2007. *Communities of the Converted: Ukrainians and Global Evangelism.* Ithaca: Cornell University Press.

Wapiński, Maciej. 2014. "The Orange Revolution and its Aftermath." Pp. 43–60 in *Maidan Uprising, Separatism and Foreign Intervention: Ukraine's Complex Transition*, edited by K. Bachmann and I. Igor Lyubashenko. Frankfurt: Peter Lang AG.

Wheeler, Lydia. 2016. "Supreme Court Denies Review of Minimum Wage Rule." Retrieved April 2, 2017 (http://thehill.com/regulation/court-battles/284982-supreme-court-denied-review-of-minimum-wage-rule-for-home-care).

White, Stephen and Ian McAllister. 2008. "Belarus, Ukraine and Russia: East or West?". *Vestnik obshchestvennogo mneniia* 3(95): 14–26.

Williams, Colin C. and John Round. 2008. "The Illusion of Capitalism in Post-Soviet Ukraine." *Debatte: Journal of Contemporary Central and Eastern Europe* 16(3): 331–345.

Wimmer, Andreas and Nina Glick Schiller. 2002. "Methodological Nationalism and Beyond: Nation-state Building, Migration and the Social Sciences." *Global Networks* 2(4): 301–334.

Wolczuk, Kataryna. 2000. "History, Europe and the 'National Idea': The 'Official' Narrative of National Identity in Ukraine." *Nationalities Papers* 28(4): 671–694.

World Bank. 2014. "Unemployment Rates, Ukraine 1999–2014." Retrieved: November 7, 2016 (https://ycharts.com/indicators/ukraine_unemployment_rate_annual).

Yushchenko, Kateryna. 2008. "The Orange Revolution and Beyond." *Journal of Democracy* 19(3): 158–161.

Yuval-Davis, Nira. 1997. *Gender & Nation.* London: Sage Publications.

Zdravomyslova, Elena. 1996. "Problems of Becoming a Housewife." Pp. 33–48 in *Women's Voices in Russia Today*, edited by A. Rotkirch and E. Haavio-Mannila. Brookfield, VT: Dartmouth Publishing Company.

Zdravomyslova, Elena. 2010. "Working Mothers and Nannies: Commercialization of Childcare and Modifications in the Gender Contract (A Sociological Essay)." *Anthropology of East Europe Review* 28(2): 200–225.

Zdravomyslova, Elena and Anna Temkina. 2013. "The Crisis of Masculinity in Late Soviet Discourse." *Russian Social Science Review* 54(1): 40–61.

Zherebkin, Sergei. 2006. "'Male Fantasies' in Ukraine: 'Fucking Women and Building Nation'." Pp. 268–279 in *Women's Movements: Networks and Debates in Post-communist Countries in the 19th and 20th Centuries*, edited by E. Saurer, M. Lanzinger and E. Frysak. Weimer: Böhlau Verlag.

Zhurzhenko, Tatiana. 2001. "Free Market Ideology and New Women's Identities in Post-socialist Ukraine." *The European Journal of Women's Studies* 8(1): 29–49.

Zhurzhenko, Tatiana. 2002. "The Myth of Two Ukraines." In *Eurozine*, September 17.

Zhurzhenko, Tatiana. 2004a. "Families in the Ukraine: Between Postponed Modernization, Neo-Familialism and Economic Survival." *Contemporary Perspectives in Family Research* 5: 187–209.

Zhurzhenko, Tatiana. 2004b. "Strong Women, Weak State: Family Politics and Nation Building in Post-Soviet Ukraine." Pp. 23–43 in *Post-Soviet Women Encountering Transition: Nation Building, Economic Survival, and Civic Activism*, edited by K. Kuehnast and C. Nechemias. Baltimore, MD: Johns Hopkins University Press.

Zhurzhenko, Tatiana. 2011. "Feminist (De)Constructions of Nationalism in the Post-Soviet Space." Pp. 173–191 in *Mapping Difference: The Many Faces of Women in Ukraine*, edited by M. J. Rubchak. New York: Berghahn Books.

Zhurzhenko, Tatiana. 2012. "Gender, Nation, and Reproduction: Demographic Discourses and Politics in Ukraine after the Orange Revolution." Pp. 131–152 in *Gender, Politics, and Society in Ukraine*, edited by O. Hankivsky and A. Salnykova. Toronto: University of Toronto Press.

Zontini, Elisabetta. 2008. "Resisting Fortress Europe: The Everyday Politics of Female Transnational Migrants." *FOCAAL* 2008(51): 13–27.

INDEX

Afineevky, Evgeny 190
Africa and Europe, 'second world' between
   65–8
Ashwin, Sarah 198
authentic identity in Ukraine 35, 40
authorized immigration to California 128–9

Babushki: double marginalization of 38–44;
   exile of *babushki* to Italy and California;
   life course of 4–5; reinvention across
   migration waves 172–82; removal of
   babushki from Ukraine 66–7
Berehynia: discourse about, political
   exploitation of 36–7; gendered migrant
   subjectivities 192, 198–9, 201; ideal in
   Ukraine of 201; rise of 198–9; symbol of
   family and nation 36–7; women's
   separate responsibilities 40
Blank, Diana 59
border controls, fears of 67–8
Bossi, Umberto 60
Bossi-Fini Law in Italy 60, 61, 88
breadwinner ideal 5–6, 35, 38, 71,110, 112,
   192–3, 201
Burawoy, Michael 18

California: authorized immigration 128–9;
   capitalism in U.S., discovery of (Dariya)
   153–63; comparison with Italy 195–7;
   demographics of Ukrainian migrants in
   18–9, 210; diaspora institutions 133–4;
   Diaspora Ukrainians 16, 128–9, 133–5,
135–6, 138, 160, 180, 188, 193, 210–1;
divided communities, migration waves
and 133–7; domestic workers in,
isolation of 67; exclusion, feelings in
exodus of 136–7; exodus, social patterns
in 187–9; exodus, subjective dimension
of 140–1; exodus, transnational social
field of 140; exodus to 196–7; exodus
to, gendered migrant subjectivities and 128;
exodus to, 'Promised Land' and 16–18;
experiences of exodus, narratives of
141–89; family reunification 128, 129–31;
family reunification, legal migration
through 127, 129–30; 'Great Migration'
from Europe to 133; green card lottery
128, 129, 130, 131, 134; green card
lottery, undocumented but playing
(Halyna) 182–7; green card winners 129,
130; homecare work in 196–7;
homecare workers in 132–3; housewife–
breadwinner family model in Ukraine,
ambivalence about 199; Immigration Act
(1990) 128; immigration laws (U.S.)
127–8, 128–32; Italy compared with
195–7; lawful permanent residence
(LPR) 128; married to U.S. state
(Viktoria) 144–53; migrant domestic
workers in 197; migration history 127;
migration waves 134–5; migration
waves, divided communities and 133–7;
nanny agencies, introductions by 129,
130; post-1991 migrants to 134;